RELIGION IN
AGING AND HEALTH

OTHER RECENT VOLUMES IN THE
SAGE FOCUS EDITIONS

RELIGION IN AGING AND HEALTH

Theoretical Foundations and Methodological Frontiers

Jeffrey S. Levin
editor

SAGE PUBLICATIONS
International Educational and Professional Publisher
Thousand Oaks   London   New Delhi

For information address:

SAGE Publications, Inc.
2455 Teller Road
Thousand Oaks, California 91320

SAGE Publications Ltd.
6 Bonhill Street
London EC2A 4PU
United Kingdom

SAGE Publications India Pvt. Ltd.
M-32 Market
Greater Kailash I
New Delhi 110048 India

Printed in the United States of America

Library of Congress Cataloging-in-Publication Data

Main entry under title:

Religion in aging and health : theoretical foundations and
  methodological frontiers / edited by Jeffrey S. Levin.
      p. cm.—(Sage focus editions ; 166)
    Includes bibliographical references and index.
    ISBN 0-8039-5438-7 (cl).—ISBN 0-8039-5439-5 (pb)
      1. Aging—Religious aspects—Study and teaching. 2. Health—
  Religious aspects—Study and teaching. I. Levin, Jeffrey S.
  BL65.A46R45   1994
  291.1'78321—dc20   93-29472
                                                                                    CIP

94 95 96 97   10 9 8 7 6 5 4 3 2 1

Sage Production Editor: Yvonne Könneker

Contents

Part II. Methodological Frontiers

To my grandfather, Harvey Goldfeder,
and to Dr. C. Eric Lincoln, teacher and colleague.

Foreword

MARTIN E. MARTY*

Religion in Aging and Health: Theoretical Perspectives and Methodological Frontiers, on first appearance, looks like a jeremiad. The jeremiad is a literary form that is at home in America, but one that has roots in ancient Israel: a literary work or speech expressing a bitter lament or a righteous prophecy. The editor and the authors have much to complain about. The healing profession and, in the present case, the social scientists and others who study attitudes toward health and illness tend to overlook a major dimension that should be in their scope: the religious involvement of people. This book would help in redirecting studies of religion and health.

It could, alternatively, be a sort of *Book of Consolations,* to borrow another name and concept from the Jewish tradition. Wherever else the essayists take the reader, they begin with and often return to words about aging, the disabled elder, or clinical epidemiology as it relates to the aged. In all cases, one finds in the chapter authors not only humanists but humane people who have regard for the needs of a population sector. They point to resources that move one beyond mourning to empathic and consoling words, without ever wandering from their scientific intentions and achievements.

*Fairfax M. Cone Distinguished Service Professor, the University of Chicago Divinity School, and Senior Scholar-in-Residence, The Park Ridge Center for the Study of Health, Faith, and Ethics, Chicago, IL.

One of the chapters even shows good humor. Sherrill and Larson invent a term to address an almost comic situation: the ATF, or anti-tenure factor. They argue that in the heart of the clinic and the academy, where all serious scholars ought to be ready for multidimensional probing, young academics or physicians who would make the field of religion and aging their specialty, for whatever demonstrable promise there is in the combination, might well find the choice of subject not only not advantageous in their tenure pursuits but positively disadvantageous. Hence a new patent on a new factor: the ATF. There is no credible scientific reason for the situation that gives rise to the need for such a term, but there it is, in the midst of the company of scientists.

This company brings up a fourth concept with which to approach the rich collection of work in this volume: It is a work of *scientia,* a contribution to knowledge. The authors here all advance knowledge; they collect and collate disparate materials, offer bibliographical comment, and guide researchers over literary terrain that far more people should know but had few chances to address until now. One hopes that this book becomes a standard item in medical school and hospital libraries and is available to those ethicists who deal with care of the aged and some of those who do the actual caring. Few of us can have known much about most of what is here; now one can know or have access to knowledge of a sort that can enhance learning and care.

Most if not all of the contributors might be embarrassed to have it said that John Calvin would have understood what they are about. The 16th-century reformer talked in a language not about healing but about salvation. He contended that one may know where salvation lies and choose not to follow. One would have thought that through and beyond the Enlightenment, when so many of the terms of scientific research were established, thoughtful people would have reckoned with resources on which the aged, sufferers, patients, and their counselors have drawn, resources that connect with words like *religion* and *spirituality.* Yet somehow the biases of the modern academy led them to screen out, overlook, forget, or even have prejudice against the use of such.

None of the authors here suggests a priori that there are positive religious addresses to all of the circumstances that they discuss; none of them is a proselyte, apologist, or advocate for a particular faith or advertiser of unmixed blessings from any or all. The authors simply show that and why dimensions of faith deserve to be explored and reckoned with.

I have had previous experience with the work of Levin and Larson, so I brought high expectations to this book of which one is editor and the other contributes two chapters. Yet these expectations were too modest, and they were more than merely met. Again and again as I read, out came the yellow marker or the red underliner to note that here are concepts that go far beyond "mere" epidemiologic accounting or bibliographical compilation.

It is hard to conceive that in the immediate future scientists or other scholars can claim to have made a well-rounded address to issues concerning the inner life of the aged, the epidemiologic implications of religion, or the formation of agendas for research on the psychology of the cared for or of those who do the caring, unless those who engage in the research have familiarized themselves with the literature so well assessed and pointed to here. I do not know whether a new discipline is being developed (comparable to, say, bioethics) or whether we need such a discipline. One can, however, easily become convinced from all the pointing that goes on here that at least a convergence or a perspective is developing, one that bids for attention and must be pursued.

Levin, up front, says that in the face of all the publications and other developments in this field, "there is no nice way to put it: Mainstream scientists and scholars seem positively oblivious to the presence of the expanding literature base of empirical data supportive of a salutary role for religion." There is something even less nice to say henceforth: If they continue to live in oblivion after these essays are easily available, the scientific character of their place in the mainstream deserves questioning. Or, more positively, it would be nice if they found a broader stream, one that merges the science they inherited with insights connected with the empirical data into which these authors would have them wade. Having wandered into these depths with them, and thanks to them, I will not be the last to say, no doubt in scholarly analogues to a colloquialism, "Come on in! The water's fine!"

Acknowledgments

I gratefully acknowledge all of the people whose hard work, assistance, and consideration brought this book into being. Dr. Kokos Markides first approached Sage Publications on my behalf and, I am convinced, helped to grease the wheel for me, no small task given the unusual topic of this book. Kokos encouraged me for many years to write a book on religion, aging, and health; I hope he'll settle for an edited volume.

Christine Smedley, at Sage, was a tremendous help to me in putting together this project and seeing it through to completion. She was always available to answer my questions, no matter how simple. I also appreciate her patience with me as I learned the ropes of editing a book and missed more than one agreed-on deadline.

Dr. Terry Davies, my department chairman, provided a comfortable and supportive environment for me to pursue this project. When researchers working in this field get together, they typically commiserate with each other about the barriers they face, the professional stigma and marginality of research on religion and health, their lack of resources, and the not-so-subtle pressure to do something more "relevant." Because of Terry's support, I have faced none of these constraints.

I must mention several other individuals who helped to train me over the years and who encouraged (and tolerated) me as I sought to establish a new field of study. These include Drs. Preston Schiller, Bert Kaplan,

Harold Vanderpool, and Jersey Liang. I am also grateful to Dr. Dave Jenkins, the director of my doctoral program at Texas, for his good cheer in the face of a student who rather obsessively spent all of his free time pursuing his vision of an epidemiology of religion instead of a more accepted area of specialization. I still recall his words of epidemiologic advice to me many years ago as he took me aside, just like in the famous "plastics scene" in *The Graduate*, and said, "Jeff, you need a disease." Well, I never did get a disease, just religion.

Finally, I would like to acknowledge the National Institute on Aging, which supported my work on this book through NIH FIRST Award Grant No. AG09462, "Religion, Health, and Psychological Well-Being in the Aged."

JEFF LEVIN

Introduction

Religion in Aging and Health

JEFFREY S. LEVIN

Over the past decade, religion has become a topic of great interest to researchers in medicine, epidemiology, gerontology, and other socio-medical disciplines. Especially significant has been an increase in empirical research linking measures of religiosity, broadly defined, to an assortment of health outcomes, notably physical health status, mental illness, health care use, adjustment to aging, and general well-being. The growth of this nascent field is exemplified by an explosion of publications, organizations, and funded research.

An abbreviated list of developments includes the inaugural issue of the *Journal of Religious Gerontology* as well as the publication of *Religion & Aging: An Annotated Bibliography* (Fecher, 1982), *Religion & Medicine: A Medical Subject Analysis and Research Index With Bibliography* (Hurley, 1985), *Religion, Health, and Aging: A Review and Theoretical Integration* (Koenig, Smiley, & Gonzales, 1988), *Religion and Prevention in Mental Health: Research, Vision, and Action* (Pargament, Maton, & Hess, 1992), *Religion and Mental Health: A Bibliography* (National Institute of Mental Health [NIMH], 1980), and the World Health Organization's *Religion, Aging and Health: A Global Perspective* (Clements, 1989). Further developments are the inclusion of chapters on religion in *The Encyclopedia of Aging* (Maddox, 1987; Markides, 1987; Palmore, 1987) and in other key edited books (e.g.,

Kart, 1987; Moberg, 1990; Taylor, 1993), the establishment of both the Forum on Religion, Spirituality, and Aging within the American Society on Aging and the private-sector National Institute for Healthcare Research, and the forthcoming publication of *Religion, Spirituality, and Aging: A Handbook* (Kimble, Ellor, McFadden, & Seeber, in press). There also have been several NIH-funded research programs addressing the interface of religion, aging, and health. These include the NIA-funded research of Levin, Taylor, Chatters, and Ainlay, and the NIMH-funded research of Sherrill. These developments "signal a maturation of research in this area and a continued acceptance of religion as a significant factor" in aging, health, and well-being (Levin & Tobin, in press).

Simultaneous to this growth, a strange paradox persists. There is no nice way to put it: Mainstream scientists and scholars seem positively oblivious to the presence of the expanding literature base of empirical data supportive of a salutary role for religion. Many erroneously conclude that after searching the literature they have determined that few such studies have ever been undertaken (e.g., Byrne & Price, 1979). Worse, others deny that religion should be studied in this way, as tacit wisdom holds that it has no bearing on health or aging; thus it is treated as an irrelevancy. Finally, still other researchers are downright hostile to the study of religious factors in any area of human life, and challenge the motives of social scientists who present data supportive of a salutary role for religion.

So what do the existing data actually reveal? According to key reviews, somewhere in the area of 400 published empirical studies dating back to the last century have investigated the effects of some aspect of religious involvement on health, illness, well-being, health care use, or other related constructs (e.g., Jarvis & Northcutt, 1987; Koenig, 1990; Levin, 1989; Levin & Schiller, 1987; Levin & Vanderpool, 1987; Schiller & Levin, 1988; Witter, Stock, Okun, & Haring, 1985). (Including psychological outcomes and health-related behaviors might add another thousand studies—no one seems to know for sure.) Despite methodological limitations and heterogeneity in religious measures, these findings point consistently, though not unanimously, to a positive, health promotive role for religion. Still, many social scientists and biomedical researchers maintain a sort of "collective amnesia" (Levin & Vanderpool, 1992, p. 84) that serves to blot out these data or to downplay their significance.

This is especially unusual in light of the strong tradition of scholarly writing on the intersection of religion and medicine. Preeminent figures in the history of modern medicine, such as Billings (1891) and Osler (1910), and leading figures of the present day, such as Frank (1973) and Dossey (in press), have argued that religion represents a rich source of sociocultural, ideological, intrapsychic, and familial influences on etiology, pathogenesis, and recovery (see Levin & Vanderpool, 1992, p. 84). For decades, applied research and writing in the area of pastoral care and counseling have explored the role of religious institutions and personal religious faith in human illness and well-being (e.g., Hiltner, 1943). Theologian Tillich (1946) wrote on this same topic nearly 50 years ago. The *Journal of Religion and Health* has published continuously for over 30 years, through its tenure presenting articles by such writers as Allport (1963). Its appearance was predated in 1957 by the first symposium of the Academy of Religion and Mental Health (1959), initiating a monograph series that later included an essay on religion and mental health by Parsons (1961). Although the recent editions of neither the *Handbook of Aging and the Social Sciences* (Binstock & George, 1990) nor the *Handbook of the Psychology of Aging* (Birren & Schaie, 1990) include material on religion, their common ancestor, the *Handbook of Social Gerontology* (Tibbitts, 1960), included an entire chapter on religion by Maves (1960). Gerontology has benefited for 40 years from the seminal work of Moberg and other pioneers such as Payne. In epidemiology, the research of Comstock and classic pieces such as Kennaway's (1948) review of religion and uterine cancer demonstrate that, although never mainstream, religion has long been the subject of provocative research.

Furthermore, within the field of religious studies, investigation of linkages between religion and medicine has been a prominent and prestigious field of study. Key books (e.g., Belgum, 1967) and articles (e.g., Vanderpool, 1977; Vaux, 1976); the establishment of the Park Ridge Center for the Study of Health, Faith, and Ethics; and the presence of a professional journal (*Second Opinion*), two fine edited volumes (Numbers & Amundsen, 1986; Sullivan, 1989), and an innovative monograph series exploring health and medicine in each of the world's major religious traditions all bear witness to the attention paid to these issues within academic religion. Nonetheless, in medicine and social science, this key intellectual discourse remains only "part of the folklore of discussion on the fringes of the research community" (Levin & Schiller, 1987, p. 10).

Why is this? One reason might lie in the antipathy to religion inherent in the modern scientific worldview. To many scientists, religion is not seen as relevant to the human condition (Levin & Vanderpool, 1992; Weaver, 1975). Perhaps it is thought that troublesome findings such as those noted above are a nuisance best ignored. As Levin and Vanderpool (1987) once remarked, "Western biomedicine, of which epidemiology is a part, is still wrestling with a body-mind dualism that defies consensus; thus, for most epidemiologists any resolution of a body-mind-spirit pluralism is simply beyond consideration" (pp. 590-591). It is difficult to gauge the salience of this explanation for the marginality of religious research in aging and health; it makes sense, but, true or false, there is not much that can be done easily and quickly to remedy the situation. Besides, there are other reasons for the persistent marginality of research on religion, aging, and health, and these reasons suggest that it is inappropriate to place the blame solely with some amorphous "scientific worldview." Sympathetic researchers themselves may be partly to blame. According to Moberg (1988),

> There are numerous findings from empirical research on the relationships between various aspects of religion and health among older people, but they are so widely scattered that most people in gerontology, geriatrics, the health and human services fields, the social and behavioral sciences, and even the religious professions are completely unaware of the predominant direction of these results. (p. x)

Furthermore, with notable exceptions, this empirical work has been mediocre, even dreadful. Although it is easy to identify examples of the many excellent and important research studies that are available (e.g., Ainlay & Smith, 1984; Anson, Antonovsky, & Sagy, 1990; Blazer & Palmore, 1976; Comstock & Tonascia, 1976; Ellison, 1991; Idler & Kasl, 1992; Krause & Tran, 1989; Mindel & Vaughan, 1978; Steinitz, 1980; Williams, Larson, Buckler, Heckmann, & Pyle, 1991), most published research, sadly, has failed to keep pace with current methodologies, psychometric innovations, and data analytic procedures and, worse, has failed to engage midrange theoretical issues. The works of Larson and Lyons have done much to document these deficiencies in religious research in general.

In his recent book, *Prolegomena to the Psychological Study of Religion,* Beit-Hallahmi (1989) summarized the views of Douglas (1963) concerning the rise and fall of the psychology of religion earlier in this century. Among the reasons offered for the demise of this field include two in particular that should sound an alarm to all those scientists and scholars involved in the study of religion, aging, and health: "The use of data collection methods and explanations was often uncritical and incompetent" and "In the desperate effort to be recognized as 'scientific,' there was an emphasis on collecting discrete facts without integrating them into a comprehensive theory" (Beit-Hallahmi, 1989, p. 25). The analogies to both religious gerontology and the "epidemiology of religion" (Levin & Vanderpool, 1987) should be apparent to those who have worked in these fields for any length of time.

The general purpose of the present volume is to address and remedy these two deficiencies—of theory and methods—and thus provide some guidance to social scientists, health professionals, and other interested researchers. The chapters in this book are written by a diverse group of social scientists and physicians—geropsychiatrists, social epidemiologists, sociologists of religion, medical sociologists, social psychologists, and social workers. Supporting material draws on an even wider range of scholarly and scientific fields.

The specific aim of this book is to explore both the theoretical foundations and methodological frontiers of research on religion, aging, and health. Certain chapters address the interface of religion and health, others address the interface of religion and aging, and some explore the interface of all three areas. This is mostly a function of the expertise and background of the chapter authors as well as the nature of the literature base pertaining to the subjects under discussion.

In keeping with the dual aim of this project, the book is divided into two parts. Part I, comprising Chapters 1 through 4, explores theoretical foundations. These chapters address the "why" of religion and health or religion and aging associations. In other words, they examine the underlying rationale for expecting religion, broadly defined, to be a meaningful and salient influence on health and well-being and in older adults. These include such possibilities as hope, forgiveness, the psychodynamics of faith and belief, and coping and stress buffering.

Levin (Chapter 1) reviews key empirical studies in this field as a whole, highlighting important recent findings. More important, he outlines a series of alternative hypotheses or explanations for statistically significant associations between religious measures and health outcomes. These include behavioral, hereditary, psychosocial, psychodynamic, and superempirical mechanisms or pathways. Finally, he describes a number of barriers experienced by researchers seeking to investigate these issues and publish in this area.

Koenig (Chapter 2) develops a Christian theology of hope for disabled elders. This is an inspiring and original exegetical study of Old and New Testament scriptures. He identifies sources of hope in medical advances, primary prevention, psychological treatments, environmental manipulations, and family and friends. Finally, he outlines 11 ways in which religious faith, from a Christian perspective, helps to ameliorate the suffering of elders.

Kaplan, Monroe-Blum, and Blazer (Chapter 3) provide a rationale for conceiving of forgiveness as an epidemiologically significant construct for the study of chronic disease. This wide-ranging piece delves into literature, philosophy, history, psychiatry, and the classical works of the early social scientists. Forgiveness is conceived of as a mechanism that accounts for and makes sense of religion's role as a source of adaptation and coping. Forgiveness, and religion in general, are thus central to the calling of social epidemiology, as characterized by Cassel, and are vital issues for empirical study.

Ellison (Chapter 4) thoroughly reviews studies of religion and psychological distress, organized by components of the life stress paradigm. This extremely comprehensive overview synthesizes social scientific research linking religion to depression, social control, stress, social resources, self-perceptions, coping, and mental health. Special attention is given to detailing specific research agendas for each of these areas. Beyond the substantive value of this overview, the author demonstrates the benefit of working from a given theoretical perspective for synthesizing findings, identifying gaps in knowledge, and generating specific hypotheses for subsequent psychosocial research.

Part II, comprising Chapters 5 through 8, explores methodological frontiers. These chapters address the "how" of studying religious factors in aging and in health. These chapters cover issues such as the conceptualization of religiosity, barriers to the study of religion, the status of religious research in the health professions, and the study of religion among African-Americans. In contrast to the diversity of subject matter addressed in Part I, in Part II all of the chapters focus to some extent on the issue of measurement. This is to emphasize the centrality of addressing and resolving conceptual and operational issues to advance empirical study of religious factors in aging and health. Without appropriate measurement, even the best study designs and analytic strategies are of little use.

Williams (Chapter 5) presents a much-needed assessment of strengths and weaknesses in current epidemiologic approaches to measuring religion. He examines both unidimensional and multidimensional measures as well as measures of subjective religiosity. Popular measures such as religious affiliation, religious attendance, and intrinsic-extrinsic religiosity are critiqued, and a variety of other creative approaches are discussed. These include tolerance of ambiguity, spiritual well-being, and religious architecture—fascinating measurement constructs not yet used in research on health. Finally, helpful suggestions are offered for prospective researchers who have little training in either religious studies or psychometrics.

Sherrill and Larson (Chapter 6) describe the professional pitfalls of studying religion, still a semiforbidden topic in some quarters. This chapter is not so much about a particular methodological approach or issue as a treatise on what they term the *anti-tenure factor* (or ATF), which has inhibited the conduct of epidemiologic and geriatric research on religiosity. The ATF is shown to have arisen from a confluence of developments, including the simplicity of early work, the idea that this research was flawed, the application of unrealistic standards, the fact that there are few researchers in this area, and the perpetuation of low-quality research. Illustrative material from epidemiology, sociology, and psychology is used to elaborate on the ATF and serve as a warning and challenge to researchers.

Larson, Sherrill, and Lyons (Chapter 7) provide an overview of their systematic review (SR) methodology—a bibliographic, meta-analytic tool for assessing both the quality and quantity of published studies of the *R* word within particular fields. The SR method is characterized as both a science and an art and consists of several sequential steps, which are illustrated in Chapter 7. Results of prior SR methodologies are presented for a number of fields, including psychiatry, family practice, gerontology and geriatrics, psychology, and pastoral care. The authors' findings are simultaneously upsetting and hopeful.

Finally, Chatters and Taylor (Chapter 8) comprehensively review studies of religion, aging, health, and psychological well-being among African-Americans. They discuss their own seminal work, offer a critique of most other key studies, and provide a very sophisticated methodological primer and agenda meant to guide the work of social scientists along the cutting edge of research design, methods, measurement, and data analysis. This tremendous and thorough overview covers patterns, determinants, and social and health outcomes of religious involvement and addresses issues ranging from midrange theory to the technicalities of covariance-structure-modeling analysis.

References

Academy of Religion and Mental Health. (Ed.). (1959). *Religion, science, and mental health: Proceedings of the first Academy symposium on inter-discipline responsibility for mental health—A religious and scientific concern.* New York: New York University Press.

Ainlay, S. C., & Smith, D. R. (1984). Aging and religious participation. *Journal of Gerontology, 39,* 357-363.

Allport, G. W. (1963). Behavioral science, religion, and mental health. *Journal of Religion and Health, 2,* 187-197.

Anson, O., Antonovsky, A., & Sagy, S. (1990). Religiosity and well-being among retirees: A question of causality. *Behavior, Health, and Aging, 1,* 85-97.

Beit-Hallahmi, B. (1989). *Prolegomena to the psychological study of religion.* Lewisburg, PA: Bucknell University Press.

Belgum, D. (Ed.). (1967). *Religion and medicine: Essays on meaning, values, and health.* Ames: Iowa State University Press.

Billings, J. S. (1891). Vital statistics of the Jews. *North American Review, 153,* 70-84.

Binstock, R. H., & George, L. K. (Eds.). (1990). *Handbook of aging and the social sciences* (3rd ed.). San Diego: Academic Press.

Birren, J. E., & Schaie, K. W. (Eds.). (1990). *Handbook of the psychology of aging* (3rd ed.). San Diego: Academic Press.

Blazer, D., & Palmore, E. (1976). Religion and aging in a longitudinal panel. *The Gerontologist, 16*(1), 82-85.

Byrne, J. T., & Price, J. H. (1979). In sickness and health: The effects of religion. *Health Education, 10,* 6-10.

Clements, W. M. (Ed.). (1989). *Religion, aging and health: A global perspective* (Compiled by the World Health Organization). New York: Haworth.

Comstock, G. W., & Tonascia, J. A. (1976). Education and mortality in Washington County, Maryland. *Journal of Health and Social Behavior, 18,* 54-61.

Dossey, L. (in press). *Healing words.* San Francisco: Harper & Row.

Douglas, W. (1963). Religion. In N. L. Faberow (Ed.), *Taboo topics.* New York: Atherton.

Ellison, C. G. (1991). Religious involvement and subjective well-being. *The Journal of Health and Social Behavior, 32,* 80-99.

Fecher, V. J. (1982). *Religion & aging: An annotated bibliography.* San Antonio: Trinity University Press.

Frank, J. D. (1973). *Persuasion and healing: A comparative study of psychotherapy.* Baltimore, MD: Johns Hopkins University Press.

Hiltner, S. (1943). *Religion and health.* New York: Macmillan.

Hurley, P. S. (1985). *Religion & medicine: A medical subject analysis and research index with bibliography.* Washington, DC: Abbe.

Idler, E. L., & Kasl, S. V. (1992). Religion, disability, depression, and the timing of death. *American Journal of Sociology, 97,* 1052-1079.

Jarvis, G. K., & Northcutt, H. C. (1987). Religion and differences in morbidity and mortality. *Social Science and Medicine, 25,* 813-824.

Kart, C. S. (1987). Age and religious commitment in the American-Jewish community. In D. E. Gelfand & C. M. Barresi (Eds.), *Ethnic dimensions of aging* (pp. 96-105). New York: Springer.

Kennaway, E. L. (1948). The racial and social incidence of cancer of the uterus. *British Journal of Cancer, 2,* 177-212.

Kimble, M. A., Ellor, J. W., McFadden, S. H., & Seeber, J. J. (Eds.). (in press). *Religion, spirituality, and aging: A handbook.* Minneapolis, MN: Fortress.

Koenig, H. G. (1990). Research on religion and mental health in later life: A review and commentary. *Journal of Geriatric Psychiatry, 23,* 23-53.

Koenig, H. G., Smiley, M., & Gonzales, J. A. P. (1988). *Religion, health, and aging: A review and theoretical integration.* New York: Greenwood.

Krause, N., & Tran, T. V. (1989). Stress and religious involvement among older blacks. *Journal of Gerontology: Social Sciences, 44,* S4-S13.

Levin, J. S. (1989). Religious factors in aging, adjustment, and health: A theoretical overview. In W. M. Clements (Ed.), *Religion, aging and health: A global perspective* (pp. 133-146). New York: Haworth.

Levin, J. S., & Schiller, P. L. (1987). Is there a religious factor in health? *Journal of Religion and Health, 26,* 9-36.

Levin, J. S., & Tobin, S. S. (in press). Religion and psychological well-being. In M. A. Kimble, J. W. Ellor, S. H. McFadden, & J. J. Seeber (Eds.), *Religion, spirituality, and aging: A handbook.* Minneapolis, MN: Fortress.

Levin, J. S., & Vanderpool, H. Y. (1987). Is frequent religious attendance *really* conducive to better health?: Toward an epidemiology of religion. *Social Science and Medicine, 24,* 589-600.

Levin, J. S., & Vanderpool, H. Y. (1989). Is religion therapeutically significant for hypertension? *Social Science and Medicine, 29,* 69-78.

Levin, J. S., & Vanderpool, H. Y. (1992). Religious factors in physical health and the prevention of illness. In K. I. Pargament, K. I. Maton, & R. E. Hess (Eds.), *Religion and prevention in mental health: Research, vision, and action* (pp. 83-103). New York: Haworth.

Maddox, G. L. (Ed.). (1987). *The encyclopedia of aging.* New York: Springer.

Markides, K. S. (1987). Religion. In G. L. Maddox (Ed.), *The encyclopedia of aging* (pp. 559-561). New York: Springer.

Maves, P. B. (1960). Aging, religion, and the church. In C. Tibbitts (Ed.), *Handbook of social gerontology: Societal aspects of aging* (pp. 698-749). Chicago: University of Chicago Press.

Mindel, C. H., & Vaughan, C. E. (1978). A multidimensional approach to religiosity and disengagement. *Journal of Gerontology, 33,* 103-108.

Moberg, D. O. (1988). Foreword. In H. G. Koenig, M. Smiley, & J. A. P. Gonzales, *Religion, health, and aging: A review and theoretical integration* (pp. ix-xi). New York: Greenwood.

Moberg, D. O. (1990). Religion and aging. In K. F. Ferraro (Ed.), *Gerontology: Perspectives and issues* (pp. 179-205). New York: Springer.

National Institute of Mental Health. (1980). *Religion and mental health: A bibliography* (DHHS Publication No. [ADM]80-964). Washington, DC: U.S. Government Printing Office.

Numbers, R. L., & Amundsen, D. W. (Eds.). (1986). *Caring and curing: Health and medicine in the western religious traditions.* New York: Macmillan.

Osler, W. (1910, June 18). The faith that heals. *British Medical Journal,* pp. 1470-1472.

Palmore, E. (1987). Religious organizations. In G. L. Maddox (Ed.), *The encyclopedia of aging* (pp. 561-563). New York: Springer.

Pargament, K. I., Maton, K. I., & Hess, R. E. (Eds.). (1992). *Religion and prevention in mental health: Research, vision, and action*. New York: Haworth.

Parsons, T. (1961). A sociological approach. In Academy of Religion and Mental Health (Ed.), *Religion, culture, and mental health* (p. 9). New York: New York University Press.

Schiller, P. L., & Levin, J. S. (1988). Is there a religious factor in health care utilization?: A review. *Social Science and Medicine, 27,* 1369-1379.

Steinitz, L. Y. (1980). Religiosity, well-being, and Weltanschauung among the elderly. *Journal for the Scientific Study of Religion, 19,* 60-67.

Sullivan, L. E. (Ed.). (1989). *Healing and restoring: Health and medicine in the world's religious traditions*. New York: Macmillan.

Taylor, R. J. (1993). Religion and religious observances. In J. S. Jackson, L. M. Chatters, & R. J. Taylor (Eds.), *Aging in black America* (pp. 101-123). Newbury Park, CA: Sage.

Tibbitts, C. (Ed.). (1960). *Handbook of social gerontology: Societal aspects of aging.* Chicago: University of Chicago Press.

Tillich, P. (1946). The relation of religion and health: Historical considerations and theoretical questions. *Review of Religion, 10,* 348-384.

Vanderpool, H. Y. (1977). Is religion therapeutically significant? *Journal of Religion and Health, 16,* 255-259.

Vaux, K. (1976). Religion and health. *Preventive Medicine, 5,* 522-536.

Weaver, W. (1975). The religion of a scientist. In L. Rosten (Ed.), *Religions of America: Ferment and faith in an age of crisis* (pp. 296-305). New York: Simon & Schuster.

Williams, D. R., Larson, D. B., Buckler, R. E., Heckmann, R. C., & Pyle, C. M. (1991). Religion and psychological distress in a community sample. *Social Science and Medicine, 32,* 1257-1262.

Witter, R. A., Stock, W. A., Okun, M. A., & Haring, M. J. (1985). Religion and subjective well-being in adulthood: A quantitative synthesis. *Review of Religious Research, 26,* 332-342.

PART I

Theoretical Foundations

1

Investigating the Epidemiologic Effects of Religious Experience

Findings, Explanations, and Barriers

JEFFREY S. LEVIN

This chapter reviews an ongoing program of empirical research on the effects of religious experience, broadly defined, on physical health status. First, this research program is briefly described and an overview is provided of key studies and papers. Overall, findings point to a generally salutary effect of religion, regardless of how religiosity is conceived or measured and regardless of which causes of morbidity or mortality are examined. Second, several possible alternative hypotheses for this summary finding are explored. These include explanations based on behavior; heredity; psychosocial effects; the psychodynamics of belief systems, religious rites, and faith; and superempirical and supernatural influences. Third, barriers are discussed that have been encountered in conducting, funding, and publishing epidemiologic and medical research on the effects of religious experience. Description of these barriers and how they were successfully overcome can serve as lessons for other scientists interested in exploring anomalous factors in health and healing.

AUTHOR'S NOTE: This chapter was presented as an invited address at TREAT V: Researching the Anomalous, Fifth Conference on Treatment and Research of Experienced Anomalous Trauma, Santa Fe, NM, March 17-21, 1993.

Overview of Selected Findings

For the past decade, I have directed a program of empirical research on patterns, predictors, and health outcomes of religious involvement, with an emphasis on developing and confirming multidimensional measurement models, operationalizing midrange theoretical perspectives, and postulating alternative hypotheses for religion-health associations. My goal has been to establish a new scientific field, which a colleague and I have termed the *epidemiology of religion* (Levin & Vanderpool, 1987). This research has proceeded in three phases.

Initial work, conducted in graduate school, consisted of a series of comprehensive review essays of existing studies of religious effects on morbidity and mortality (Levin & Schiller, 1987), health care use (Schiller & Levin, 1988), and psychological well-being (Levin, 1989) and a review of the health effects of attendance at religious services (Levin & Vanderpool, 1987). The second phase of this work consisted of a series of modest secondary analyses of data sets available to me in graduate school. This included a series of papers on religious effects on health and well-being in three generations of Mexican-Americans (Levin & Markides, 1985, 1986, 1988), in older Anglo whites and Mexican-Americans (Markides, Levin, & Ray, 1987), in white air traffic controllers (Levin, Jenkins, & Rose, 1988), and in black and white adults from rural West Virginia (Levin & Schiller, 1986).

Currently, my research is supported by two NIH grants. One is a 5-year FIRST Award titled "Religion, Health, and Psychological Well-Being in the Aged." The second grant, on which I serve as Coprincipal Investigator with Taylor (who is the Principal Investigator) and Chatters (of the Institute for Social Research at the University of Michigan), involves studying social-structural variation in racial differences in religious experience. My FIRST Award grant supports secondary analysis of several large, national, random probability surveys (the National Opinion Research Center's General Social Survey, the National Survey of Black Americans, the Quality of American Life study, the Myth and Reality of Aging study, and the Americans' Changing Lives study). The goal of this research is to validate multidimensional measurement models of religious behaviors, attitudes, and experiences and then incorporate them in multifactorial structural models of physical health status and psychological well-being. Recent research in medical sociology and social gerontology has suggested that health status is a three-dimensional construct containing an objective or clinical dimension, a functional dimension, and a subjective dimension (Liang & Whitelaw, 1990). Accordingly, my research investigates the effects of religiosity on indicators of each of these dimensions, including chronic disease, functional disability, and subjective perceptions of overall health. This research also focuses on variations in patterns, predictors, and health outcomes of religiosity by age, race, ethnicity, gender, social class, religious denomination, and other social and psychological factors.

This research program has produced a considerable number of published studies, too many to describe in detail (for an overview, see Levin & Vanderpool, 1992). The following is a summary of selected highlights of the reviews and empirical investigations mentioned above.

1. Over the past 150 years or so, more than 250 published empirical studies in medicine and epidemiology have explored the effects of one or more religious measures on indicators of nearly every cause of morbidity and mortality imaginable (Jarvis & Northcutt, 1987; Levin & Schiller, 1987). Statistically significant associations have been found linking religion and health variables in the areas of cardiovascular disease, hypertension and stroke, cancer (especially uterine cancer), colitis and enteritis, overall and site-specific mortality, general health status, physical symptomatology, and self-rated health as well as dozens of other illnesses. Regardless of the religious measures used or the health outcomes under study, the results across all of these studies are remarkably consistent, although not universal, and point to two basic findings. First, in studies that make comparisons between two or more groups on the basis of religious affiliation, there is greater health and less morbidity and mortality among adherents of what might be termed behaviorally strict religions and denominations (e.g., Seventh-Day Adventists and Mormons) compared with other religious groups and unaffiliated individuals. Second, in studies in which at least ordinal-level measures of religiosity are used (e.g., religious attendance, subjective religiosity, and various other behaviors and attitudes), the greater the intensity or degree of religiousness, the better the health and the less of whatever illness is being investigated. These results are especially pronounced for hypertension (Levin & Vanderpool, 1989) and for studies examining the effects of frequent religious attendance (Levin & Vanderpool, 1987).

What is especially fascinating about this body of findings is that until reviews began to appear, few scientists, it seems, knew this collection of data existed. That is, many of the studies themselves were well known, but because few were designed to focus on religion, significant findings linking religious variables to health outcomes were never collated across studies. In typical epidemiologic fashion, the investigators of these studies of, for example, atherosclerosis, stroke-related mortality, tuberculosis incidence, colitis, cervical cancer, or symptomatology collected tons of data on many more social, psychological, and biological variables than were ever intended to be explicitly studied. Serendipitously, then, a stray religion variable or two would make a discrete guest appearance, and some sort of statistical result bearing on the health effects of these variables would end up buried in a table with dozens of other results. Only after an exhaustive 5-year effort of searching the literature, reading, and collating did the full picture emerge.

2. In recent years, gerontologists and geriatricians especially have focused on the health and mental health effects of religious involvement. This is probably the result of an acknowledgment that religion, as both a social institution and a source of existential meaning, is a profoundly important personal resource for older adults in terms of the provision both of services and fellowship and of an intrapsychic means of coping and adaptation with issues of daily life, change, loss, and death. Reviews of empirical studies of the effects of religious indicators on health and well-being in older adults support and elaborate on the epidemiologic findings noted above (Koenig, 1990; Levin, 1989; Witter, Stock, Okun, & Haring, 1985). Namely, as adults age, formal or organizational religious involvement is strongly predictive of better health, happiness, and life satisfaction. Similarly, nonorganizational or private expressions of religiosity as well as positive subjective religious attitudes or beliefs are also promotive of health, especially when formal or public participation is lessened because of declining health.

3. Findings from the National Survey of Black Americans reveal that each of these dimensions of religious expression is significantly associated with physical health and/or psychological well-being (Levin, Chatters, Taylor, & Jackson, 1989). In fact, religiosity is shown to be predictive of well-being even after controlling for the effects of health status, and the magnitude of this effect is at least as great as that of health itself on well-being. This is notable, as it has been tacitly held for years that one's health is the best predictor of one's well-being. Furthermore, controlling for the effects of a variety of sociodemographic indicators does not eliminate the predictive salience of religious involvement for well-being. In other words, the prevailing materialist conception of life satisfaction and happiness as being determined mainly by such things as health and finances, as opposed to one's engagement of the sacred,

may be false. Whereas this may not be surprising to religious scholars or psychologists or philosophers, it is quite counterintuitive to many social and biomedical scientists.

4. Using data from the General Social Survey, an effort was made to update the work of Greeley (1975), who provided a profile of the lifetime prevalence of *psi,* or mystical, experiences in the general population. In the nearly two decades since Greeley's findings were published, it appears that mystical experience has been on the rise (Levin, 1993). Reports of ESP, déjà vu, clairvoyance, spiritualism, and numinous experience in general have increased considerably with successive age cohorts. In fact, as many Americans now report ever having had contact with the dead (about 40%) as attend church every week. Furthermore, whereas organizational religiosity is negatively associated with mystical experience, both private and subjective religiosity are strongly and positively associated with these experiences. In other words, mystical experience is not necessarily a replacement for traditional religion. Rather, it appears to be a reflection of a heightened intensity of subjective religious feelings and of private expressions of religious commitment, such as prayer, Bible study, and saying grace.

In addition to my own research, which is primarily based on survey-research and epidemiologic methodologies, work from within an experimental paradigm has also begun to explore how religious expression affects health. The most notable example of this is the study by Byrd (1988), which demonstrated the effect of prayer on cardiac patients. This study, which has become quite celebrated (or notorious, depending on one's perspective), was a double-blind, randomized clinical trial—a "drug trial," in essence—in which the therapy was distant, intercessory prayer. In a nutshell, it worked. Prayed-for patients (who, in double-blind fashion, did not know that they had been prayed for), had fewer symptoms and were less frequently intubated than patients who did not receive prayer. The prayer givers had no contact with the patients; they were selected from among the membership of Catholic and evangelical Protestant prayer groups who met and prayed outside of the hospital. The letters column of the *Southern Medical Journal* (the journal that had the foresight to publish this landmark study) subsequently resembled the letters column of *Sports Illustrated* following their annual swimsuit issue, when angry parents write in to complain and berate the editor and cancel their subscriptions. Byrd's success has been encouraging to many researchers in this field, and another study of prayer and health is about to be published in the same journal, although it is an observational study and does not provide experimental findings (Levin, Lyons, & Larson, in press).

Alternative Hypotheses
for Salutary Religious Effects

In light of these and numerous other similar findings from epidemiology and the sociomedical sciences, a list of alternative hypotheses or explanations was developed (Levin & Vanderpool, 1989) for why statistically significant associations might be observed between religion and health indicators. This work was guided by the following considerations:

> Although considerable in number and suggestive of a general trend, these findings nonetheless do not constitute proof of a consistent, salutary effect of religious belief or spiritual forces on [health]. This is the case because "religion" incorporates many variables that frequently are not identified and measured. Beliefs and/or spiritual or supernatural forces or influences, for example, need to be disentangled from various social, psychological, and biological characteristics and functions of religious groups and religious group membership, many of which have been found to influence health. Several of these characteristics and functions are rather mundane, in that while they are characteristic of religious groups, they are not exclusive to these groups or to some particular religious system of belief. (Levin & Vanderpool, 1989, p. 72)

In other words, the following alternative hypotheses for why religious experience appears to influence health are meant to explain this influence in the sense of elucidating its pathways and mechanisms, not in the sense of "explaining it away." The latter would imply an operational definition of the influence of religion only in supernatural terms—as some sort of divine or ineffable force or spirit—which exemplifies a type of reductionism. Religion, as a social institution, and religiosity, as a component or dimension of our psychological makeup and interpersonal life, are real phenomena—as real as any other psychosocial construct. Just as medical scientists speak of biomarkers of certain phenomena, it is possible to establish *psychosociomarkers* (a poor term, admittedly) of religious experience and then measure their effects on health. On the other hand, this is not to deny that the empirical findings reviewed earlier may also provide evidence of a benevolent divine force. The following alternative hypotheses are described in greater detail elsewhere (Levin & Vanderpool, 1989).

Behavior. Certain health promotive lifestyles or health related behaviors are sanctioned by particular religions or religious denominations. These proscriptions and prescriptions govern alcohol, tobacco, drugs, diet, exercise, and general hygiene (Spector, 1979) and help to explain why morbidity and mortality rates are lower among certain religious groups (e.g., Mormons and Seventh-Day Adventists).

Heredity. Morbidity and mortality might be higher (or lower) in a particular religious group owing to genetic risk (or protection) for certain diseases specific to religioethnic groups. For example, Tay Sachs disease seems to be most incident among Ashkenazi (i.e., Eastern European) Jews; hypercholesterolemia disproportionately strikes Dutch Reformed Afrikaaners; and sickle-cell anemia is likely to be more prevalent among members of the National Baptist Convention of America (which is predominantly black) than among members of the Southern Baptist Convention (which is predominantly white). These certainly represent distinctly religious differences in morbidity, yet are likely attributable to genetic characteristics of religious group membership as opposed to, religious differences in theology or polity or worship practices.

Psychosocial Effects. More frequent religious involvement and more intense or committed religious experience may be associated with better health due to religion's promotion of social support, a sense of belonging, and convivial fellowship. An entire tradition of research in social epidemiology has demonstrated the salutary nature of social relationships (House, Landis, & Umberson, 1988), which serve to buffer the adverse effects of stress and anger, perhaps via psychoneuroimmunological pathways.

Psychodynamics of Belief Systems. The operant beliefs of particular religious traditions may engender peacefulness, self-confidence, and a sense of purpose; alternatively, they may lead to guilt and self-doubt. These sorts of beliefs, in turn, have been shown to be related to health beliefs and, indirectly, to health itself. Indeed, certain religious beliefs or theological worldviews seem quite convergent with respective health beliefs or personalities. For example, descriptions of the well-known Protestant work ethic are quite similar to descriptions of the Type A behavioral pattern, long believed to put individuals at risk for myocardial infarction (Levin et al., 1988). In addition, scales that measure the construct of internal locus of control, a predictor of positive health related action, also appear to tap a "free-will" theological perspective (Levin & Schiller, 1986). *Psychodynamics of Religious Rites.* Engagement in the public and private cultic rituals of religious worship and spiritual practice may serve to ease anxiety and dread, defeat loneliness, and establish a sense of being loved and appreciated. These psychological outcomes of religious practice as well as the actual physiological markers of emotional arousal during worship are believed to be associated with healing and health and well-being. These salutary effects could be described as psychic beta-blockers or emotional placebos.

Psychodynamics of Faith. Even if all of the above is not true, the mere belief that religion or God is health enhancing may be enough to produce measurable effects. In other words, significant findings between religion and health outcomes, especially in prospective studies, may, in part, present evidence akin to a placebo effect. Various scriptures promise victory or survival to the faithful (e.g., Isaiah 54:17), and the physiological effects of expectant beliefs such as this are now being documented by mind-body researchers.

Multifactorial Explanation. Most likely, a combination of some or all of the above explanations helps to clarify statistically significant relationships between religion and health. For example, many studies show that Seventh-Day Adventists are considerably healthier than the members of other religious groups, especially in regard to hypertension. Taking into account the hypotheses outlined above, in order, this distinct advantage may be attributable to the following confluence of factors:

> The avoidance of meat (leading to low levels of dietary fat and cholesterol); the discouragement of intermarriage (supporting a trend toward selecting out of the population those persons predisposed to hypertension); an emphasis on family solidarity and religious fellowship (buffering the adverse physiological consequences of life stress and anxiety); a theological emphasis on self-responsibility and positive health-directedness (encouraging self-care and beneficial health-related behavior); a sense of trust and peace engendered both through expectations of God's directly transforming the world and through ritual experience of transformation through divine power (preventing or ameliorating state anxiety, hassles and uplifts, anger, etc.); and a sense of purpose and well-being because the worldview and piety of Adventists is believed to be promotive of health (reinforced by the relative lack of hypertension-related morbidity among co-religionists). (Levin & Vanderpool, 1989, p. 75)

Superempirical Force. Whereas the above hypotheses engage social, psychological, and biological phenomena or processes fairly well accepted by scientists, this hypothesis suggests that religious practice or belief or worship in some way taps or accesses a pantheistic, discarnate force or power. The term *superempirical* is used to distinguish it from the supernatural, which by definition cannot be measured because it is outside of nature. Superempirical is used to denote those realms that, ultimately, are not supernatural at all but are currently subject to controversy or mystery. Such a force or power goes by various names (prana, chi, orgone, odyle, etc.), and its existence and operation are central to such health related phenomena as the function of the chakras and nadis, the state of the etheric and astral bodies, the efficacy of pranayama exercises and Reiki healing, and so on. Some individuals (e.g., Motoyama, 1991), have reported success in measuring these superempirical forces, so perhaps they are no longer superempirical but empirical.

Supernatural Influence. The last possible hypothesis for religion-health associations is a supernatural explanation. In other words, a transcendent being who exists fully or partly outside of nature chooses when and why to endow or bless individuals with health or healing, presumably on the basis of their faithfulness. Whereas superempirical hypotheses can be scientifically explored, even if such research evokes controversy, this hypothesis, by definition, is outside the reach of humans, except when it is possible to rule out or control for all of the other hypotheses and still have a significant association remain. However, for the sake of completeness, this hypothesis must be listed alongside of other possible explanations.

What is so interesting about the Byrd study mentioned earlier is that his results clearly and without qualification point to one of these latter two explanations. Byrd, who is a devout Christian, believed that his results were convincing evidence of a supernatural influence. This is not true, for a superempirical explanation is also logically possible: His results may have been obtained not because God answered prayer but because the praying individuals unknowingly practiced absent healing by creating or accessing and then sending an energy to the patients, which promoted what Dossey (1989) has termed "nonlocal healing." Nonetheless, if Byrd's (1988) study and its findings were accurately portrayed in his article, then the true explanation for his results is indeed definitely one or the other (or both) of these two explanations.

Barriers to Research on
Religious Factors in Health

Despite the current success of this research program in terms of external funding, refereed publications, and publicity, many barriers were met during the formative stages of this work. These barriers involved some extraordinarily hostile reactions by anonymous journal referees and, in general, discouragement—even disparagement—from more senior scientists over pursuing this research. On the other hand, several mentors were extremely supportive and certain journals have been wide open to this work. Furthermore, despite the commonly heard complaint among many New Age scientists that the medical establishment will wickedly impede and prevent research that violates the tenets of current paradigms, the National Institutes of Health (NIH) have generously funded my religious research and the work of several others in this emergent field.

In the early days of this work (the early to middle 1980s), it was not unusual for review essays collating the hundreds of studies found in the literature to be rejected on the grounds that "everybody knows that religion doesn't affect health." The irony is that many of the studies reviewed had been published in the very journals that rejected the review papers on the basis that no such studies existed. The most humorous example came in a rejection by a preeminent epidemiology journal. In lieu of the conventional boilerplate in the cover letter, the editor felt the need to add his two cents' worth in a two-page, single-spaced commentary, the gist of which was that not only was our review unacceptable but the mere idea of an epidemiology of religion was "execrable." This is awfully strong language for what should have been a polite form letter. It was even more unusual considering that one of the two anonymous referees was very enthusiastic and recommended acceptance without revision.

This story is not told here out of sour grapes—every successful scientist can paper a wall with manuscript rejections. Rather, the ferocity that these anomalous findings provoked underscores the resistance in some quarters to new ideas. The irony is that the idea of a religious effect on health is not new at all, as evidenced by the hundreds of positive findings published over the years. It is as if mainstream epidemiology and allopathic medicine were in the throes of some sort of collective amnesia. Even though the health effects of religion have been considered in numerous studies and have been found to be significant, many scientists would rather not acknowledge these results and instead have taken a shoot-the-messenger approach.

> More frequently, though, religion goes unconsidered; epistemologically speaking, the domain and effects of "religious commitment" are believed to be unknowable or unreal or both. Western biomedicine, of which epidemiology is a part, is still wrestling with a body-mind dualism that defies consensus; thus, for most epidemiologists any resolution of a body-mind-spirit pluralism is simply beyond consideration. (Levin & Vanderpool, 1987, pp. 590-591)

Other barriers to the study of religious factors in health can be identified. Many of these barriers can be generalized to the study of the health effects of anomalous factors. Each of the following barriers has either been personally experienced by me or been recorded in the scientific literature.

Religion Is Unimportant. The idea that religion is unimportant represents a conflict of worldviews. In other words,

> struck by religion's seemingly nonsensical claims, and often escaping from or growing beyond the religious orientations of their childhoods, many researchers and medical professionals may feel that since religion means little to them personally, it must not be a very salient force generally. (Levin & Vanderpool, 1992, p. 87)

This disregard can precipitate disinterest, and the lack of basic religious knowledge can reach comic proportions. Once while I was in graduate school, a senior professor, curious about my research and about my Jewish beliefs and weekly trips to synagogue to study gematria with the rabbi, expressed amazement that a scientist could possibly be religious. "You mean you believe in Jesus and Mary and the Bible and all that?" Years later, I am still speechless.

Religion Is Not Real. The view that religion is not real is a patronizing approach. Here, the physician or scientist admits that although religion may matter to people, it is mainly a nuisance to be accommodated. In no way, though, could it actually promote healing or do anything other than get in the way. This particular attitude is simply wrong, scientifically. Hundreds of published studies demonstrate this to be so. Furthermore, this attitude also points out a reductionistic view of religion as something solely supernatural or otherworldly. Yet, as noted earlier, religion and religiousness impact various aspects of the natural history of disease—risk, etiology, diagnosis, treatment, and prognosis—by way of various behavioral, social, psychological, and biological processes. A physician or scientist need not profess belief in a supernatural being to acknowledge that religious experience impacts health status, for better or worse. Bertrand Russell, Albert Ellis, and Paul Kurtz, for example, although personally nonbelievers in religion, have noted the salience of religiosity in human life and the importance of studying its influences.

This Is Bad Science. Scientists who claim that "this is bad science" are apparently confusing what they believe as people, or what the current state of their discipline holds to be so, with the foundations of the scientific method. This leads to assertions, for example, that the mere asking of certain questions is "execrable." One letter writer responded to the *Southern Medical Journal*'s publication of the Byrd study by claiming that publicizing findings like these represents "an attempt to return medicine to the Dark Ages." In fact, Byrd's study represents just the opposite: It is a laudable effort to subject a widely held folk belief to scientific scrutiny, using the strictest experimental design. If hypotheses can be posited and tested, constructs defined and operationalized, and studies designed and conducted, then the study of anomalous factors such as religiosity is just as scientific as anything else.

This Goes Against My Training. To state that such studies go against one's training is not much of an argument, but it can be a formidable barrier. I once made an informal review of the various study guides used by medical students to prepare for their board exams. There are separate guides for each specialty or field, and several companies publish a full series of guides. An examination of the index of every study guide on behavioral science, psychiatry, and preventive medicine and public health turned up a single reference to religion—one mention of religion in one of these study guides. In this guide, *religiosity* was present in a list of clinical signs of psychopathology. It is little wonder that most of the research described in this paper would be considered strange or threatening. It bears mentioning, however, that any new, paradigm-challenging discovery or knowledge almost has to have gone against the prevailing wisdom, by definition.

This Will Only Encourage the Clergy. There is some fear that publicizing findings such as these will lead to changes in approaches to prevention, health care delivery, and patient care (as if the current health care system were in no need of change). This has some people very worried, and even the activities of hospital chaplains have been described in adversarial terms. One program was expressly set up to address physicians' concern over the clergy's "inability to respond adequately when confronted with a hospital stress situation" because certain acute problems may "affront their orthodoxy" (Kasanof, 1970, p. 211). Pastors were taught to be "careful not to exceed their duty and enter the physician's domain" (p. 214). It is debatable just whose orthodoxy was being affronted.

Conclusion

Despite the barriers that were encountered, I was ultimately successful in establishing a program of research. Two key reasons for this success were perseverance and an upgrading of methodological and statistical knowledge. Through an NIH-funded postdoctoral fellowship, I was trained in a variety of high-tech, multivariate causal modeling procedures, principally covariance structure modeling (or LISREL analysis). This training enabled me to speak the language of the most sophisticated social scientists and survey researchers.

A major problem with prior research on religion and health has been a prevailing weakness, even ineptitude, of study design, methods, and data analysis. These problems detract from the substantive value of the studies and allow findings to be easily dismissed. Accordingly, this field would benefit from more attention to issues such as measurement error, formulation of sound midrange theories and hypotheses, specification of multifactorial models, and use of prospective and panel designs (Levin, 1989). (These issues are described in greater detail in Chapter 8.) As these advances have begun to be made, especially in gerontological studies of religion and health, the perceived marginality and anomalousness of this research has begun to fade. The most visible outcome has been a proliferation of excellent publications in top-line aging journals by a growing cadre of researchers.

Another result of the growing methodological sophistication of researchers in this area has been the ability to secure external funding from NIH for empirical research. Both the National Institute on Aging and the National Institute of Mental Health have funded studies of the effects of religious involvement on physical and mental health, psychological well-being, and other social and psychological processes or outcomes related to the aging process or to older adulthood. My FIRST Award grant was funded on its initial submission after review by a specially convened ad hoc study group. This submission was successful for three reasons.

First, I worked hard and persevered for several years before submitting the proposal, often sacrificing nights and weekends. I also published many review essays and speculative pieces that established my credibility as a candidate for an NIH grant in this area. Second, by upgrading my methodological and statistical skills, I demonstrated to NIH that whatever publications were produced by this study promised to be no less sophisticated and rigorously prepared than the state of the art of current research in the sociomedical sciences. Finally, my proposal was not solely pitched as a study of religion and health. Rather, it addressed current NIH initiatives and areas of interest, such as minority aging, and health and effective functioning in older adults. Therefore, although certain of the substantive issues broached in my research may be unusual, the project itself is squarely in the mainstream of aging research. Furthermore, in my publications from this project, the statistical associations reported between religion and health are described with explicit reference to their social and health services applications (Levin & Vanderpool, 1992).

It is presumtuous to believe that NIH or NSF are duty-bound to fund basic research on every poorly conceived or unsubstantiated alternative concept or therapy that someone somewhere thinks might benefit health or promote healing. Furthermore, it does little good to blame NIH or the AMA or the FDA or the pharmaceutical industry for the perceived marginality of certain unusual areas of medical research. The burden is on the prospective investigator to establish the appropriate credentials and track record, design a credible study, and state clearly the clinical or practical applications of expected findings. The remaining chapters in this book provide some theoretical and methodological guidelines for researchers seeking to advance this field.

References

Byrd, R. C. (1988). Positive therapeutic effects of intercessory prayer in a coronary care unit population. *Southern Medical Journal, 81,* 826-829.

Dossey, L. (1989). *Recovering the soul: A scientific and spiritual search.* New York: Bantam.

Greeley, A. M. (1975). *The sociology of the paranormal: A reconnaissance.* Beverly Hills, CA: Sage.

House, J. S., Landis, K. R., & Umberson, D. (1988). Social relationships and health. *Science, 241,* 540-545.

Jarvis, G. K., & Northcutt, H. C. (1987). Religion and differences in morbidity and mortality. *Social Science and Medicine, 25,* 813-824.

Kasanof, D. (1970, March 2). Clergy can be bad medicine. *Medical Economics*, pp. 211-215.

Koenig, H. G. (1990). Research on religion and mental health in later life: A review and commentary. *Journal of Geriatric Psychiatry, 23*, 23-53.

Levin, J. S. (1989). Religious factors in aging, adjustment, and health: A theoretical overview. In W. M. Clements (Ed.), *Religion, aging and health: A global perspective* (pp. 133-146). New York: Haworth Press.

Levin, J. S. (1993). Age differences in mystical experience. *The Gerontologist, 33*, 507-513.

Levin, J. S., Chatters, L. M., Taylor, R. J., & Jackson, J. S. (1989, July 13). *Religiosity, health, and life satisfaction in black Americans.* Paper presented at the Annual Meeting of the American Psychological Association, New Orleans.

Levin, J. S., Jenkins, C. D., & Rose, R. M. (1988). Religion, Type A behavior, and health. *Journal of Religion and Health, 27*, 267-278.

Levin, J. S., Lyons, J. S., & Larson, D. B. (in press). Prayer and health during pregnancy: Findings from the GLOWBS study. *Southern Medical Journal.*

Levin, J. S., & Markides, K. S. (1985). Religion and health in Mexican Americans. *Journal of Religion and Health, 24*, 60-69.

Levin, J. S., & Markides, K. S. (1986). Religious attendance and subjective health. *Journal for the Scientific Study of Religion, 25*, 31-40.

Levin, J. S., & Markides, K. S. (1988). Religious attendance and psychological well-being in middle-aged and older Mexican Americans. *Sociological Analysis, 49*, 66-72.

Levin, J. S., & Schiller, P. L. (1986). Religion and the multidimensional health locus of control scales. *Psychological Reports, 59*, 26.

Levin, J. S., & Schiller, P. L. (1987). Is there a religious factor in health? *Journal of Religion and Health, 26*, 9-36.

Levin, J. S., & Vanderpool, H. Y. (1987). Is frequent religious attendance *really* conducive to better health?: Toward an epidemiology of religion. *Social Science and Medicine, 24*, 589-600.

Levin, J. S., & Vanderpool, H. Y. (1989). Is religion therapeutically significant for hypertension? *Social Science and Medicine, 29*, 69-78.

Levin, J. S., & Vanderpool, H. Y. (1992). Religious factors in physical health and the prevention of illness. In K. I. Pargament, K. I. Maton, & R. E. Hess (Eds.), *Religion and prevention in mental health: Research, vision, and action* (pp. 83-103). New York: Haworth Press.

Liang, J., & Whitelaw, N. A. (1990). Assessing the physical and mental health of the elderly. In S. M. Stahl (Ed.), *The legacy of longevity: Health and health care in later life* (pp. 35-54). Newbury Park, CA: Sage.

Markides, K. S., Levin, J. S., & Ray, L. A. (1987). Religion, aging, and life satisfaction: An eight-year, three-wave longitudinal study. *The Gerontologist, 27*, 660-665.

Motoyama, H. (1991). *The correlation between psi energy and ki: Unification of religion and science.* Tokyo: Human Science Press.

Schiller, P. L., & Levin, J. S. (1988). Is there a religious factor in health care utilization?: A review. *Social Science and Medicine, 27*, 1369-1379.

Spector, R. E. (1979). *Cultural diversity in health and illness.* New York: Appleton-Century-Crofts.

Witter, R. A., Stock, W. A., Okun, M. A., & Haring, M. J. (1985). Religion and subjective well-being in adulthood: A quantitative synthesis. *Review of Religious Research, 26*, 332-342.

2

Religion and Hope for the Disabled Elder

HAROLD G. KOENIG

To know how to grow old is the master work of wisdom and one of the most difficult chapters in the great art of living.

—Henri Amiel

Ann and Sally

"Oh, what a beautiful morning!" exclaimed Ann, as she stepped lightly onto the trail that would take her through the forest, down the hill, around the lake, and back to her home. Her morning walk was a special time. It typically began about 5 a.m. just before the sun came up. The world was so serene and peaceful at this time of the day. As Ann walked briskly along, she could see several stars and a crescent moon hanging just above the horizon; they became dimmer and dimmer as the light of dawn filled the sky. She could hear the crow of a rooster at a nearby farmhouse, the rustle of squirrels chasing each other in the underbrush, and the chatter of blue jays in the old oak trees along the path. She loved these early morning sounds. They carried her back to childhood days.

AUTHOR'S NOTE: Funding was provided by the Center for the Study of Aging and Human Development, Duke University Medical Center under Grant No. AG00371 and by the Geriatric Research, Education, and Clinical Center, Durham, NC.

As Ann emerged from the forest, a ray of sunlight burst forth on the horizon and lit the rolling hills with an orange, misty hue. She felt invigorated as she strolled briskly along the 2-mile route. Her mind was full of making plans for the day.

"I mustn't forget to take the turkey out of the freezer," she said aloud to herself, as she thought of the family gathering that was planned that afternoon. Her son and two daughters were coming for supper. Along with them would be four grandchildren, who always brightened her day with their seemingly inexhaustible store of energy. Although preparing for them was a lot of work, she enjoyed it immensely. After supper, they would beg her to tell them stories about what the world was like back in the days when she was a young girl. Robert, her husband, was a great help on days like this. He would pitch in with cleaning up the house, setting the table, and clearing the dishes after supper while Ann went off with the grandchildren. Because he was more of a night person than his wife, Robert was still in bed this morning. He preferred an early evening jog to a morning walk. Both Robert and Ann were in their middle 70s, in good health, financially secure, with many friends and three children who lived nearby. Until he retired 5 years earlier, Robert had worked for the government. His pension, along with a healthy savings they had accumulated over the years, allowed them to live quite comfortably.

Ann picked up her pace. It was Sunday, and she didn't want to be late for church that morning. The sermon would probably be long and boring, but she looked forward to having brunch with their friends after church. She rounded the bend and came in view of the home place. Their house was about 20 years old, had four bedrooms, a sunken living room, formal dining room, and spacious screened-in back porch; it was ideal for entertaining guests, as they were accustomed to doing. They owned the 5 acres surrounding the house, and Ann had planted a large garden that year with sweet corn, beans, and tomatoes, some of which she would now pick for the family supper. After gathering the vegetables, she entered into the kitchen where her husband was drinking coffee and reading the morning paper. She set the corn and tomatoes down, and fell into the chair next to Robert. "Oh what a beautiful morning," she repeated somewhat breathlessly. She kissed her husband lightly on the cheek.

Robert was preoccupied reading the obituary column, but responded to his wife's presence by a loving pat on her hand. "Good morning, Ann. How was your walk?" Not waiting for a response, he continued. "Did you know that Sally Jackson died yesterday?"

"No!" Ann exclaimed, her mind suddenly filling with thoughts and emotions. After a moment, in a low voice, she said, "I guess it's a blessing."

Sally and Ann had been friends since their teens. They were the same age, attended the same high school, and were members of the same church. After graduation, they had both married and raised families. Their husbands were also good friends, and they frequently went out as couples. Over the past 10 years, however, things had changed.

Sally had not been as fortunate as Ann in her later years. Bill, her husband of 45 years, had died 10 years earlier of a heart attack, leaving Sally a widow at the age of 64. They had two children and several grandchildren, but the family was not close. Both children lived in distant cities, were preoccupied with their own affairs, and only infrequently visited or called. Sally did not cope well with the loss of her husband, whom she had depended on heavily throughout their marriage. Handling finances and keeping things up around the house and yard were difficult for her. After Bill's death, Sally reduced her social activity because things just weren't the same without him. Although her old friends kept inviting her to go places with them, most were still married and she felt out of place (and perhaps a bit envious). Sally spent most of her time alone at home, listening to music, reading, watching television, or working in the garden. She, like Ann, enjoyed early morning walks. The beauties of nature would help take the edge off the loneliness since her husband's death. Sally was also an avid bird-watcher, a hobby she and Bill shared together for many years.

About 6 years after Bill's death, soon after turning age 70, Sally's health began to fail. Her eyesight dimmed—"macular degeneration" the doctor had called it. He had told her that this eye disease was common in later life and did not have a cure. Soon she could no longer see well enough to read the paper or her favorite magazines. Bird-watching became difficult and the moon and stars in the early morning sky became a blur. Finally, her doctor said she would have to stop driving. This news shocked and upset her. How would she get her groceries and other supplies needed around the house? How could she get to church each week and maintain her social relationships there?

Not long after this, Sally's hearing also began to deteriorate. As a young adult, she had worked in a local cannery where the noise level was high and ear plugs were scarce. The hearing specialist had told her that this noise exposure and just getting older were probably responsible. The hearing problem continued to worsen. Sally eventually stopped going to church. In addition to having transportation problems, she could no longer hear the preacher well enough to follow the sermon; furthermore, she could not understand conversational speech well enough now to participate in the social hour after the service. As the hearing deficit worsened, she began to have difficulty distinguishing the bird calls in the forest from other background noises. When Ann would visit, Sally would ask her, "Why is all this happening to me?"

Ann would respond, "We're getting older."

As if the problems with sight and hearing were not enough, Sally then began having increasing pain from arthritis in the shoulder and knee. This limited activity at home made gardening difficult and restricted her morning walks. Despite arthritis medicine, the joint pains gradually worsened and disability increased to the point that she became essentially homebound. Sally continued to live independently, however, by hiring an aide to help with the housework, laundry, and meal preparation.

As time passed, Sally's financial situation gradually worsened. The doctor bills, cost of medication, occasional hospitalizations, and the in-home help drained a meager savings that her husband, Bill, had left her. Soon she could no longer afford to hire an aide to come in each day. Unable to maintain her house, she sold it and moved into a low-cost apartment. The move was hard. Sally had lived in the old house for almost 40 years; she had raised her children there. The apartment she moved into had two rooms, a kitchen, and a combination bedroom-living room. She seldom left the apartment. Her arthritis and dimming vision made it difficult for her to get out, even for shopping; a local store, however, made an arrangement to deliver her groceries. For a while, Sally was able to manage. Life was not easy, though. It became increasingly difficult to bathe and dress herself. Sally had trouble standing in the shower because of the discomfort in her knees and hips. She would struggle with the buttons on her clothes. Sally could no longer bend to put on her socks and tie her shoe laces. Because of shoulder pain, even combing her hair and brushing her teeth became uncomfortable chores. Life was a battle from the moment she got up in the morning until the moment she retired at night.

Sally's world was rapidly shrinking. She became further isolated from others. There was little contact with her children. Even calls from them on Christmas and Easter were frustrating because she had to struggle to understand their speech. Her ability to live independently was becoming less and less feasible, and she had no close relative or friend willing to take her in. Because of her poor vision and worsening arthritis, she spent most of each day sitting in a sofa chair by the window. A social worker came to visit one day. She found the apartment a mess and Sally unkept and smelling of urine. Arrangements were made for admission to a local nursing home.

At the nursing home, life was different from anything Sally had ever experienced. She shared a room with another elderly woman with advanced Alzheimer's disease, who would go through her clothes and mess up her bed, unaware of what she was doing. At this point, Sally could do little for herself and was almost totally dependent on the nursing staff for bathing, dressing, and transfer in and out of the wheel chair. Nevertheless, she was still alert and aware of her surroundings. It was in this dismal state that Sally had been for the past 2 years. Ann and Robert would visit her on occasion but did not stay long because of the difficulty communicating with her. They also felt somewhat uneasy for another reason. Sally reminded them of their own increasing vulnerability. Nevertheless, Ann and Robert kept coming, because they knew she had few other visitors.

Every day was the same for Sally: morning bath, sit up in the day room, lunch, back to bed for several hours, up in the wheelchair, supper, and back to her room. When the home was short-staffed, she might be left sitting for hours in the wheelchair suffering pain and stiffness from lack of movement. One day the nursing staff discovered a bed sore on her backside. They urged her to do more for herself. She tried, but just didn't seem to have the energy and will to move about when it was so difficult and all so meaningless. Some staff members said she didn't try hard enough, that she really wasn't in all that much discomfort, and that she exaggerated her complaints. This attitude bothered her more than anything; she was burdened not only with the limitations of her condition but also with the insensitivity of caretakers who treated her like she was lazy and faking her symptoms. At night she would lie awake, thinking about the past and dreading her future. She had lost all sense of control and self-determination. She was helpless and dependent. Other people told her when to eat, when to sleep, when she had to bathe, when to sit up and lie down. There was nothing to look forward to anymore.

Sally's despondency deepened as her hope for a better life slowly extinguished. She became bitter and lost all desire to help herself. Her doctor, diagnosing depression, prescribed an antidepressant; she could not tolerate the side effects, however, so it was discontinued. She was admitted to the hospital for electroconvulsive therapy. Sally responded for brief periods, but each time she returned to the home, her symptoms reappeared. She longed for an end to it all. Sally's will to live was gone. The physical and emotional pain had become too much to bear. She begged God to let her die. She was a burden on others and served no useful purpose in this world. On Saturday, her wish was granted. Indeed, her death was a blessing, as Ann had observed.

Sovereign my master the old age is here, senility has descended in me, the weakness of my childhood is renewed, so I sleep all the time. The arms are weak, the legs have given up following the heart that has become tired. The mouth is mute, it can no longer speak, the eyes are weak, the ears are deaf, the nose is blocked, it can no longer breathe. The taste is completely gone. The spirit is forgetful. It can no longer remember yesterday. The bones ache in the old age, getting up and sitting down are both difficult. What was nice has become bad. (Ptah Haty, 7th century B.C., quoted in Loza & Milad, 1989)

Problems in Later Life

The stories of Ann and Sally contrast the lives of two older adults, one who appeared to be successfully aging and the other who was not. The many different circumstances in which elderly persons find themselves, however, make neither of these two stories that uncommon. Let us now take a look at just how prevalent disease and disability are in later life and explore psychosocial and medical sources of hope.

Studies have shown that later life is a time characterized by tremendous physical and psychological heterogeneity. Indeed, some elders experience little physical disability or hardship. They remain active, financially secure, socially involved, and surrounded by loving family members, fully enjoying their retirement years. In fact, the majority of persons age 65 or over are healthy (66% with no disability that affects a major activity), married (75% of men; 45% of women), and financially secure (Neugarten, 1968).

On the other hand, a very large number of elders are beset with disability, chronic medical or neurological illnesses, and/or psychosocial difficulties. Neurological changes in the brain with aging result in a loss of 30% to 60% of cortical neurons at a rate of about 1% per year after the age of 60 (Anderson, Hubbard, Coghill, & Slidders, 1983; Henderson, Tomlinson, & Gibson, 1980; Victoroff, 1991). Consequently, age-associated declines may appear in attention, memory, language, and spatial performance (Binks, 1989; Kirasic & Allen, 1985; Plude &

Hoyer, 1985). The changes associated with normal aging are accentuated by the changes in cognitive functioning from illness. A recent community study indicated that among elders living beyond age 85, almost 50% had Alzheimer's disease (Evans et al., 1989).

Physical function also declines as a consequence of both aging and disease. According to reports from the National Institute on Aging, more than 32% of people over age 75 are unable to climb stairs, 40% are unable to walk two blocks, 7% cannot walk across a small room, and 22% cannot lift 10 pounds. Among elders hospitalized with medical illness, Hirsch, Sommers, Olsen, Mjullen, and Winograd (1990) found that 76% needed help or supervision with four or more activities of daily living, including 51% with incontinence of either stool or urine. Of special concern was that by discharge, 67% showed no improvement and 10% experienced further deterioration. In 1985, the National Nursing Home Survey found that among institutionalized elders, more than 90% require help with bathing, 76% with dressing, 62% with transfer from bed to wheel chair, 51% with toileting, and 38% with eating (Wiener, Hanley, Clark, & Van Nostrand, 1990). Although only 5% of elders are currently living in nursing homes, 20% to 25% of persons who survive to age 65 will spend some time there; almost 50% of women will do so, who represent 75% of all nursing home patients (American Association of Retired Persons [AARP], 1989a).

Financial hardship often compounds and complicates health disabilities, particularly among women and minority groups such as blacks. Nearly 50% of women over age 65 are widows (U.S. Bureau of the Census, 1989a). For women age 65 or over, the median income (including earnings, Social Security, pensions, and assets) in 1987 was $6,734 (just more than half the median income of elderly men); for elderly black women, median yearly income was only $4,691 (U.S. Bureau of the Census, 1989b). A total of 35% of elderly unmarried women depend on Social Security for 90% or more of their income (Grad, 1988). In 1986, Medicare paid for only 33% of the total health care expenditures for unmarried women over age 65 (compared with about 50% for elderly men) (Older Women's League, 1987). Approximately 75% of informal caregivers are women, who average 46 years of age (AARP, 1989b).

The costs of long-term care can quickly dissipate even the most comfortable retirement savings. In 1989, Americans spent $48 billion on skilled nursing home care, which on the average cost $30,000 per year (AARP, 1991a). Medicaid paid about $20.6 billion of this figure, private health insurance about $500 million, and private sources and government programs about $1.9 billion. Medicare paid less than $4 billion, and nursing home residents and their families paid the remaining $21.3 billion (AARP, 1991a). Thus, contrary to most persons' expectations and beliefs, as long as the elders have any money at all left, the great bulk of nursing home costs rests on them and their families. By the year 2030, the need for skilled nursing care will double—reaching an annual cost of nearly $100 billion.

Social resources also diminish with aging, as family members and friends die or move away. A total of 30.5% of all older households are made up of elderly persons who live alone. Among persons age 75 to 84, 38.2% live alone; among those age 85 or older, 47% live alone (AARP, 1991b). Elderly women make up 78% of those who live alone. The problem of finances adds to social isolation among those who live alone, especially older blacks (72% living below 125% of poverty) and elders in rural areas (45% below 125% of poverty). When such persons become ill or are no longer able to care for their needs independently, they rely heavily on other family members, particularly children. In today's mobile society, however, adult children often move away from parents. Approximately 43% of elderly persons who live alone have no children living nearby, and 27% have no living children at all (AARP, 1991b). When they become disabled, there is often little choice but to move to a nursing home.

Psychological Reactions
to Physical Disability

Loss of physical function often has an enormous psychological impact. Perhaps only those actually experiencing loss of health and independence can appreciate this. Losses at this time, even though expected, can be especially distressing because they are frequently permanent and irreversible. Thus a stroke may forever take away the ability to garden or perform other activities that gave life meaning and joy. Loss of hearing can prevent a person from ever enjoying the sound of their favorite song again; it can destroy communication, impair ability to socialize, and isolate the individual from loved ones and friends. An eye disease can irreversibly impair sight and eliminate the ability to read, watch television, or enjoy the sights of nature ever again. These losses are imposed at a time when the elder is often struggling with other issues. Achieving integrity, the final Eriksonian life task, may already be impaired because of unsuccessful resolution of earlier psychological tasks. Health problems only complicate the situation. Although many elders manage to cope amazingly well in spite of these obstacles, others have a difficult time doing so. The amount of suffering can be great, and the conclusion that there is little hope for better times in the future may be a realistic fact.

Consequently, it is not surprising that more than 25% of older adults living in the community (Blazer, Hughes, & George, 1987) and almost 50% of those hospitalized or living in nursing homes (Koenig, Meador, Cohen, & Blazer, 1988; Parmelee, Katz, & Lawton, 1989) experience some degree of depression. Among institutionalized elders, severe despondency and withdrawal in the form of a major depression occurs in 12% to 16% of patients (Koenig et al., 1991; Parmelee et al., 1989; Rovner, 1991; Weissman, Bruce, Leaf, Florio, & Holzer, 1991). These rates would be even higher in nursing homes if it were not for the fact that nearly 50% of residents have severe cognitive impairment that interferes with their ability to appreciate the dismal nature of their circumstances. Thus, whereas old age may represent the "golden years" for some, this is clearly not the case for many others. What sources of hope are there for elders like Sally?

Sources of Hope

Medical Advances

Advances in medical research offer hope for treating visual, hearing, and other functional problems associated with aging. New pain medications and treatments that halt or reverse the progression of arthritis or stroke may someday provide relief to those suffering from these conditions. Medical science hopes to achieve a "rectangularization" of the survival curve, by which people would live relatively free of disease until a certain age (85 or 90 years), at which time they would experience massive organ system failure over a short period and die (like the one-horse sleigh that fell apart completely in one moment of one day). Lingering with chronic illness would be a rarity. The postponement of illness until just before death, however, is a highly optimistic goal. In reality, effective medical treatments for many chronic conditions are a long way off, and many of us alive today will never see them. Some illnesses may, in fact, be untreatable. For example, despite $120 million per year spent on Alzheimer's disease research in this country, progress has been slow and disappointing.

Even when new treatments are discovered, there is no guarantee that their cost will be in the range affordable to most elders. Already, one-third of the U.S. health budget is spent on care for the elderly, and lawmakers are searching for ways to cut costs and limit expenditures, not expand services to this age group (U.S. Senate, 1987-1988). Given that the number of persons age 65 or over in this country will double in the next 25 to 30 years, it is doubtful that all older persons will have unlimited health care and full access to new, expensive treatments. Thus older persons are likely to experience chronic illness and suffer irreversible functional disability for a long time to come.

Primary Prevention

If disability and chronic illness cannot be cured or delayed, perhaps they can be avoided. Healthy behaviors in earlier and later life may help prevent functional disabilities or at least postpone them to some extent. For instance, cessation of smoking, healthy eating habits, attention to weight and cholesterol level, and regular relaxation and exercise may help to lessen the chances of stroke and stroke-related cognitive decline. Avoidance of heavy alcohol or drug use may also reduce the likelihood of adverse late-life sequelae such as liver disease and alcohol-related dementia. Nevertheless, many diseases are hereditary, degenerative, immunological, or infectious in origin (Alzheimer's disease, Parkinson's disease, arthritis, and some cancers); individual behaviors probably have little impact on these conditions. Likewise, everyone probably knows at least one person who exercised, ate a balanced diet, and compulsively watched his or her cholesterol, who was diagnosed with cancer or had a heart attack in their mid 50s or 60s or developed cognitive impairment at an early age. Thus, although having a healthy lifestyle can reduce the chances of disability in late life, it can by no means eliminate them.

Psychological Treatments

If we are unable to cure or prevent many disabling conditions, then elders for now must learn to cope with these conditions the best way they can. Because of an inherited vulnerability, unresolved conflicts from earlier life, and/or severe current life stressors, some may become overwhelmed to the point that they require outside assistance. Psychological therapies help in such circumstances. Psychiatrists, psychologists, or social workers can help elders change their attitudes, negative thought patterns, and/or self-destructive behaviors; elders can be taught to reframe difficult situations in a more positive light (Sadavoy & Leszcz, 1987; Thompson, Gallagher, & Breckinridge, 1987). Psychological therapies, however, often take time to be effective, may not always work, and are not always acceptable to older adults. Likewise, they can be quite expensive; the typical cost of outpatient treatment is about $100 per hour, thus reserving most of such therapy for only the rich or those with insurance.

Environmental Manipulations

Much of the suffering from chronic disability can be relieved by correcting weaknesses in the current system of long-term care. Institutional personnel, caretakers, and family members can be taught the importance of giving patients as much control and self-determination as possible. If able to make even small decisions about their care, elders will experience increased self-esteem and satisfaction with life. Being able to determine when a bath will take place, when and how long to sit up in a chair, when to go to bed at night and get up in the morning, can give the elder at least a minimal sense of autonomy and self-direction. Indeed, allowing the patient to make such decisions should be considered a vital aspect of medical treatment, as important as administering a daily heart pill or insulin injection. Again, however, pressure to limit expenditures has caused a shortage of nursing home staff, making it impractical to allow patients to make such decisions. When there is a single nursing aide for 30 or 40 patients and 90% need a bath, 40% need to be fed, 80% need to be put up in a chair, and all the beds have to be made, even the most dedicated and responsible staff member will be hard pressed to find time for inquiring about or instituting patient preferences.

Family and Friends

Loved ones are frequently a source of hope for many disabled elders. Often the key to an older person remaining in his or her home is the presence of a concerned family member willing to provide the necessary assistance and physical care. This often ends up being a daughter or daughter-in-law who may have children and a family of her own or may even be elderly and frail herself. Because many older persons are upset over being dependent and frustrated by their disabilities, they may be irritable and difficult to care for. Thus relatives not infrequently burn out or become overwhelmed by the responsibilities that are thrust on them. This usually results in nursing home placement. Elders may then become angry at loved ones for abandoning them and cut them off psychologically. Visits from family members are then met with bitter resentment or silence, discouraging any further efforts by relatives to be supportive. Alternatively, endless complaints may be made in an attempt to elicit pity or guilt to increase the frequency of visits.

Most complaints by disabled elders are legitimate and without malice or intention to manipulate others. Many discuss their troubles in an attempt to find someone who understands and can help them carry the truly enormous burdens they may have to shoulder. After a while, however, family and friends frequently get tired of hearing the elder's complaints, and either decrease visits or discourage the patient from discussing their problems. Some patients are aware of this and, there-fore, tend to avoid talking about their illnesses. They come to realize that it is futile to complain about their suffering to others, because others have only limited interest in their problems and may be driven away by a rehearsal of woes. In fact, caretakers may accuse patients of exaggerating their pain; this is often done to relieve the anxiety and helplessness that caretakers feel when exposed to such suffering. This frequently has the desired effect of decreasing further discussions. To listen and empathize with another's pain means to share in and take on oneself some of the burden of that pain. While relatives and friends typically make truly heroic efforts in this regard, many others are not willing to do so.

In the end, neither medical advances, healthy lifestyles, psychologi-cal therapies, environmental manipulations, nor even the support of loved ones can make up for the tremendous physical and social losses that can occur with aging and illness. Much of the burden remains on the older adult. It is a burden that must be carried every waking moment of every day. Many elders like Sally need a source of hope greater than that which either health professional or family can provide.

Elders like Sally in this world demand a response. Mental health professionals are often called on to provide that response, whether they are prepared to do so or not. Although physical health problems provide the background for Sally's demise, psychological issues play a distinct role in directing her downward course. To address problems like hers, we need to uncover all resources, explore all possible avenues of help.

One resource, perhaps the oldest and most often used throughout history, is religion.

Religion and Hope

What does religion have to offer the Sallys of this world? A great deal, I believe. The degree of hope and emotional strength afforded by religion to some older adults may far exceed that obtainable from other sources. This is particularly true in situations in which health, wealth, or love of others is lacking or insufficient to meet needs. Through a system of beliefs and ritual activities, religion provides a mechanism by which attitudes can be changed and life circumstances reframed. Furthermore, the activation of religion's positive effects is more dependent on the person's own will than on the actions or intentions of others.

When persons encounter suffering of the magnitude experienced by Sally, however, some may turn away from God in frustration or anger. Rather than seek him for support, a common first reaction is to blame God. Indeed, it is difficult to understand the reason for the tremendous difference in fortune that befalls elders like Ann and Sally in this world. Feelings of anger and of being deserted by God are a natural and normal part of the grieving process; they must be discussed and gotten out in the open. However, if an elder gets stuck in his or her anger against God by dwelling on the "why," this can prevent him or her from experiencing the tremendous comfort that religion can provide.

Suffering and the
Judeo-Christian Tradition

Nowhere does the Bible underestimate the difficulties of growing old. Here are some aspects of the Judeo-Christian religions that make them especially relevant to the elder who is suffering from a physical disability:

1. Emphasis on interpersonal relations
2. Stress on seeking forgiveness
3. Provision of hope for change
4. Emphasis on forgiving others and oneself
5. Provision of hope for healing
6. Provision of a paradigm for suffering
7. Provision of role models for suffering
8. Emphasis on sense of control and self-determination

9. Promise of life after death
10. Promise of ready accessibility
11. Provision of a supportive community

Interpersonal Relations

There is a natural tendency for those overwhelmed by emotional or physical pain to either withdraw from or cling desperately to others. Judeo-Christian teachings encourage balance in interpersonal relations and provide guidelines to bring this about. The proscription is the following: " 'Love the Lord your God with all your heart, and with all your soul, and with all your mind.' This is the first and greatest commandment. And the second is like it, 'Love your neighbor as yourself' " (Matthew 22:37-39).[1] The order presented here is crucial. The first and most important command is to love God. If this first step is skipped or neglected, it may be difficult to accomplish the second. Although the command to love others as oneself is given almost equal importance to the first command ("the second is like it"), it still comes after the command to love God.

It is very, very difficult for a person to give love to or receive love from another, unless he or she has at least a rudimentary level of self-esteem (i.e., thinks well of himself or herself). Paradoxically, however, to have esteem for oneself a person must have experienced the love of another person; such love out of which self-esteem grows is conveyed in early life by a parent or parentlike figure. People who have not had this experience, and consequently do not feel good about themselves, spend most of their energy and time trying to manipulate others into providing them with this feeling. These people have no sense of worth independent of how others see them. Because of an exaggerated, urgent need for approval and acceptance by others, they are unable to function well in interpersonal relationships that require a balance of giving and receiving. The Judeo-Christian scriptures indicate that whether or not an individual has received love from another person, he or she can always obtain emotional fulfillment from a relationship with God. Having been made complete, the person becomes freer to give to others without requiring something in return. Loving others then becomes an act of worship and obedience to God, rather than a desperate attempt to affirm one's own lovability. Caring in this way, rather than depleting one's emotional resources, generates more love to give. Now, how can these ideas bring hope to disabled elders?

Much of the emotional pain associated with severe disability is the result of the actual or perceived loss of love, esteem, and value by others. Disabled elders may see themselves (and be seen by others) as no longer being able to do their share. The hard and basic fact is that they can no longer produce, and productivity in this society is equivalent to value. Take, for instance, the partially deaf elder who has difficulty communicating with others. Eventually, others may stop including that person in their social group because of the effort required to interact with him or her. Another example is the elder with a stroke who must depend on others to help him or her get about. Because the disabled persons cannot participate fully in the relationship, they are less likely to be asked by their friends to go out to dinner or go to a public event—unless that person can provide something in the relationship that equals or makes up for the effort required by others to include them (i.e., pay for the dinner, provide a car for transportation to the event, offer pleasant companionship, and so forth). If the disabled persons cannot provide such compensation (because of their level of dysfunction or because of depression or discouragement), then others will not include them on a regular basis unless those persons are motivated by other concerns (altruism, guilt, a previously established emotional bond, or family ties). What does a person like Sally have to offer others for the love and esteem that she desperately needs? When she came to the conclusion that she indeed had nothing to offer and was only a burden on others, she decided that life was not worth living. Sally lost all hope of ever again obtaining the love and esteem of others that she needed to feel worthwhile and to give life meaning. This is where religion can be of assistance. No matter how disabled or dependent an elder is, as long as he or she has cognitive awareness and a sense of will, that person can always turn his or her thoughts toward God and establish a loving relationship with him. Acting out the first commandment, then, can be a powerful source of love and self-esteem.

Recall that according to Judeo-Christian scriptures, this is the first step before individuals can truly love themselves or others in an unconditional manner. Out of a love relationship with God, then, the elder may begin to feel that he or she is worthwhile and is an important and vital part of this world. *World* here can even be a small room in a crowded nursing home. Scripture gives a true basis for value that is independent of personal productivity. Feeling valued by the creator of the universe, then, may provide a sense of self-worth that may enable elders to reach out and love others.

There are many acts of love that even the most dependent and functionally disabled elder can perform. Opportunities to minister surround the person on every side: a kind word of thanks and a heartfelt smile to an overworked nursing aide who has just given the daily bath, a kind word or gesture to a visitor or a relative, and taking a moment to listen to the complaints of or encourage a fellow patient. When one feels that he or she has purpose and meaning, opportunities for love and kindness start opening up everywhere, whether in a nursing home, an acute care hospital, or at home. Such actions strongly reinforce themselves. Acts of love, support, or encouragement toward others distract the elder from his or her own problems. Rather than drive caretakers away, such behaviors act as a magnet to draw people closer and make their work easier. Such actions further give a sense of purpose and meaning to existence, and truly make the elder less of a burden on others—even if severely disabled and completely dependent. Caregiver stress seldom results from the actual physical burden of care; rather it results from the emotional distress brought on by continual contact with someone who is bitter, complaining, or ungrateful.

As noted before, however, the capacity to love and give to others—especially when these actions do not come naturally—depends heavily on experiencing and receiving God's love. According to scriptures, God's love can be experienced during times of intimate communication during prayer or worship. Reading passages from scripture that speak of the tremendous value of each person to God, can be uplifting and help convey a sense of worth and self-esteem independent of functional ability (see, e.g., Acts 20:24; Deuteronomy 14:2, 23:5, 31:6, 32:10-13, 33:3; Ephesians 3:17-19; Exodus 4:21, 19:4-6, 29:4-5; Ezekiel 34:29-31, 36:24-28, 37:26-28; Galatians 4:6; Genesis 50:24; Hebrews 13:5; Isaiah 43:1-4, 49:14-15; James 1:18, 3:9; I John 3:1, 16-18, 4:10; Leviticus 26:12; Luke 12:6, 15:4-10; Matthew 10:29, 30; Psalms 8:4-8; Romans 8:15). These scriptures provide a true and constant basis for human value—a value that is not easily achieved in a purely secular system that views humans as highly evolved animals in a world where only the fittest survive.

Closer Than a Brother (Winter, 1973) is a contemporary revision of the 17th-century classic, *Practicing the Presence of God*. It provides instructions in simple language about how to train oneself to turn one's thoughts to God throughout the day to experience God's love on a more constant basis:

> And I practice this all the time—thinking of God, reminding myself of his goodness, love, and holiness. . . . Think of God as often as you can. Cultivate

the habit, by degrees, of turning consciously to him at every opportunity, no matter how briefly. Make these small, holy acts of worship and prayer. (Winter, 1973, pp. 59, 83)

These acts are especially useful for disabled elders because they are entirely cognitive in nature and are not dependent on physical health or the cooperation of others. The value of religious cognitions is evident from their frequency of use among elders coping with stressful life events (Koenig, George, & Siegler, 1988) and their association with successful adaptation (Koenig et al., 1993; Koenig, Kvale, & Ferrel, 1988; Koenig, Siegler, & George, 1989).

What about elders with cognitive impairment? It is true that a certain degree of awareness is necessary to pray or even think about God. However, religious cognitions can be quite simple and often involve deeply ingrained psychological functions such as trust and dependence. Memories involving religious experiences and religious symbols—perhaps because they are affectively charged—are among the last memories lost in dementing illnesses. Religious rituals (such as the sacrament of communion) often retain their meaning and significance to religious elders despite advanced cognitive impairment.

Another important point is that the suffering associated with progressive loss of intellectual functioning seems to be greatest in those who have the most insight into their illness and awareness of their surroundings. Studies have shown that as cognitive impairment advances, suffering and depression actually decrease (Reifler, Larson, & Hanley, 1982; Reynolds et al., 1986). A certain minimum level of cognitive function, then, is required for both suffering and religious experience. Religious cognitions, then, are most accessible to precisely those people who need them (the ones with insight).

Seeking Forgiveness and
Providing Hope for Change

Many elders are emotionally disabled because of regrets over wrong decisions or guilt over negative interactions with parents or children that occurred long in the past. The Judeo-Christian scriptures provide a mechanism by which forgiveness can be obtained. There is the promise that through a humble and sincere confession of past sins or wrongdoings and a resolve to sin no more, God will completely forgive the person: "Though your sins are like scarlet, they shall be as white as snow; though they are red as crimson, they shall be like wool" (Isaiah 1:18). Regardless of age, there is always a possibility for starting over. The parable of the prodigal son drives this point home. Despite having squandered his inheritance and ruined his life, when he decided to return to his father's house, his father receives him with great thanksgiving and joy; indeed, his father gave him the same status as his older brother, who had never left the father's side (Luke 15:11-32). The notion that people can change (and indeed must change) is a central concept in Judeo-Christian theology. The approach taken to bring about such change is a cognitive-behavioral strategy, which has behind it the forces of tradition, culture, and personal faith that are available to younger and older adult alike. This is quite unlike the philosophy of some mental health professionals who have maintained that older people are too rigid to change and that the investment of the professional's time and energy to accomplish this end is not worth the effort at this stage of life. According to Jones (1948), Freud notes the following:

> With persons who are too far advanced in years, [the psychoanalytic method] fails because, owing to the accumulation of material, so much time would be required so that the end of the cure would be reached at a period of life in which much importance is no longer attached to nervous health. (p. 245)

The effectiveness of religious strategies to induce change, then, is not diminished by age. For some people, in fact, it is not until later life—when other resources are not available to fall back on—that change by this route becomes possible. The busyness of youth, the responsibilities of family, and many other competing interests and activities frequently push spiritual concerns out of awareness. As one grows older, however, he or she has more time to think about these things. Negative life events may revive existential concerns and stimulate a review of the meaning and purpose of life. Old age, then, is a ripe time for a reorientation toward spiritual concerns and, in some cases, a complete change in direction.

In a study of religious change among 850 elderly hospitalized men (Koenig, in press), 33% had a life-changing religious experience at some time in their lives; among those with such an experience, more than 40% reported that this event occurred after they had reached the age of 50. In the longitudinal portion of the study, one patient in his late 80s claimed during several early evaluations that he had no religious affiliation or interest. When hospitalized in the intensive care unit on a later admission, however, he reported a religious experience that changed his life—the experience of God's presence at his bedside accompanied by a sense of complete relief from concern and worry. Over the next 12 months he repeatedly drew our attention back to that experience and the tremendous impact it had on his life.

That God does not desert those who are aging is a message declared repeatedly throughout scripture. Furthermore, there is an expectation that the religious person will continue to prosper even late in life: "They will still bear fruit in old age, they will stay fresh and green, proclaiming, 'The Lord is upright; he is my Rock' " (Psalms 92:14-15), and "Even to your old age and gray hairs I am he, I am he who will sustain you. I have made you and I will carry you. I will sustain you and I will rescue you" (Isaiah 46:3-4).

Out of the love from a relationship with God, even the most disabled person can prosper or bear fruit in his or her old age. Again, *fruit* can consist of the smallest acts of kindness or gratefulness shown by a bedridden patient toward a caregiver or nurse's aide. In fact, to God such acts are probably equal in value to the most heroic acts of self-sacrifice performed by zealous missionaries or charismatic religious leaders. Speaking directly to this point, Jesus contrasts the gifts of the rich to the two small copper coins offered by the poor widow to the temple offering: " 'I tell you the truth,' he said, 'this poor widow has put in more than all the others. All these people gave their gifts out of their wealth; but she out of her poverty put in all she had to live on' " (Luke 21:3-4). Indeed, then, it is not the size of act that counts, but the circumstances under which it is performed.

Forgiving Others and Oneself

Some elders, rather than being disabled by guilt or regrets, are imprisoned by bitterness and resentfulness over past wrongs done to them by others. Unresolved anger can place an enormous drain on both psychological and physical energy, thus interfering with the experience of joys and satisfactions in life; likewise, such harborings can disrupt physical health (see below). Much neurotic illness, depression, and unhappiness in later life (as well as at every other age) has a lack of forgiveness at its core. If people were able to forgive others and renew relationships, many psychiatrists would be out of business today. Psychiatrist Menninger once said in a talk that if all persons were somehow able to forgive and let go of their resentments, 75% of patients in psychiatric hospitals could be discharged.

The Judeo-Christian scriptures place great importance on forgiveness and, as noted earlier, provide clear directions on how to do this. Because of God's own mercy and forgiveness toward humanity, he expects the same action from individuals toward their neighbors. Scriptures equate a state of unforgiveness with either imprisonment or death and indicate that this condition may seriously affect one's relationship with God (Mark 11:25). Apparently, God cannot and will not forgive those who have not forgiven others. In the Lord's Prayer (Luke 11:2-4) God is asked to "forgive us our sins, for we also forgive everyone who sins against us," implying that forgiveness is received during the process of forgiving others. This point is again exemplified in the parable of the two debtors (Matthew 18:23-35). The story goes that a money-lender forgave a man of a large debt; despite receiving mercy himself, this man later demanded what was due him from someone else who owed him money and threw him into prison when he didn't pay. When the king found out about this, he was furious and turned him (the man whose debt had been forgiven) over to the "torturers" until he could pay back every cent. The final sentence of the parable crystallizes the meaning: "This is how my heavenly Father will treat each of you unless you forgive your brother from your heart" (Matthew 18:34).

Indeed, we imprison ourselves by failing to forgive. Perhaps there is no emotion that has more destructive effects on the human psyche than resentment. Resentment is a direct consequence of unforgiveness. Psychodynamically, it represents the presence of unexpressed anger at another person (from the present or the past). Such anger may destroy mental well-being and have negative health consequences; the latter has been eloquently outlined by Williams (1989), who won the award for the best medical book of 1990. The book describes the destructive influences of anger on the cardiovascular system. Given that the two leading causes of death in later life are stroke and heart disease, the potential impact of pent-up anger on the elder's physical health is clear. The religious prescription to love and forgive one's neighbor is not just another meaningless, burdensome platitude; it expresses a principle that has profound consequences on emotional and physical well-being.

There are basically two ways that the deep-seated negative emotion of resentment can be done away with. First, one can openly express anger toward the person or in some other way achieve revenge. This may not be possible, however, if the person can no longer be contacted due to geographical relocation or perhaps because of death. Secular psychotherapy can assist with the expression of such anger. Most mental health professionals would advocate that the appropriate and timely expression of anger is healthy; however, this is often not easily achieved. The second way to deal with bitterness and resentment is to forgive. Forgiveness in this sense does not mean to suppress feelings of anger. It means literally to give up or let go of the anger, so that it is no longer present either consciously or unconsciously. Like timely and appropriate expression of anger, forgiving is seldom an easy accomplishment, even for the most determined and religiously motivated individual. Having a relationship with God, however, helps make this process possible. The experience of God's love and recognition of his mercy allows a person, in turn, to release others of their unpaid debts (as in Luke 7:41). Because God operates outside of space and time, forgiveness can take place even if the person to be forgiven is not immediately present or even alive. Again, however, the power to forgive is predicated on the experience of God's love and forgiveness; without this, true forgiveness becomes difficult because both the motivation and ability to forgive are less.

Hope for Healing

Judeo-Christian scriptures focus on the topic of healing. Physically ailing religious elders have hope that God will someday heal them of their infirmity—whether in this life or the next. Jesus healed the man with the crippled hand (Mark 3:5), the paralytic brought to him through the roof of the house (Mark 2:3-12), the crippled person waiting for 38 years at the Pool of Bethesda (John 5:2-15), the woman with chronic gynecologic problems (Mark 5:25-34), the leper (Luke 5:14), the insane man in the cemetery (Luke 8:26-39), and the blind men (John 9:1-34; Luke 18:35-43), among others. Thus there is always the hope that through some natural or supernatural process, disability may improve or be reversed. This notion is particularly relevant for chronic illnesses in later life that may have a psychosomatic origin or influence (asthma, hypertension, coronary artery disease, and gastrointestinal problems). MacNutt (1974) makes a case for the importance of believing in God's miraculous power to heal. He argues that sickness is not sent from God and should be vigorously resisted. His point is that sickness or disability should never be passively accepted as God's will.

There is a story about a missionary who worked with the natives in central Africa. While he was out in the jungle one day, he came across a hungry lion. The missionary fell to his knees and prayed, "Please dear God, let this be a Christian lion—but I want thy will to be done."

The lion then suddenly stopped, sat up, and prayed, "Thank you, oh Lord, for these thy gifts which I am about to receive."

The moral of the story is that one should pray directly and specifically for healing, believing that it will be accomplished. However, there does come a time when everything medically, psychologically, and spiritually possible have been done to reverse an illness; at that time, acceptance of one's cross perhaps yields greater benefits than a painful struggle against it.

A Paradigm for Suffering

Much of the Judeo-Christian scriptures directly address topics of suffering, disability, and sickness (James; Job; Psalms). For many elders, these scriptures provide comfort and give hope that suffering need not be useless or meaningless. Scriptures indicate that troubles and sufferings are an important means by which character is refined and a person is brought closer to God (James 1:2-4, 12; I Peter 2:19-20, 4:1, 12-13, 5:9-10; Revelations 3:17-19; Romans 5:3-4; see also Kung, 1976). This claim has aroused much debate and disagreement. Suffering can also be quite destructive of moral and spiritual values, and it is often the relief of suffering that enhances faith.

Nevertheless, the argument that suffering can have a sanctifying value goes as follows. When life is running smoothly and peacefully, there is often little that motivates a person to seek religious truths. According to Lewis (1962), "God whispers to us in our pleasures, speaks in our conscience, but shouts in our pains: it is his megaphone to rouse a deaf world" (p. 93). It is only in times of confusion and suffering that people are shocked out of complacency and forced to question their current view of the world ("in their misery they will earnestly seek me," Hosea 5.15). Brother Lawrence echoes Lewis in saying that infirmities may come directly from God:

> Such things come to us from the hand of God, as a means which he uses to make us more completely his, and that *rightly accepted and borne* they bring great sweetness and consolation into our lives. This illness is not, then, an enemy to be fought but an ally in the spiritual warfare to be gladly received

and used. . . . Of course you can't expect those who do not believe in God to see things in this way. You cannot ask an unbeliever to suffer as a Christian. He considers illness as an enemy of life and nature, and finds nothing in it but grief and distress. The Christian, however, sees it as coming from the hands of God. (quoted in Winter, 1973, p. 132, emphasis added)

It is an interesting fact that religion is both now, and has always been, more common among the uneducated, the socioeconomically deprived, the chronically ill, women, the elderly, and minority groups such as blacks. Why? Is it because these people are less knowledgeable, more superstitious, or more out of touch with popular trends in society? I don't think so. Rather, it is because these people are more likely to be suffering some persecution or hardship, and that is precisely where scripture predicts God will be—with the underprivileged and those in pain.

Recent developments in the former Soviet Union exemplify the importance of religion to those who are oppressed. Pravda was the giant and very official Communist party publishing house in Moscow. For more than 70 years, it forbade the publication and spreading of religious literature by anyone—Communist or non-Communist. On August 10, 1991, Pravda's deputy director, Mikhail Troschin, made the no less than astounding announcement that it would begin publishing the Bible (Pravda, 1991). The reason for this remarkable turnabout? Between 1990 and 1991, Pravda's major news publication dropped in circulation from 10 million to 5 million. According to Troschin, "Business is business. . . . The demand for the Bible is very great" (quoted in Pravda, 1991). This has been a time of tremendous economic hardship and social upheaval for the people of Russia and other republics. In the midst of these troubled times, the importance of religion has apparently skyrocketed. Many Russians are now finding consolation in the Bible, which the Communist party itself had begun distributing before its disbandment.

Thus, when a disabled elder turns to scripture for encouragement, the benefits to him or her should not be underestimated or misinterpreted. These verses were written by those who were themselves suffering and often felt deserted by both humanity and God. There are perhaps things that the person in pain can understand in scripture that those unacquainted with suffering simply cannot comprehend. Miller (1988) says it this way:

Our deepest wounds are not the problem but the answer, that they can teach us things not to be learned through any easier pedagogy, and that the key to wisdom is not at all to recover from them but to let them speak even if at first they do so in the inarticulate tongue of anguish. (p. 11)

Knowledge, then, may be gained from suffering that cannot be acquired in any other way. If the scriptures are correct, then being comfortable and at peace without struggle during life is not the primary goal of existence. If the goal is to come into a deeper knowledge of and relationship with the creator, then suffering and pain are our closest allies. The decision to carry one's burden of suffering as a sacrificial offering to God may convert meaningless pain into an act of worship with eternal value (Colossians 1:24; I Corinthians 15:58). Brother Lawrence suggests the following:

> Offer him your pains. They come from him, or by his permission, so turn them into an offering to lay at his feet—his will for you accepted and carried through. Ask him for the strength you will need to bear them. And, above all, continually lift your thoughts away from the pain you feel and towards him, who loves you as a father his favorite child. (quoted in Winter, 1973, p. 138)

Role Models for Suffering

Scripture provides role models for those who are suffering. Indeed, Jesus himself was described as "a man of sorrows and familiar with suffering" (Isaiah 53:3; see also I Peter 2:21-24) and felt deserted by God at the moment of his death ("Eloi, Eloi, lama sabachthani?" Matthew 27:46). Job (Job 3:20-26, 7:4-5, 16), Hannah (Samuel's mother; see I Samuel 1:5-18), David (Psalms 6:2-6, 13, 31:9-13, 102:1-11), Elijah (I Kings 19:4-10), and Jonah (Jonah 4:1-10) all suffered severe depression over the circumstances that befell them. Jeremiah (Jeremiah 20:7-18) and Isaiah (Isaiah 38:13-16) suffered over the plight of their people. Human traits and weaknesses are stressed in these portrayals. David (Psalms 10:1-4, 22:1-2, 39, 44:23-26) and Job (Job 23:8-9) both vehemently accused God of deserting them when they needed him most. Job, in particular, expressed anger toward God for being treated unfairly. Thus negative feelings toward God are seen as inevitable human reactions that need not arouse undue guilt. The assurance that God is aware of what is happening ("the very hairs of your head are all numbered," Luke 12:7), knows what he is doing, and is in fact suffering right along with the sufferer ("In all their distress he too was distressed," Isaiah 63:9) can provide emotional comfort to those enduring pain and disability.

Sense of Control and Self-Determination

Issues of control, self-determination, and autonomy are especially relevant for disabled elders like Sally who become progressively more dependent on others for their basic needs. These "others" may or may not have the elder's best interests in mind or be able to meet his or her emotional or physical needs. The belief in an omnipotent God outside of oneself who cares and responds to prayer can give the elder a sense of control over his or her situation. Although there may be nothing more that medical professionals can do to cure illness or relieve suffering, the elder is assured by scripture that he or she can still influence his or her circumstances by praying to God, who has the power to heal and make the elder completely well; even if he does not do so, this too could be seen as being in the person's best interest:

> We find it very hard to believe that God knows all, and therefore that what he plans for us is best. We prefer to follow our fallen reason, or our own defective sight. But "we walk by faith, not by sight." What we can see, and what we can understand is *very, very limited*. God knows and sees all. (Winter, 1973, p. 148, emphasis added)

Scriptures promise that good can result from even the most dismal of circumstances: "And we know that in all things God works for the good of those who love him, who have been called according to his purpose" (Romans 8:28). This is a powerful verse that when combined with faith can make an enormous impact on how a person views his or her situation and can directly counteract feelings of helplessness and hopelessness. Although religious elders may appear to be relying on an external locus of control (i.e., God), studies have shown that devout religious belief is actually associated with a greater internal locus of control (Kivett, 1979). Although religious elders may not have much immediate control over their situations, their belief is that they can positively influence their conditions by praying to a God who cares about them and is responsive to their pleas; in effect, this obviates the need to depend on other external sources of control and provides a vicarious type of internal control. Indeed, the Judeo-Christian religions teach that problems in life are not due to chance or to the actions of powerful other persons, nor is the individual instructed to be passive (characteristics of those with an external locus of control). Rather, these religions encourage believers to do everything they can possibly do to solve their problems, while praying to God for help and trusting him to do his part.

Life After Death

Not the least important of Christian teachings is that there is a better life to come. Scriptures stress that troubles and difficulties are to be expected in this world, but that if these crosses are carried in good faith, then there will be a reward in the life after death. The hope of eternal life that religion offers should not be underestimated in its effect on morale. Imagine the psychological impact that the following passage might have on the elder who is disabled with impaired vision, loss of hearing, or painful musculoskeletal or neurological problems that have forever robbed him or her of youthful independence:

> In the same way, our earthly bodies which die and decay are different from the bodies we shall have when we come back to life again, for they will never die. The bodies we have now embarrass us for they become sick and die; but they will be full of glory when we come back to life again. Yes, they are weak, dying bodies now, but when we live again they will be full of strength. They are just human bodies at death, but when they come back to life they will be superhuman bodies. For just as there are natural, human bodies, there are also supernatural spiritual bodies. . . . Oh death, where then your victory? Where then your sting? (I Corinthians 15:42-44, 55)[2]

It is easy to see how such beliefs might help relieve the fear associated with death, because the threat of nonexistence of the self is removed and the transition at death can now be viewed as a positive one. On the other hand, the prospects of hell may induce anxiety in those who are uncertain about whether they have lived up to standards. Even for these individuals, however, the Christian tradition gives an opportunity to repent and receive total forgiveness (Hebrews 10:22; I John 2:2; Romans 8:38-39). Some elders, however, may believe that they cannot be forgiven, believing that they have committed an unforgivable sin (Matthew 12:31) in their past life. Such notions may arise from either a misunderstanding of scripture or, more often, from a form of pathological guilt seen in mental disorders such as delusional depression or other late-life psychosis.

Ready Accessibility

Unlike philosophies of life that are accessible only to the intellectually gifted, the physically healthy, or economically advantaged, religion is available to all—the poor, the homeless schizophrenic, the homesick soldier, the isolated prisoner, the fearful small child, the depressed middle-aged housewife, the older man with disabling arthritis, or the elderly woman who has recently lost her husband. Thus it is potentially available to all persons, regardless of their education or position, providing hope and meaning in their lives.

Elders can always wait—wait for future medical advances to cure their conditions; wait for the weekly or monthly visit from a friend, relative, or psychotherapist to relieve their loneliness or wait for the time when their environment improves or caregivers show more understanding. They do not have to wait, however, for the comfort that religion can offer; it is immediately available and largely dependent on the person's own will. When the pain gets bad and no one is around, when it's in the middle of the night and he or she cannot sleep, when discouragement and hopelessness become overwhelming, the elder can always turn his or her thoughts to God in a silent prayer for help or perform an act of worship by consciously bearing the discomfort for God and thanking him for whatever good things still remain in life.

Idealism versus Realism. Is the approach taken here too idealistic? When someone is actually caught up in the grips of suffering, it is often difficult for him or her to experience God's presence; in fact, he may seem unusually distant at that time. Recall the Lewis quote (presented earlier) on the value of suffering, which comes out of a book that this British theologian and widely known defender of Christianity wrote in 1940 titled *The Problem of Pain* (1962). In that volume, Lewis argued that suffering and pain were God's method of bringing humans closer to him and emphasized the good that could come out of this type of experience. Several years after writing this book, his wife died, causing him great emotional turmoil and pain. During that time, he wrote another book, titled *A Grief Observed* (1961), expressing his thoughts and feelings at the time. The following excerpts come from that volume:

> But go to Him when your need is desperate, when all other help is vain, and what do you find? A door slammed in your face, and sound of bolting and double bolting on the inside. After that, silence. You may as well turn away. The longer you wait, the more emphatic the silence will become. There are no lights in the windows. (p. 9)

> Not that I am (I think) in much danger of ceasing to believe in God. The real danger is of coming to believe such dreadful things about Him. The conclu-

sion I dread is not, "So there's no God after all," but, "So this is what God's really like." Deceive yourself no longer. (p. 10)

There is no answer. Only the locked door, the iron curtain, the vacuum, absolute zero. "Them as asks don't get." I was a fool to ask. (p. 11)

What reasons have we, except our own desperate wishes, to believe that God is, by any standard we can conceive, "good"? Doesn't the prima facie evidence suggest exactly the opposite? (p. 25)

I wrote that last night. It was a yell rather than a thought. Let me try it over again. Is it rational to believe in a bad God? Anyway, in a God so bad as all that? The Cosmic Sadist, the spiteful imbecile? (p. 26)

Some people experience this sense of distance from God as even more distressing than the emotional or physical discomfort they suffer from their illnesses. This sense of distance from God may be partly a result of the effects of mental disorder itself (i.e., depression). In a depressed state, the person feels like no one cares and may feel unworthy of being cared for; it is easy to understand how one might include God among those who don't care. Some of this sense of distance from God may also result from the frustration and anger of chronic suffering that becomes directed either consciously or unconsciously at God, who is perceived as having let the sufferer down.

Despite the forces that interfere with one's turning to God during these inordinately painful moments, the scriptures promise that persistent efforts in this direction will bear fruit (Luke 18:1-8). Although Judeo-Christian attitudes toward suffering and disability may be difficult to achieve fully, they are nonetheless, in my opinion, quite realistic as goals to be sought after. Without a goal and a vision, there can be no hope. Take the pilot who flies his or her plane during a storm that impairs his or her vision. In this circumstance, the pilot relies on information from the control tower and from the instrument panel to navigate the plane; it would be treacherous for the pilot to rely on his or her own judgment that is based on incomplete information. For the religious person, the promises of God in scripture represent his or her control tower and instrument panel. They assure the sufferer that God is not absent or disinterested. Until the time that God's presence is felt again, however, one may have to rely on faith alone, in the absence of feelings. It is during this time that support from one's faith community is vitally important, because God's hands are often those of his people.

A Supportive Community

Judeo-Christian scriptures strongly emphasize the importance of helping the less fortunate and those who are sick. To the Christian, they indicate that God himself identifies with such persons:

> Come, you who are blessed of my Father, take your inheritance, the kingdom prepared for you since the creation of the world. For I was hungry and you gave me something to eat, I was thirsty and you gave me something to drink, I was a stranger and you invited me in, I needed clothes and you clothed me, I was sick and you looked after me, I was in prison and you came to visit me. . . . I tell you the truth, whatever you did for one of the least of these brothers of mine, you did for me. (Matthew 25:34-36, 40)

It is clear that caring for the disabled elderly is not an option (Galatians 6:2). Because of the heavy burden of support that lies on caregivers in private homes and staff in nursing facilities, there is a need for individuals from the community to volunteer time to minister to older persons disabled with physical illness. Organized religion represents a potential source of informal support for elders (Sherwood & Bernstein, 1985-1986; Tobin, Ellor, & Anderson-Ray, 1986). This is especially so because older adults are more likely to be involved in church groups than in all other voluntary social groups combined (Cutler, 1976; Mayo, 1951). A study of elderly patients attending a geriatric medicine clinic found that for the majority of the sample, at least four out of their five closest friends were members of their local church congregation (Koenig, Moberg, & Kvale, 1988).

The functions served by the religious community parallel in many ways those of community mental health centers as outlined by Dewald (1971, pp. 306-308). The religious community can play an important role in supporting the disabled elderly by visits that counteract isolation, prevent disengagement, and dilute intense relationships between them and their caregivers. The church or synagogue is a ready source of age-matched peers with similar value systems. As health deteriorates and family members die, opportunities for socialization often decrease. As their social skills atrophy from disuse, elders begin to feel uncomfortable in social settings, which then further reinforces a tendency toward withdrawal and disengagement. Religious communities can counteract such tendencies by encouraging members to reach out to elders and draw them back into the mainstream of church life. Participation in religious services can provide structure, nurturance, and catharsis and enable persons to sublimate their feelings through singing, praising, and even shouting (as occurs in some conservative, fundamentalist, or African-American church congregations).

In addition to meeting the mental health needs of elders with coping problems or less severe neuroses, religious organizations also play an important role in helping those with severe mental illness. Older persons with chronic mental disorders often have needs that exceed the resources of any one individual. In the religious community, these needs can be distributed among different members so that no one person is overburdened.

Thus religious bodies could be a ready source of volunteers to serve the needs of (1) the homebound, (2) elders in nursing homes or chronic psychiatric facilities, and (3) elders hospitalized with acute illness. American churches, however, have yet to effectively meet this challenge. It is difficult to motivate people—even those who claim to be religious—to break out from their own comfortable worlds to help others. Furthermore, ministering to the needs of elders in one's own home or in the home down the street, is often more difficult and less exciting than other forms of service.

One possible answer is the Shepherds' Center approach. Shepherds' Centers are innovative and rapidly spreading programs that take advantage of the often dormant talents and abilities of healthy older adults to fulfill the needs of the sick elderly in the community (Koenig, 1986). A Shepherds' Center is entirely supported by donations from businesses and churches in the local community and has no governmental affiliations or funding. Services include respite care, education and health information, meals on wheels, transportation for medical visits, and exercise and health maintenance. The most attractive aspect about Shepherds' Centers is that they are operated and managed entirely by older volunteers. In addition to serving a vital need, these programs give healthy elders a feeling of purpose and self-esteem as they serve their neighbors in the community and nursing homes. The original Shepherds' Center was started in 1972 in Kansas City, Missouri; that particular center is now supported by 26 churches and synagogues and currently serves more than 6000 older adults through 400 elderly volunteers. Over the past 20 years, centers have spread into 75 communities in 24 states.

Summary

Chronic illness and physical disability are common in later life. They are frequently associated with emotional distress, as the elder's sense of control and self-determination are threatened. Although advances in the medical and psychological sciences, improvements in health care delivery, and the love and support of family and friends may go a long way to enhance quality of life and lessen the pain of disability, much of the burden will remain on the older person himself or herself. In addition to providing a community of believers to help shoulder this burden, religion through its belief system and rituals offers the disabled elder a source of comfort that is as powerful and endurable as any other resource available. It can infuse the most dismal life with meaning and purpose. It can enable the sufferer to transcend circumstances that cannot be altered, and may teach truths about life that can be understood only by those who are suffering. Religion is not a resource that cannot be afforded or must be waited for. It is immediately accessible to elders regardless of disability or circumstance, as long as they have retained the cognitive capacity to believe and have faith. According to Erickson, the ability to trust is the first psychosocial capacity learned by the infant; it is also among the last to go at the other end of the age spectrum.

Notes

1. All biblical quotes are from the New International Version, except when noted.
2. This quote is from the Living Bible.

References

American Association of Retired Persons. (1989a). *Facts about older women: Twelve powerful statistics on older women.* Washington, DC: Author.

American Association of Retired Persons. (1989b). *A national survey of caregivers.* Washington, DC: Author and the Travelers Foundation.

American Association of Retired Persons. (1991a). *Fact sheet: The cost of long-term care* (Public Policy Institute FS5). Washington, DC: Author.

American Association of Retired Persons. (1991b). *Fact sheet: Elderly people who live alone* (Public Policy Institute FS2). Washington, DC: Author.

Anderson, J. M., Hubbard, B. M., Coghill, G. R., & Slidders, W. (1983). The effect of advanced old age on the neuron content of the cerebral cortex. *Journal of the Neurological Sciences, 58,* 235-244.

Binks, M. (1989). Changes in mental functioning associated with normal aging. In T. Chichester (Ed.), *The clinical neurology of old age* (pp. 27-39). New York: Wiley.

Blazer, D. G., Hughes, D. C., & George, L. K. (1987). The epidemiology of depression in an elderly community population. *The Gerontologist, 27,* 281-285.

Cutler, S. J. (1976). Membership in different types of voluntary associations and psychological well-being. *The Gerontologist, 16,* 335-339.

Dewald, P. A. (1971). *Psychotherapy: A dynamic approach.* Oxford: Blackwell.

Evans, D. A., Funkenstein, H. H., Albert, M. S., Scherr, P. A., Cook, N. R., Chown, M. J., Hebert, L. E., Hennekens, C. H., & Taylor, J. O. (1989). Prevalence of Alzheimer's disease in a community population of older persons. *Journal of the American Medical Association, 262,* 2551-2556.

Grad, S. (1988). *Income of the population 55 or older in 1986.* U.S. Department of Health and Human Services, Social Security Administration, Office of Research, Statistics, and International Policy. Washington, DC: U.S. Government Printing Office.

Henderson, G., Tomlinson, B. E., & Gibson, P. H. (1980). Cell counts in human cerebral cortex in normal adults throughout life using an image analyzing computer. *Journal of the Neurological Sciences, 46,* 113-136.

Hirsch, C. H., Sommers, L., Olsen, A., Mullen, L., & Winograd, C. H. (1990). The natural history of functional morbidity in hospitalized older patients. *Journal of the American Geriatrics Society, 38,* 1296-1303.

Jones, E. (Ed.). (1948). *Sigmund Freud, collected papers* (Vol. 1). London: Hogarth.

Kirasic, K. C., & Allen, G. L. (1985). Aging, spatial performance, and spatial competence. In N. Charness (Ed.), *Aging and human performance* (pp. 191-224). Chichester, UK: Wiley.

Kivett, V. R. (1979). Religious motivation in middle age: Correlates and implications. *Journal of Gerontology, 34,* 106-115.

Koenig, H. G. (1986). Shepherds' Centers: Elderly people helping themselves. *Journal of the American Geriatrics Society, 34,* 73.

Koenig, H. G. (in press). *Aging and God.* New York: Haworth.

Koenig, H. G., Cohen, H. J., Blazer, D. G., Pieper, C., Meador, K. G., Shelp, F., Goli, V., & DiPasquale, R. (1992). Religious coping and depression in hospitalized elderly medically ill men. *American Journal of Psychiatry, 149,* 1693-1700.

Koenig, H. G., George, L. K., & Siegler, I. C. (1988). The use of religion and other emotion-regulating coping strategies among older adults. *The Gerontologist, 28,* 303-310.

Koenig, H. G., Kvale, J. N., & Ferrel, C. (1988). Religion and well-being in later life. *The Gerontologist, 28,* 18-27.

Koenig, H. G., Meador, K. G., Cohen, H. J., & Blazer, D. G. (1988). Depression in elderly hospitalized patients with medical illness. *Archives of Internal Medicine, 148,* 1929-1936.

Koenig, H. G., Meador, K. G., Shelp, F., Goli, V., Cohen, H. J., & Blazer, D. G. (1991). Major depressive disorder in hospitalized medically ill patients: An examination of young and elderly veterans. *Journal of the American Geriatrics Society, 39,* 880-891.

Koenig, H. G., Moberg, D. O., & Kvale, J. N. (1988). Religious activities and attitudes of older adults in a geriatric assessment clinic. *Journal of the American Geriatrics Society, 36,* 362-374.

Koenig, H. G., Siegler, I. C., & George, L. K. (1989). Religious and non-religious coping: Impact on adaptation in later life. *Journal of Religion & Aging, 5*(4), 73-94.

Kung, H. (1976). *On being a Christian.* Garden City, NY: Doubleday.

Lewis, C. S. (1961). *A grief observed.* New York: Seabury.

Lewis, C. S. (1962). *The problem of pain.* New York: Macmillan.

Loza, N., & Milad, G. (1989). *Old age in the history of ancient civilization in Egypt.* Unpublished manuscript.

MacNutt, F. (1974). *Healing.* South Bend, IN: Ave Maria Press.

Mayo, S. C. (1951). Social participation among the older population in rural areas of Wake County, N.C. *Social Forces, 30,* 53-59.

Miller, J.A. (1988). The way of suffering: A reasoning of the heart. In J. A. Miller (Ed.), *The geography of crisis* (p. 11). Washington, DC: Georgetown University Press.

Neugarten, B. (1968). *Middle age and aging: A reader in social psychology.* Chicago: University of Chicago Press.

Older Women's League. (1987). *The picture of health for midlife and older women in America.* Washington, DC: Author.

Parmelee, P. A., Katz, I. R., & Lawton, M. P. (1989). Depression among institutionalized aged: Assessment and prevalence estimation. *Journal of Gerontology: Medical Sciences, 44,* M22-M27.

Plude, D. J., & Hoyer, W. J. (1985). Attention and performance: Identifying and localizing age deficits. In N. Charness (Ed.), *Aging and human performance* (pp. 47-99). Chichester, UK: Wiley.

Pravda. (1991). Bible may be the answer to Pravda's prayers. *Greensboro News & Record, 101*(222), 1.

Reifler, B. V., Larson, E., & Hanley, R. (1982). Coexistence of cognitive impairment and depression in geriatric outpatients. *American Journal of Psychiatry, 139,* 623-629.

Reynolds, C. F., Kupfer, D. J., Hock, C. C., Stack, J. A., Houck, P. R., & Sewitch, D. E. (1986). Two-year follow-up of elderly patients with mixed depression and dementia. *Journal of the American Geriatrics Society, 34,* 793-798.

Rovner, B. W. (1991). Much major depression in nursing homes said to be overlooked. *Clinical Psychiatry News, 19*(5), 12.

Sadavoy, J., & Leszcz, M. (1987). *Treating the elderly with psychotherapy: The scope for change in later life.* New York: International Universities Press.

Sherwood, S., & Bernstein, E. (1985-1986). Informal care for vulnerable elderly: Suggestions for church involvement. *Journal of Religion & Aging, 2*(1-2), 55-67.

Thompson, L. W., Gallagher, D., & Breckinridge, J. S. (1987). Comparative effectiveness of psychotherapies for depressed elders. *Journal of Consulting and Clinical Psychology, 55,* 385-390.

Tobin, S. S., Ellor, J., & Anderson-Ray, S. M. (1986). *Enabling the elderly: Religious institutions within the community service system.* Albany: State University of New York Press.

U.S. Bureau of the Census. (1989a). *Current population reports: Series P-20, No. 433: Marital status and living arrangements, March 1988.* Washington, DC: U.S. Government Printing Office.

U.S. Bureau of the Census. (1989b). *Current population reports: Series P-60, No. 162: Money income of households, families, and persons in the United States, 1987.* Washington, DC: U.S. Government Printing Office.

U.S. Senate Special Committee on Aging. (1987-1988). *Aging America: Trends and projections.* Washington, DC: U.S. Government Printing Office.

Victoroff, J. I. (1991). Neurological evaluation. In J. Sadavoy, L. Lazarus, & L. Jarvik (Eds.), *Comprehensive review of geriatric psychiatry* (pp. 199-200). Washington, DC: American Psychiatric Press.

Weissman, M. M., Bruce, M. L., Leaf, P. J., Florio, L. P., & Holzer, C. (1991). Affective disorders. In L. N. Robins, & D. A. Regier (Eds.), *Psychiatric disorders in America: The Epidemiologic Catchment Area Study* (p. 53-80). New York: Free Press.

Wiener, J. M., Hanley, R. J., Clark, R., & Van Nostrand, J. F. (1990). Measuring the activities of daily living: Comparisons across national surveys. *Journal of Gerontology: Social Sciences, 45,* S229-S237.

Williams, R. (1989). *The trusting heart.* New York: Times Books.

Winter, D. (1973). *Closer than a brother.* Wheaton, IL: Shaw.

3

Religion, Health, and Forgiveness

Traditions and Challenges

BERTON H. KAPLAN
HEATHER MUNROE-BLUM
DAN G. BLAZER

Introduction

The extent of the ability to bond and to create socially cohesive systems of interrelationships is the characteristic which most differentiates humans from other group-living creatures. At any given time and place in human history, the larger group or culture preempts many bonding possibilities by channeling individual bonding propensities toward particular classes of individuals, objects, or goals. Nevertheless, whatever the particular instance, there is a fundamental set of sociophysiological mechanisms through which most societal forces must work. (Barchas & Mendoza, 1984, p. xi)

Two characteristics of anthropological work on religion accomplished since the second world war strike me as curious when such work is placed against that carried out just before and just after the first. One is that it has made no theoretical advances of major importance. It is living off the conceptual capital of its ancestors, adding very little, save a certain empirical enrichment, to it. The second is that it draws what concepts it does use from a very narrowly defined intellectual tradition. There is Durkheim, Weber, Freud, or Malinowski, and in any particular work the approach of one or two of these transcendent figures is followed, with but a few marginal corrections necessitated by the natural tendency to excess of seminal minds or by the expanded body of reliable descriptive data. But virtually no one even thinks of looking elsewhere—to philosophy, history, law, literature, or the "harder" sciences—as these men themselves looked, for analytical ideas. And it occurs to me, also, that these two curious characteristics are not unrelated. (Geertz, 1973, pp. 87-88)

Our organizing questions are as follows. First, what are the "expanded" classic commentaries on religion and adaptation? Second, how does religion fit into the stress and adaptation paradigm? Third, how does the concept of forgiveness highlight a strategic but neglected problem in the stress, religion, and adaptation paradigm?

With these three organizing questions, we have chosen to use these two introductory quotations as preamble. Barchas and Geertz set a useful framework for our work. Barchas's work (1984) requires us to examine three fundamental interlocking processes: the human necessity to bond, the characteristics of human groupings, and the sociophysiological mechanisms necessary for biosocial life. Geertz (1973) reminds us to look for fresh ideas beyond the founding figures in the social anthropology (psychology and sociology) of religion for expanding our understanding of religious expression and bonds. Our basic task then is to examine a selected but expanded view of the classical questions in the study of the interrelationships of religion, social health, and one neglected coping topic, the process of forgiveness. As an integrating question, is the "forgiving heart" (Kaplan, 1992) a critical process at the intersection of social bonds, psychological healing, and health?

Classical Formulations: An Overview

We accept the editor's invitation to explore new ground and to be free to share intuitions and speculations. Therefore, we seek to extend the classical canon, to extend the range of religion and health adaptive issues, to be selective yet (we hope) provocative, and to be strategic but not exhaustive. With these goals in mind, we will sequentially examine the ancient nature of our subject in three ways: (1) Jaspers's concept of *axial age,* (2) paradise motifs, and (3) literature and religion. For the usual canon, we will comment briefly on Durkheim, James, Weber, Freud, and Malinowski—we hope to emphasize neglected points in these seminal works. For the neglected empirical study of religion and adaptation, we have chosen three areas to highlight: existential psychiatry and religion, the dark side of religion, and Bowker's treatment of suffering as core to the study of religion and adaptation. Whatever the time perspective, these selected classical perspectives on religion illustrate the particular and universal ways in which religious traditions mirror the ancient questions of the adaptive processes involved in stress and health (Elliott & Eisdorfer, 1982). Indeed, all civilizations deal with the nature of reality and the nature of society.

Taking our cue from Geertz (1973) and from personal observations, we will expand on the usual list of classical formulations. Others may add or subtract. With the perspectives of ancient time, first take Jaspers's concept of axial age, or breakthroughs. In Schwartz (1975), we encounter the classical issues on the broadest historical scale:

> It has been observed by Karl Jaspers and others that the first millennium before Christ (perhaps more accurately the first seven or eight hundred years before Christ) witnessed the emergence within the orbit of the "higher civilizations" of certain major spiritual, moral, and intellectual "breakthroughs." In the Middle East we see the rise of classical Judaism through the prophets and the beginnings of rabbinical Judaism; in Persia the rise of Zoroastrianism; in India the transition from the Vedas to the Upanishads, Buddhism, Jainism, and other heterodox sects; in China Confucianism, Taoism, and the "hundred schools," and in Greece the evolution from Homer and Hesiod to pre-Socratic and classical philosophy. Jaspers uses the term "axial age" to characterize these momentous developments. (Schwartz, 1975, p. 1)

What significance does Jaspers's concept of axial age and Schwartz's amazing essay have for understanding religion and adaptation? For Schwartz (1975), the answer lies in the concept of transcendence. To what does transcendence refer? His usage has a generic meaning: "A kind of standing back and looking beyond—a kind of critical, reflective questioning of the actual and a new vision of what lies beyond" (Schwartz, 1975, p. 3). Schwartz has other criteria: for example, (1) the function of wisdom and doubt on the conscious life; (2) ethical ideas that put constraints on the negative (e.g., pride and passions); (3) the function of centuries of development and crises requiring a spiritual breakthrough offering new formulations and foundations; and (4) the small but very influential elite of philosophers, thinkers, moral leaders, and prophets (pp. 3-4).

For us, Jaspers's concept of the axial highlights the religious breakthroughs that produce big impacts on subsequent history, notably the Vedas and then Upanishads. For example, our understanding of the evolution of the Hebrew prophets and rabbinic Judaism, the Confucian harmony and order ethic, the philosophic Taoism, and Buddhist discipline and renunciation forces us to understand more of the impact of the past on present religious ideas. Do the concepts of axial age and the transcendent open fresh questions for inquiry today? We think so.

Out of our antiquity, it could be further argued that the classical questions about religion and adaptation are suggested and modeled by the concepts of paradise, terrestrial and celestial. Manuel and Manuel's (1972) work is very thought provoking:

> A revealing way to examine the psychic life of Judeo-Christian civilization would be to study it as a paradise cult, isolating fantasies about another world as they found expression in sacred texts, in commentaries upon them, and in their secular adaptation. Grand enterprises of Western man, among them the propagation of Christianity, the Crusades against Islam, millenarian revolts during the Reformation, the overseas explorations of the sixteenth century, and the settlement of the American continent, drew sustenance from the body of this myth. In visions of paradise terrestrial and celestial, men have been disclosing their innermost desires, whether they thrust them backward into the past, projected them forward into the future on earth, or raised them beyond the bounds of this sphere. As in dreams, men displaced themselves in time and space and compressed their manifold wishes into an all-embracing metaphor—the "golden race" of Hesiod, the "garden eastward in Eden" of Genesis, the "World to Come" of the rabbis, the "city of the living God" of the Epistle to the Hebrews, the "ineffabile allegrezza" of Dante's *Paradiso*. (p. 83)

The terrestrial and celestial models of paradise have motivated a great deal of the history of religious thought about basic adaptation issues. The reader may think immediately of the mythic Garden of Eden, the Elysium, various religious and secular images of the messianic and utopian, Rousseau, Thomas More's *Utopia,* and even Marx and Teilhard (Manuel & Manuel, 1972). Indeed, for example, the Confucian model of harmony is still a vital value to understanding Chinese civilization.

As Manuel and Manuel (1972) point out, for an ancient source, Hesiod's *Works and Days* images of paradise are still with us: existence described by happiness, serenity, bounty automate, peace, and a conquest over old age and death. Sound familiar? In any case, our point is this: Any serious student of religion and adaptation must come to understand the powerful function of secular and sacred models of paradise and the utopian, rooted in the knowledge that this concept is ancient and contemporary. Certainly, the tradition of studying the universal in religious messianic myths links us to an even larger set of adaptive issues, such as meaning, hope, suffering, and "explanations" (Campbell, 1988; Frazer, 1922; Jung, 1959; Levi-Strauss, 1962). As we take a very broad view of classical traditions in the study of religion, we would include literature and religion. One of the functions of religion is to provide a literature (Alter & Kermode, 1987) for spiritual thought, action, and speculation. Indeed, as Alter and Kermode (1987) argue, the Bible expresses a broad range of literary voices and motifs of the Judeo-Christian *explanatory* literature. Literature offers hypotheses about the spiritual journey in all cultures. For example, Dostoyevsky (1880/1960) offers this "theory" of religion:

This is the significance of the first question in the wilderness, and this is what Thou hast rejected for the sake of that freedom which Thou hast exalted above everything. Yet in this question lies hid the great secret of this world. Choosing "bread," Thou wouldst have satisfied the universal and everlasting craving of humanity—to find some one to worship. So long as man remains free he strives for nothing so incessantly and so painfully as to find some one to worship. But man seeks to worship what is established beyond dispute, so that all men would agree at once to worship it. For these pitiful creatures are concerned not only to find what one or the other can worship, but to find something that all would believe in and worship; what is essential is that all may be together in it. This craving for community of worship is the chief misery of every man individually and of all humanity from the beginning of time. For the sake of common worship they've slain each other with the sword. They have set up gods and challenged one another, "Put away your gods and come and worship ours, or we will kill you and your gods!" And so it will be to the end of the world, even when gods disappear from the earth; they will fall down before idols just the same. (p. 263)

Pasternak (1958) offers this brief "theory" of religion:

Now what is history? It is the centuries of systematic explorations of the riddle of death, with a view to overcoming death. That's why people discover mathematical infinity and electromagnetic waves, that's why they write symphonies. Now you can't advance in this direction without a certain faith. (p. 10)

One of our favorite books on literature and religious themes is Kaufmann's (1961) *Religion From Tolstoy to Camus*. The literature and religion tradition is so ancient and huge. For example, we could start with the Gilgamesh epic literature, or the Vedas. We will focus, rather, on Wilson's (1992) recent use of great literature to focus on the thesis that religion is a form of leisure.

Wilson's major points force us to think of the intersection of leisure and religious experience:

1. Our cultural values of rationality erode the religious concerns with tragedy, enchantment, philosophic doubt, the mysterious, and existential uncertainty.
2. Leisure values facilitate religious experiences that prize sentiments of wonder, praise, the unknowable, contemplation, and especially silence.

In Wilson's thesis, our greatest contemporary Western value is placed on rationality, not the mysterious and transcendental. For Heschel (1963), the biblical creation story nurtures our ability to contemplate both time and space. For a linguistic clue, he notes that the Hebrew *Hemdat Yamin* refers to the Sabbath as a day to be coveted (Heschel, 1963, p. 91). Leisure is coveted. So Wilson's thesis finds expression in ancient Israel.

Now, we turn to the usual classical sources. Durkheim (1912/1961) was interested in the nature of the sacred, in how religion expressed basic functions of solidarity, and how the defects in social attachment (illustrated in religious groupings) represented types of social risk for suicide. In *The Elementary Forms of Religious Life,* Durkheim (1912/1961) focused on how religious rituals, practices, and symbols provide a social projection of the inner and social realities of life. In the Durkheimian tradition, scholarship focused on social bonding, rituals, sentiments, and functions. One of Durkheim's (1912/1961) major interests is expressed thus:

> The general conclusion the reader has before him is that religion is something eminently social. Religious representations are collective representations which express collective reality; the rites are a manner of acting which take rise in the midst of the assembled group and which are destined to excite, maintain, or recreate certain mental states in these groups. So if the categories are of religious origin, they ought to participate in this nature common to all religious facts; they too should be social affairs and the product of collective thought. At least—for the actual condition of our knowledge of these matters, one should be careful to avoid all radical and exclusive statements—it is allowable to suppose that they are rich in social elements. (p. 22)

In James's (1958) *The Varieties of Religious Experience* there is a section on religion and neurology. James was interested in the interface between religious experience, psychophysiology, and mental response. Of special interest was James's religion of the healthy minded and the religion of the sick soul. James (1958) defines the religious sentiments that encourage the religion of the healthy soul and, in contrast, the religion of the sick soul:

a. The Healthy Soul: If, then, we give the name of healthy-mindedness to the tendency which looks on all things and sees that they are good, we find we must distinguish between a more involuntary and a more voluntary or systematic way of being healthy minded. In its involuntary variety, healthy-mindedness is a way of feeling happy about things immediately. In its systematical variety, it is an abstract way of conceiving things as good.

b. The Sick Soul: Now in contrast to such healthy minded views as these, if we treat them as a way of deliberately minimizing evil, stands a radically opposite view, a way of maximizing evil if you please so to call it, based on the persuasion that the evil aspects of our life are of its very essence, that the world's meaning most comes home to us when we lay them most to heart.

So much for melancholia in the sense of incapacity for joyous giving, a much worse form of it is positive and active anguish, a sort of psychic neuralgia wholly unknown to healthy life. Such anguish may partake of various characters, having something more the quality of lowly; sometimes that of irritation and exasperation; or again of self-mistrust and self-despair; or of suspicion, anxiety, trepidation, and fear. (pp. 21-38)

It is hard to find an empirical tradition in James's religion of the healthy soul and of the sick soul (Kaplan, 1976). Yet his works are listed in any of the classical canons, and rightly so.

Malinowski's work is also listed in the usual canon (Geertz, 1973). Besides Malinowski's (1925/1948) provocative and well-known delineations of the differences between magic, science, and religion, he also offers a religion-as-coping hypothesis, that religion helps one deal with "situations of emotional stress" (p. 67). Nadel (1957) refers to Malinowski, in this regard, as proposing a "theology of optimism." We will let Malinowski (1925/1948) speak to this: Religion provides for stress management by "opening up escapes from such situations and impasses as offer no empirical way out except by ritual and belief into the domain of the supernatural" (p. 67).

Another classic is Weber's (1958a) *The Protestant Ethic and the Spirit of Capitalism.* From Weber's work, it is reasonable to look on the Protestant work ethic as a learned coping style. In Weber's scheme, Protestantism (especially Calvinism) nurtured the rise of capitalism. In this case, Weber was interested in how religion structured social life and the motivations for capitalism. Yet, there is a larger scholarly tradition in Weber's (1952, 1958b, 1964) study of the sociology of religion, his classic books on religious "rational" orders that came with Confucianism, philosophical Brahmanism, and ancient Judaism. Weber's major historical scholarship is famous, yet not fully appreciated as the work on the Protestant ethic and capitalism. Take Weber's derived concept of "disenchantment" that followed the rational ordering cited above. With rational ordering, as Geertz (1973) phrases it, "the locus of sacredness was removed from the rooftrees, graveyards, and road-crossings of everyday life and put, in some sense into another realm where dwelt Jahweh, Logos, Tao, or Brahman" (p. 174). So Weber's (1952, 1958b, 1964) problem of "disenchantment" is with the loss of spiritual immediacy created by "rational" ordering of religious thought. Do we confront this disenchantment in our time? In our time, for example, the work of Bellah, Madsen, Sullivan, Swidler, and Tipton (1991) examines the tensions between individualism, even alienation, and a sense of community and the morality of virtue (Hauerwas, 1981) and the common good (MacIntyre, 1984).

Marx (1963) is often left out of the classic citation list, the fount of our research tradition. Marx is well known for his commentaries and severe criticism of how religion can serve to legitimize oppressed status in the ordering of social groups. Furthermore, as Bowker (1970) documents, Marx offered a social model for understanding suffering in the classical religious way, and suffering as a function of the social order. For Marx, the industrial revolution had created intense human suffering. For Marx, there is a social solution, one thread of which is much alive—that labeled social democracy. Bowker (1970, p. 137) argues that Marx's (1963) critiques were rooted in the Western religious traditions.

Freud's observations on religion are often cited (Galanter, Larson, & Rubenstone, 1991). Freud (1927/1961) expressed his skepticism and his views on the illusionary and neurotic in religion. On the other hand, Jung (1959) emphasized the vital importance of religion in psychic life. In any case, Freud and Jung continue to be vital stimuli for studying how religion influences mental health and psychiatric pathologies. Freud's (1927/1961) continuing provocative hypothesis is about the parallels between personal and collective rituals.

In the spirit of extending our sense of the classical for the purpose of stimulating fresh research questions, let us turn to what, for illustration, Cohen (1961) termed "the dark side of religion." Indeed, it is hard to read the usual classics on religion without the inference that the term *religion* is synonymous with altruism, compassion, and benevolence. In our opinion, the usual literature reviews have a religion-is-good-for-you bias.

As noted earlier, James (1958) reminds us of the concept of the religion of the healthy and the sick soul. Cohen (1961) details these dark sides or destructive aspects of religious history: (1) superstitions, demonic possession, and opposition to science; (2) historical crusades of war and hatred sanctioned by religion; (3) the "sacrifice" of heretics (e.g., during the Inquisition); (4) absolute claims that other faiths are heresy, in error, or "outside," as well as religious wars and justification of slavery; (5) the church normally siding with the powerful; and (6) inflicted spiritual agonies and terrors. Cohen does not exclude the positive side of religion, but argues we cannot ignore the destructive in religion. For example, how well do we understand the ways in which certain religious practices become learned sources of crippling fears and anxieties? Other obvious questions follow.

In keeping with James (1958) and Cohen (1961), we asked the help of Ellison in thinking about what could be called the religion-is-good-for-you bias in the literature. Ellison confirms only a handful of studies on the undesirable consequences of religion (Ellison, 1991). In our view, Pargament et al.'s (1988) attempt to study religious coping in both destructive (passive) and constructive (dynamic) ways offers clues for future research on the positive and negative aspects of religion. In future research, let us not neglect Cohen's and James's classic questions and observations on the destructive potential of certain types of religious experience (e.g., crippling and impossible expectations).

There is yet another current tradition vital to studying religion and health. Existential psychiatry is concerned with the structure of meaning and consequent adaptations, successful or unsuccessful. For example, the work of Frankl (1963) and May (1977) pioneered this tradition. The current expression of "the existential" and the process of finding meaning is reviewed in Yalom's (1980) important book. Yalom (1980) focuses on the vital ways we cope with death, freedom, isolation, and meaninglessness—the existential imperatives. In the full richness of these four existential issues, our conviction is that the study of religion and health has not fully addressed these coping imperatives.

In an overlooked work, Bowker (1970) focuses on the concept of suffering as one of the fundamental religious problems. Each of the world's great religions offers a foundation, a process, a language, a ritual, and an ideology within which inevitable suffering (death, sickness, oppression, injustice, etc.) finds expression and even proposed resolution. For Bowker (1970), the range of thinking on the problem of suffering is quite exceptional: for example, Judaism, Christianity, Islam, Buddhism, Hinduism, Marxism, Jainism, Manichaeism, and Zoroastrianism. Bowker's work should trigger a new era in the study of coping with suffering.

In summary, the above is not exhaustive, and our sense is that the classical canon needs expansion. The usual seminal figures of Marx, Freud, James, Durkheim, Malinowski, and Weber are still vital sources of ideas. But so are the concepts of axial age, paradise models, and literary insights. Perhaps a much larger canon is in order. More precision of concepts is needed. There are also neglected issues, such as how religions vary as to how to cope with suffering and other existential questions. There is a neglect of the dark side or the potential sick sentiments nurtured by religion. Religious experience, indeed, mirrors the full range of human experience. Just as religious assumptions are central to understanding various civilizations so they are central to understanding adaptive failures and successes. This leads us to a brief review of the place of religion in the current stress and adaptation paradigm for health and illness.

The Place of Religion in the Stress Paradigm

The above expanded views of the classical formulations relate to the stress paradigm set forth by Cassel (1976). We have chosen Cassel's summary as still basic and pivotal. To be sure, there are other cognate points of view (Elliott & Eisdorfer, 1982). Cassel makes a clear case for issues of control, threat, predictability, supportive feedback, and perception of meaning as key concepts in understanding host susceptibility. The same concepts are central to religious systems. But religion is absent from Cassel's (1976) classic formulation of a general model that relates social stress and support to host susceptibility. As we shall now suggest, religious aspects of stress, coping, and support are just beginning to be examined in today's stress and health paradigm. Religious structure is strategic to an understanding of social order in general. As the poet Stevens (1950) put it, we "rage for order" (p. 660).

Let us look at recent reviews of the place of religion in the stress, coping, and adaptation literature. In Elliott and Eisdorfer's (1982) edited work, an Institute of Medicine sponsored review of stress and health, there are no bibliographic references to religious belief, behavior, and the stress model. In Lazarus and Folkman's (1984) work, there is no reference to religion in their model, although there is a brief reference to the coping functions of cults and beliefs (pp. 64-65). If you consider Frankl's (1963) existential work or May's (1977) book as religious, then you have exhausted the references to religion in Lazarus and Folkman's review of the state of the art.

Cohen and Syme's (1985) edited work provides a thorough review of the support and health hypothesis. Support is a critical question for the study of religion and health, yet religion as support is not noted in titles, topics, or contents. There are references to Banfield (1958) about social integration, and to Comstock and Partridge's (1972) much-cited early paper. However, there are no other references to religion mentioned as a fundamental category for supportive strategies.

Let us next consider the use of religious variables in the social ties and health literature. In one example (Zuckerman, Kasl, & Ostfeld, 1984), religion is measured in an index of religiousness based on three questions concerning religious attendance, subjective religiousness, and religion as a source of strength. The authors found that religion had a protective effect only among those in poor health. In contrasting this work with a recent paper by Schoenbach and associates (1986), two measurement traditions are apparent:

1. Religion as an item in social ties indices (e.g., Schoenbach, Kaplan, Fredman, & Kleinbaum, 1986) following the example of Berkman and Syme (1979).
2. Religion as the exposure/independent variable (e.g., Comstock & Partridge, 1972; Levin & Vanderpool, 1991; Zuckerman et al., 1984).

Larson, Pattison, Blazer, Omran, and Kaplan (1986) set out to ask how attentive psychiatric research has been to measuring religious behavior as adaptation. They reported as follows:

> The authors conducted a systematic analysis of quantitative research on religious variables found in four psychiatric journals between 1978 and 1982. Of the 2,348 psychiatric articles reviewed, 59 included a quantified religious variable. In this research, the religious variable chosen was most often a single static measure of religion rather than multiple dynamic measures. In addition, other available religious research was seldom cited. Comparison with systematic analyses of religious research in psychology and sociology suggests that psychiatric research lacks conceptual and methodological sophistication. The data suggest that the academic knowledge and skills needed to evaluate religion have not been absorbed into the psychiatric domain. (p. 329)

More recently, Idler and Kasl (1992) lament the rare examination of Durkheim's work in the study of religion and health relationships. They note that "despite its importance in Durkheim's work, the subject of religion's influence on health and well-being is rarely addressed in contemporary sociological research" (p. 1052). Given that the extant literature is scant, the remainder of this chapter can be considered a development in the incorporation of religion into the stress and coping paradigm.

In a recent paper Ellison (1991; see also Chapter 4) synthesizes the relationship between religion and subjective well-being and several bodies of evidence:

1. *Social integration* focuses on social relations among those with shared values, through formal and informal networks, via the promotion of values that enhance well-being, and by rituals of shared meaning.

2. *Divine interaction* focuses on the ancient observations of relations that Buber (1958) refers to as I-thou, personal-divine identification, and dialogue.

3. *Existential certainty* focuses on issues such as coherence, order, meaning, and interpretation schemes. Our evolving understanding of existential certainty and health is a critical problem (Ellison, 1991, p. 82).

4. *Promotion of healthy practices and lifestyles* focuses on religiosity, denominational variations, relationships, and health habits that affect health (Ellison, 1991, pp. 81-83).

It is important to quote Ellison's (1991) caution about the quality of the current evidence: "Researchers remain far from a consensus on which specific dimensions of religiosity contribute to psychological well-being and subjective perceptions of life quality" (p. 80). Indeed, it is our position that there has been insufficient research to date to draw conclusions regarding the specific nature of the relationships among these variables. There is every indication that such investigation is warranted with different health outcomes (Levin, 1989; Levin & Vanderpool, 1987, 1991).

We now turn to broader attempts to suggest a framework for religion and health inquiries. From Kaplan's (1976) earlier review and the study by Graham et al. (1978), we focus on some possible hypotheses about religion as a source of stress. Our framework (Kaplan, 1976) is based on James's (1958) concepts that religion can promote the sick or healthy soul (see Table 3.1).

In an earlier review of the literature on religion and cardiovascular response, Kaplan (1976) suggested the following hypotheses about religion and coping:

Table 3.1   Preliminary Set of Religious Risk and Protective Behaviors

---

Risk Behaviors

1. James's sick soul, promotive of excessive guilt, self-doubt, sexuality fears, anxiety over personal worth, and so on.
2. Excessive demands of the work ethic.
3. Conflicts over systems of meaning and belief.
4. Conflicts over beliefs, feelings, and action.

Protective behaviors

1. Prohibitions against smoking.
2. Encouragement of physical fitness.
3. Early/preventive medical care ethos.
4. Regulation of excessive alcohol usage.
5. Socioemotional support.
6. Crisis resources.
7. Religious therapy (e.g., external sources of control, counseling, belief, and healing).
8. Reduction of anxiety/despair through systems of meaning and ritual release.

The following religious social mechanisms probably contribute to the maintenance of *hope*, the regulation of depression/fear/anxiety problems, and the protection of social-personal integration:

1. Ritual behavior—contributions to a sense of personal community and meaning, emotional "warmth," release of fear/anxiety, and a personal language of stress and healing.
2. Interpersonal provisions of support—social activities, "brothers and sisters," surrogate extended family, and crisis support.
3. Coping models—the extent to which religious teachings and models represent effective models for dealing with threat, anxiety, and despair: for example, providing predictability, models for coping with the finite and infinite, models of ideal attachments (personal and theological), anticipatory coping skills, emergency threat management, effective information, self-esteem protection, insulation from dangerous feelings, not giving up, and hope. Above all, the maintenance of hope and the regulation of fear are probably related to a variety of arousal responses. Many of the Psalms speak of this hypothesis, for example, the 27th.

In our most recent work, we have also attempted to summarize the basic research agenda in the study of stress, religion, and adaptation. In a forthcoming chapter (Kaplan & Blazer, in press), we quote a heuristic device to stimulate new research:

Religion addresses some of the fundamental *questions* of adaptation:

1. Time: between birth and death. The *meaning* of time is an essential problem to solve, or at least to find some personal comfort. How do we deal with forever?
2. "Community"—larger sense: Religions address the question of a personal and comfortable source of a sense of "community" and coherence.
3. Attachment and Separation Models: In the individual or social sense, religions (varying in response) deal with fundamental issues of social bonding and with the individual's degrees of freedom. Similarly, religions (varying again) deal with the meaning of separation and loss. There are no doubt a variety of religious *ultimate* models of attachment and loss. Ultimate refers to however we attach ourselves to our conception of God.
4. Relational Supplies/Rituals: Religions likewise deal with relational supplies of comfort, sociability, symbols and values, and ritual for handling the problems of living.
5. Rewards and Punishment: In dealing with the "problems" of living, religions have, usually, some model of rewards and punishments for conduct in an ethical context.
6. Meaning: Religions inevitably address these basic questions of life's meaning that address these classic problems:
   a. Life Problems/Burdens—how to manage?
   b. Values—how to find meaning?
   c. Tragedy/Injustice—how to deal with suffering?
   d. Death—how to give meaning to the ultimate "stressor"?
   e. Experience—how to give meaning to the human endeavor?
7. Wisdom—problem solving for "living" issues: Religions are accumulated wisdoms on how to deal with life. How well do they work?
8. Place in Cosmos/Nela: For the Greeks, we live in a cosmos, an order; for the Hebrews, we live with nela, the *mystery* of the universe.
9. Religious *sources* of sufferings can come in personal or social terms. There are no doubt religious sources of suffering, e.g. excessive guilt. How is this kept from being destructive? On the other hand, religion can be a major source of managing, and giving meaning to suffering.
10. Religion and the Social Order: As Durkheim and Weber originally pointed out, religion asks questions and provides "models" of social order.

Religions no doubt vary in how the above questions are answered, and how successfully for each group or individual. Although not exhaustive, these key questions are found in the various religious traditions and in the anthropology, sociology, and psychology of religion.

Our synthesis is from our reading of this vast literature. Our inquisitiveness leads us to choose one neglected coping process: forgiveness.

Forgiveness:
A Neglected Source of Research Ideas

We have selectively touched on the basic classical ideas that have driven the sociology, anthropology, and psychology of religion. We have linked these motivating ideas to the stress and adaptation paradigm, with an emphasis on the relative neglect of religious processes in our understanding of health and illness. We wish to focus on one neglected concept that links religion to human adaptation: the process and mechanisms of forgiveness. Arendt's (1958) conception of forgiveness is a powerful statement for our scientific purposes:

> Without being forgiven, released from the consequences of what we have done, our capacity to act would, as it were, be confined to one single deed from which we could never recover; we would remain the victims of its consequences forever, not unlike the sorcerer's apprentice who lacked the magic formula to break the spell. Without being bound to the fulfillment of promises, we would never be able to keep our identities; we would be condemned to wander helplessly and without direction in the darkness of each man's lonely heart, caught in its contradictions and equivocalities—a darkness which only the light shed over the public realm through the presence of others, who confirm the identity between the one who promises and the one who fulfils, can dispel. Both faculties, therefore, depend on plurality, on the presence and acting of others, for no one can forgive himself and no one can feel bound by a promise made only to himself; forgiving and promising enacted in solitude or isolation remain without reality and can signify no more than a role played before one's self. (p. 237)

We will approach the concept of forgiveness in three ways: (1) as the dynamic link between revenge and forgiveness, (2) as the link between forgiveness and the philosophy of religion, and (3) as the beginning proposals for a research agenda on forgiveness and health (Kaplan,

1992). In regard to the first point, we are guided by Jacoby (1983), in which she traces a history of the evolution of revenge. In regard to the second point, we are guided by the most recent attempt by Murphy and Hampton (1988) to provide an exhaustive look at the philosophy of forgiveness. Finally, we will draw on Kaplan's (1992) recent attempt to link the concept of forgiveness to our social health and to hostility and heart disease. In this regard, there is very little scientific literature (Fitzgibbons, 1986; Hope, 1987) on forgiveness as coping and as a biosocial health question. Indeed, Williams's (1989) focus is on trust for treating chronic hostility.

Jacoby (1983) provides a series of observations on forgiveness in the classical literature. As noted in Arendt (1958), forgiveness is a process central to understanding human social functions. As you examine the variety of ways of thinking about forgiveness, you are forced to take a look at one of the alternate responses: revenge. In this context, Jacoby (1983) ties the question of forgiveness to the larger literature on revenge in literature, religion, and law.

This work is very hard to summarize other than by listing Jacoby's major points relevant to our inquiry into the forgiveness process. Take the cliché forgive and forget; however difficult or impossible, it is more acceptable than the next step of private or public revenge (Jacoby, 1983, p. 1). Publicly, we accept justice; however, we have historically evolved transitions to create institutions to deal with revenge, for example, God, art, the law, and religion (Jacoby, 1983). Jacoby's basic point is that revenge is a robust theme in literature from the earliest Semitic and Greek epics (p. 15) to the present. Epps (1969) emphasizes that the Greeks thought revenge to be the most powerful and predictable response to injury. Forgiveness is not a significant concern in the Greek epics (Epps, 1969).

For example, according to Jacoby's (1983) admirable synthesis, in religion we find contradictory themes. God and prophets of mercy and love-versus-vengeance themes abound (pp. 66-67). As Jacoby points out, all Western religions reject human revenge but approve vengeance to serve God's purpose (p. 68). Jacoby's classic example is that Christianity created a mythic story that asserted that the Jews were to suffer revenge for Christ's death, the oldest revenge story in history (pp. 68-69). Religion institutionalized vengeance for itself. It is at the institutional level that revenge is legitimate and controlled. For example, Paul's promise is "vengeance is the Lord's and He will repay" (Jacoby, 1983, p. 83).

Jacoby (1983) must be quoted on the subject of forgiveness. She offers us much to ponder and to clarify:

So it is with forgiveness and vindictiveness, which touch reciprocal chords within the injured spirit, as well as between the sufferer and the agent of suffering. This reciprocity lies at the heart of the evolution of revenge. It is central to the resolution of both private and public conflicts; it informs spiritual and temporal passions. Unlike revenge, forgiveness has rarely exerted so forceful an influence on human affairs as to require the restraints of law and religion. Forgiveness is seen as an expression of the noblest possibilities of human nature, revenge of the basest—and we have become all too accustomed to the ascendancy of the base.

This perceived opposition between forgiveness and revenge omits at least two crucial elements of the moral equation. The first is a willingness to acknowledge culpability on the part of the man or woman who has wrought the suffering of others. The second goes beyond culpability and involves the offender's degree of remorse; "I did it and I'm glad" is not an admission of responsibility calculated to inspire forgiveness. A third factor comes into play when the injury is a public matter—the pressure applied by society to restore some sort of equilibrium between victim and victimizer. This equilibrium is called justice, and it is far from irrelevant even in private spheres of existence which cannot be reached by law. Fairness is to private disputes as justice is to public ones. Even in the context of profound love—affording compassion far beyond the point where it is extended or expected in other social contexts—forgiveness becomes impossible if a basic sense of fairness is repeatedly assaulted: the act is meaningless unless both parties realize there is something to forgive. (p. 332)

Jacoby focuses our attention on better understanding the powerful dynamics at the intersection of the value of forgiveness processes that invoke also the revenge response. Let us now turn our remaining remarks to the forgiveness process. Murphy and Hampton (1988) offer the most recent attempt to summarize the classical forgiveness questions. We will deal with the key commentaries of each author, first with Murphy's critical chapter. Murphy's use of Butler's definition of forgiveness sets his theme: "Forgiveness, Bishop Butler teaches, is the forswearing of resentment—the resolute overcoming of the anger and hatred that are naturally directed toward a person who has done one an unjustified and non-excused moral injury" (Murphy & Hampton, 1988, p. 15). Butler's definition is utilitarian: It is a practical and useful way to control resentment (e.g., the bad consequences of personal revenge), and it is distinct from the issue of forgetting. For Murphy, forgiveness serves self-esteem, perceptions of worth, and reciprocities of what is owed (p. 16). Given these orienting definitions of Butler and Murphy, we will list the key considerations of forgiveness in Murphy's theory

of forgiveness and resentment (Murphy & Hampton, 1988, pp. 14-34).
Then we will summarize Hampton's basic arguments.
Murphy's major themes for our purposes are as follows:

1. Resentment can be a barrier to restored moral order. Forgiveness heals.
2. There is a betrayal side to the processes of resentment. Murphy quotes
   Cosmus, the duke of Florence: "You shall read that we are commanded to
   forgive our enemies: but you never read that we are commanded to forgive
   our friends" (p. 17).
3. Murphy cautions that forgiveness can be a vice when given at the cost of
   human dignity, to play the doormat, or as Horney's morbid dependency
   (pp. 18-19).
4. What is forgiveness? It is not an excuse, a justification, or mercy (p. 20).
5. How are we to solve Butler's puzzle: the command to love and the human
   passion of resentment? And do we forget? So for Murphy forgiveness
   involves one of these moral grounds:
   a. "he repented or had a change or heart"
   b. "he meant well (his motives are good)"
   c. "he has suffered enough"
   d. "he has undergone humiliation (perhaps some ritual humiliation, e.g.,
      the apology ritual of 'I beg forgiveness')"
   e. "for old time's sake ('He has been a good and loyal friend to me in
      the past')" (p. 24).

Let us now turn to Hampton's commentary on forgiveness, resentment, and hatred (Murphy & Hampton, 1988, pp. 35-87). Perhaps her
introductory quote is special food for thought:

Sir Joshua told us a curious particular of Dr. Adam Smith. He had taken a
resolution that he would hate nobody, and if he knew himself, there was
nobody in the world whom he hated. This was a new thought to me for the
moment, and I am afraid it is new to most people in actual practice. But it is
an essential principle of Christianity. Let me try it. But it does not exclude a
certain degree of aversion to some compared to others. (James Boswell,
quoted in Murphy & Hampton, 1988, p. 35)

Hampton's theses force us to think more clearly about the uses of the
term *forgiveness*. First, both Hampton and Murphy are sympathetic to
Nietzsche's observation that forgiveness, in some limited circumstances,
can be harmful, a vice; indeed, Nietzsche thought of Christianity as
promoting repressed resentment. "So we face the following puzzle: how

can forgiveness be a duty when it seems to involve overcoming a useful, even therapeutic emotion in a way that can do harm to the forgiver?" (Murphy & Hampton, 1988, pp. 35-36). Second, Hampton finds the biblical model for forgiveness useful: The Hebrew words for forgiveness are revealing: *kipper,* "to cover"; *nasa,* "to lift up, or carry away, or cleanse"; and *salach,* "to let go" (Murphy & Hampton, 1988, p. 37). Hence the wronged lets go of being the victim, of feeling wronged. Jesus' use of the Greek word *aphiemi* refers to forgiveness as "to remit, send away, or liberate" as well as to forgive (Murphy & Hampton, 1988, p. 37). Both biblical themes are identical in that forgiving focuses on the actions of the wrongdoer first—as preparatory (p. 38); one then overcomes a point of view that permits forgiveness. The Hebrew concepts of *kippur, nasa,* and *salach* cover the same semantic range as the Greek word *aphiemi* (p. 37).

Hampton's major task becomes this: For the forgiver, what is required to "let go of" (Murphy & Hampton, 1988, p. 43)? From this evolves Hampton's conception of forgiveness. So let us note Hampton's required actions in the forgiveness processes:

1. Being insulted and being degraded (p. 43). Hampton's basic response to this question falls into four aspects of a theory of human worth: (a) What are the conceptions of human values? (b) How are human values ranked? (c) What is the evidence of value and rank? (d) How do humans lose or gain value? (pp. 48-49). For example, in this framework, an assessment of insult or hurt takes place (e.g., rape, insult, and slight).

2. Resentment and indignation. Hampton insists on thinking about resentment as more than rage or defensive anger; resentment "is an idea-ridden response" (p. 54). How do we assess the cognitive processes involved?

3. Resentment and hatred. Resentment focuses on the act or actions; hatred is directed toward the person (p. 60).

4. The functions of not hating are as follows:
   a. to establish a sensible moral basis for not seeking revenge
   b. to hate is self-defeating (p. 79)

5. Moral hatred and forgiveness. Hampton's essential conclusion (for our reflection) is captured in the following summary:

   To define forgiveness adequately we must capture the forgiver's change of heart (as distinct from his psychological preparations for it), and analyze it as some kind of absolution from guilt, while still making clear how it is not what Kolnai called condonation. The preceding analysis proposes that the first stage of the forgiving process, namely, the psychological preparation for this change of heart, involves regaining one's confidence in one's own worth despite the immoral action challenging it. This is accomplished by overcoming, in the sense of "giving up" or "repudiating," emotions such as spite or malice, and "overcoming" in the sense of "transcending" resentment. But even after one has overcome these emotions, indignation at the action and some degree of moral hatred towards the wrongdoer may remain. I want to propose that these are the emotions which, when they are overthrown, enable the following change of heart to take place:

The forgiver who previously saw the wrongdoer as someone bad or rotten or morally indecent to some degree has a change of heart when he "washes away" or disregards the wrongdoer's immoral actions or character traits in his ultimate moral judgement of her, and comes to see her as still *decent, not* rotten as a person, and someone with whom he may be able to renew a relationship.

When one has a change of heart towards one's wrongdoer, one "reapproves" of her, so that one is able to consider renewing an association with her. The change of heart is the new understanding of the wrongdoer as a person one can be "for" rather than "against." (p. 83)

Hampton (Murphy & Hampton, 1988, pp. 86-87) closes on several challenges that any scientific approach to forgiveness must consider. First, Judaism and Christianity consider self-forgiveness to be hard to accomplish. Both turn to God for certain basic sources of atonement. Second, how does the process of avoiding self-loathing work? Third, how does forgiveness serve to protect self-worth? Fourth, when can forgiveness sometimes be a bad thing?

Summary and Research Agenda

In summary, we come back to our three originating questions. It is obvious that Geertz is correct: We must expand the research agenda on religion and health in terms far richer than those of Freud, Durkheim, James, Weber, Malinowski, and Marx, however vital they were at the time. For example, there are still key questions to explore around James's (1958) concept that religion is humankind's basic way of coping with solitude. There are vital research questions linked to an understanding of the axial age in religious thought.

First, over time, how does religious creativity work? In the great literature of history, there are other triggering questions. For example, Pasternak links religious concerns to a wish for cosmic understanding. Dostoyevsky views religion as the "need" to worship, yet emphasizes the destructive consequences of religions that need heretics by simply being outside a "truth" community. Cohen (1961) reminds us of the dark side of religious history and of religion as a potentially destructive force. The existential tradition emphasizes how various groups and cultures come to explain death, meaningfulness, freedom and choice, tragedy, and injustice. Coping with suffering is central to all religious traditions. Where is the cutting edge inquiry into religion and coping with suffering (Bowker, 1970)? In the area of specific diseases, coping with cancer is certainly a cognate literature (Broadhead & Kaplan, 1991). But there is far more to do.

Second, the foregoing pose questions for our understanding of the stress and adaptation paradigm: For example, how does religion offer coping resources? How does religion, in contrast, pose impossible expectations? It is clear that the stress and adaptation paradigm requires greater study of James's hypotheses about the religion of the healthy soul or the religion of the sick soul. Indeed, religious systems model the data for all the basic stress and adaptation paradigm themes. For example, Slater's (1966) neglected hypothesis is that group processes evolve microcosms of basic religious concepts. Slater's (1966) title is revealing: *Microcosm: Structural, Psychological and Religious Evolution in Groups.*

These first two questions have been areas of a great deal of scholarship. In regard to our third question, we will pay special attention to expanding our understanding of forgiveness as a coping and healing process. We will, therefore, sketch out several areas for research on forgiveness as a basic support, coping, and healing process. We must first confront the problems of definition. The following serve to illustrate a range of definitions:

1. After Butler, Murphy and Hampton (1988) argue that to forgive is to foreswear resentment, and to overcome anger for moral reasons.
2. Nietzsche argued that a truly strong person does not need to forgive. There is no resentment involved. The strong person is not hurt (Murphy & Hampton, 1988, pp. 35-36).
3. Socrates argued that a good person cannot be injured. Self-esteem is, therefore, protective against a resentment response (Epps, 1966, pp. 1-7).

4. Williams (1989) offers a definition with a treatment goal:

> One final strategy for reducing hostility and having a more trusting heart. . . . Simply *forgive* those who have mistreated and/or angered you. Rather than blame those who have mistreated you, rather than continuing to resent them and to seek revenge, try to understand the emotions of the one who has wronged you. By letting go of the resentment and relinquishing the goal of retribution, you may find, as psychiatrist Richard Fitzgibbons suggests, that the weight of anger lifts from your shoulders, easing your pain and also helping you to forget the wrong. (p. 195)

5. Ornish (1990, pp. 214-222) devotes eight pages to the topic of altruism, compassion, and forgiveness in his book. He provides examples of altruism, compassion, and forgiveness as therapeutic but gives no precise definitions of the three concepts.

Given the unresolved problems of the range of definitions, the forgiveness process invokes basic questions for further study:

1. To foreswear resentment (forgive) is a complex process. Why?
2. Forgiveness involves different audiences: for example, yourself, friends, family, and the Ultimate. Are these different processes?
3. For forgiveness and social justice in daily life, how does forgiveness enable the resolution of feeling victimized?
4. How does forgiveness enable the problems of isolation to lead to social comfort?
5. In Wechsler's (1990, p. 140) summary, how do various religious traditions facilitate, or interfere, with his five dimensions of repentance: remorse, recantation, renunciation, resolution, and reconciliation?
6. Following Jacoby (1983), why is revenge rather than forgiveness the more likely response to injury?

The works of Hope (1987) and Fitzgibbons (1986) suggest therapeutic applications. For the sake of illustration, several issues seem key:

1. How does the Alcoholics Anonymous tradition of using forgiveness as a skill work?
2. Hope (1987) asks patients to consider the consequences of not forgiving. How does this work as a therapeutic tactic?
3. Forgiveness is central to Judeo-Christian religious ritual. How do these rituals actually work as to efficacy?

4. Hope (1987) points out that in Zen "forgiveness is an attitude of lavishness and utter openness" (p. 243). Indeed, how are we to study forgiveness cross-culturally?

5. Fitzgibbons (1986) urges the uses of forgiveness to treat anger. How does this work?

In a recent paper, Kaplan (1992) put forward the idea that to learn to be more forgiving, several social skills are essential as hypotheses:

1. To be more accepting of human frailty in self and others.
2. To balance healthy humility with sense of humor.
3. To balance appreciation of gifts and limitations.
4. To balance expectations with realization.
5. To protect self-esteem skills.
6. To seek interpersonal diversity and openness.

In another recent paper, the result of a 5-year seminar at the University of Washington, Enright, Gassin, and Wu (1992) provide an exceptional review of a developmental perspective on forgiveness. They propose that the dominant Kohlberg tradition of studying justice and moral development be expanded to focus on forgiveness. They suggest two paradigms for research on forgiveness and moral development: (1) the cognitive stages of justice and forgiveness and (2) factors in the psychological process of forgiveness as a therapeutic aim.

As closing questions, Murphy and Hampton (1988) suggest at least four troubling enigmas:

1. What are the advantages of turning over certain retributions and equity to God, or creator?
2. How do we deal with the "unforgivable"?
3. How do we deal with forgiveness if that means being a doormat?
4. When is forgiveness not in order?

To put the above in another way, from Dostoyevsky (1880/1960): "One can love one's neighbours in the abstract, or even at a distance, but at close quarters it's almost impossible" (p. 246).

In conclusion, the critical human yearning for meaning, a major motive in religious behavior, is brilliantly expressed by Santayana:

Any attempt to speak without speaking any particular language is not more
hopeless than the attempt to have a religion that shall be no religion in
particular. . . . Thus every living and healthy religion has a marked idiosyn-
crasy. Its power consists in its special and surprising message and in the bias
which that revelation gives to life. The vistas it opens and the mysteries it
propounds are another world to live in; and another world to live in—whether
we expect ever to pass wholly over into it or no—is what we mean by having
a religion. (quoted in Geertz, 1973, p. 87)

Does the forgiveness process open us to the language of healthy
religion and to fresh vistas in the study of religion and health?

References

Alter, R., & Kermode, F. (Eds.). (1987). *The literary guide to the Bible.* Cambridge, MA:
Harvard University Press.
Arendt, H. (1958). *The human condition.* Chicago: University of Chicago Press.
Banfield, E. C. (1958). *The moral order for a backward society.* Glencoe, IL: Free Press.
Barchas, P. R. (Ed.). (1984). *Social hierarchies.* Westport, CT: Greenwood.
Barchas, P. R., & Mendoza S. P. (Eds.). (1984). *Social cohesion.* Westport, CT: Green-
wood.
Bellah, R. N., Madsen, R., Sullivan, W. M., Swidler, A., & Tipton, S. M. (1991). *The good
society.* New York: Alfred Knopf.
Berkman, L. F., & Syme, S. L. (1979). Social networks, host resistance, and mortality.
American Journal of Epidemiology, 109, 186-204.
Bowker, J. (1970). *Problems of suffering in religions of the world.* Cambridge: Cambridge
University Press.
Broadhead, W. E., & Kaplan, B. H. (1991). Social support and the cancer patient. *Cancer,
67,* 794-799.
Buber, M. (1958). *I and thou* (2nd ed., R. Smith, Trans.). New York: Scribner's.
Campbell, J. (1988). *The power of myth.* New York: Doubleday.
Cassel, J. (1976). The contribution of the social environment to host susceptibility.
American Journal of Epidemiology, 104, 107-123.
Cohen, S., & Syme, L. (Ed.). (1985). *Social support and health.* New York: Academic
Press.
Cohen, M. (1961). The dark side of religion. In W. Kaufman (Ed.), *Religion from Tolstoy
to Camus* (pp. 279-297). New York: Harper & Row.
Comstock, G. W., & Partridge, K.B. (1972). Church attendance and health. *Journal of
Chronic Diseases, 25,* 665-672.
Dostoyevsky, F. M. (1960). *The brothers Karamazov* (C. Garnett, Trans.). New York:
Random House. (Original work published 1880)
Durkheim, E. (1961). *The elementary forms of the religious life.* New York: Collier Books.
(Original work published 1912)

Ellison, C. G. (1991). Religious involvement and subjective well-being. *Journal of Health and Social Behavior, 32,* 80-99.

Elliott, G. R., & Eisdorfer, C. (Eds.). (1982). *Stress and human health.* New York: Springer.

Enright, R. D., Gassin, E. A., & Wu, G. R. (1992). Forgiveness: A developmental view. *Journal of Moral Education, 21,* 99-113.

Epps, P. (1969). *Thoughts from the Greeks.* Columbus: Missouri University Press.

Fitzgibbons, R. P. (1986). The cognitive uses of forgiveness in the treatment of anger. *Psychotherapy, 23,* 629-633.

Frazer, J. (1922). *The golden bough.* New York: Macmillan.

Frankl, V. E. (1963). *Man's search for meaning.* New York: Washington Square Press.

Freud, S. (1961). *The future of an illusion* (J. Strachey, Trans.). New York: Norton. (Original work published 1927)

Galanter, M., Larson, D., & Rubenstone, E. (1991). Christian psychiatry. *American Journal of Psychiatry, 148,* 90-95.

Geertz, C. (1973). *The interpretation of cultures.* New York: Basic Books.

Graham, T. W., Kaplan, B. H., Cornoni-Huntley, J. C., James, S. A., Becker, C., Hames, C., & Heyden, S. (1978). Frequency of church attendance and blood pressure elevation. *Journal of Behavioral Medicine, 1,* 37-43.

Hauerwas, S. (1981). *A community of character.* South Bend, IN: University of Notre Dame Press.

Heschel, A. J. (1963). *The sabbath.* Philadelphia: Jewish Publication Society of America.

Hope, D. (1987). The healing paradox of forgiveness. *Psychotherapy, 24,* 240-244.

Idler, E. L., & Kasl, S. V. (1992). Religion, disability, depression, and the timing of death. *American Journal of Sociology, 97,* 1052-1079.

Jacoby, S. (1983). *Wild justice.* New York: Harper & Row.

James, W. (1958). *The varieties of religious experience* (7th ed.). New York: Mentor Books.

Jung, C. G. (1959). The archetypes and the collective unconscious. In C. G. Jung, *Collected works* (Vol. 9, Pt. 1, pp. 79-91). New York: Routledge & Kegan Paul.

Kaplan, B. H. (1976). A note on religious beliefs and coronary heart disease. *Journal of the South Carolina Medical Society, 15* (5, Suppl.), 60-64.

Kaplan, B. H. (1992). Social health and the forgiving heart. *Journal of Behavioral Medicine, 15,* 3-14.

Kaplan, B. H., & Blazer, D. G. (in press). Religion in the stress and adaptation paradigm. In P. Barchas (Ed.), *Essays in sociophysiology.* New York: Oxford Press.

Kaufman, W. (1961). *Religion from Tolstoy to Camus.* New York: Harper Torchbooks.

Larson, D. B., Pattison, E. M., Blazer, D. G., Omran, A. R., & Kaplan, B. H. (1986). Systematic analysis of research on religious variables in four major psychiatric journals, 1978-1982. *American Journal of Psychiatry, 143,* 329-334.

Lazarus, R. S., & Folkman, S. (1984). *Stress, appraisal, and coping.* New York: Springer.

Levin, J. S. (1989). Religious factors in aging, adjustment, and health: A theoretical overview. In W. M. Clements (Ed.), *Religion, aging and health: A global perspective* (pp. 133-146). New York: Haworth.

Levin, J. S., & Vanderpool, H. Y. (1987). Is frequent religious attendance *really* conducive to better health? Toward an epidemiology of religion. *Social Science and Medicine, 24,* 589-600.

Levin, J. S., & Vanderpool, H. Y. (1991). Religious factors in physical health and the prevention of illness. *Prevention in Human Services, 9,* 41-64.

Levi-Strauss, C. (1962). *The savage mind.* Chicago: University of Chicago Press.

MacIntyre, A. C. (1984). *After virtue.* South Bend, IN: University of Notre Dame Press.

Malinowski, B. (1948). *Magic, science, and religion.* Garden City, NY: Doubleday. (Original work published 1925)

Manuel, F. E., & Manuel, F. R. (1972). Sketch of a natural history of paradise. *Daedalus, 101,* 83-128.

Marx, K. (1963). *Das Kapital* (rev. ed.). Chicago: University of Chicago Press.

May, R. (1977). *The meaning of anxiety* (rev. ed.). New York: Ronald.

Murphy, M. G., & Hampton, J. (1988). *Forgiveness and mercy.* New York: Cambridge University Press.

Nadel, S. F. (1957). Malinowski on magic and religion. In R. W. Firth (Ed.), *Man and culture* (pp. 189-208). New York: Harper & Row.

Ornish, D. (1990). *Reversing heart disease.* New York: Ballantine.

Paragament, K. I., Kennell, J., Hathaway, W., Grevengoed, N., Newman, J., & Jones, W. (1988). Religion and the problem-solving process: Three styles of coping. *Journal for the Scientific Study of Religion, 27,* 90-104.

Paternak, B. (1958). *Doctor Zhivago.* New York: Pantheon.

Schoenbach, V. J., Kaplan, B. H., Fredman, L., & Kleinbaum, D. (1986). Social ties and mortality in Evans County. *American Journal of Epidemiology, 123,* 577-591.

Schwartz, B. I. (1975). The age of transcendence. *Daedalus, 104,* 1-9.

Slater, P. E. (1966). *Microcosm: Structural, psychological and religious evolution in groups.* New York: Wiley.

Stevens, W. (1950). The idea of order at Key West. In F. O. Matthiessen (Ed.), *The Oxford book of American verse.* New York: Oxford University Press.

Weber, M. (1952). *Ancient Judaism.* Glencoe, IL: Free Press.

Weber, M. (1958a). *The Protestant ethic and the spirit of capitalism* (T. Parsons, Trans.). New York: Scribners.

Weber, M. (1958b). *The religion of India.* Glencoe, IL: Free Press.

Weber, M. (1964). *The religion of China.* New York: Macmillan.

Wechsler, H. J. (1990). *What's so bad about guilt?* New York: Simon & Schuster.

Williams, R. (1989). *The trusting heart.* New York: Random House.

Wilson, R. N. (1992). *The courage to be leisured.* Unpublished manuscript.

Yalom, I. D. (1980). *Existential psychotherapy.* New York: Basic Books.

Zuckerman, D. M., Kasl, S. V., & Ostfeld, A. M. (1984). Psychosocial predictors of mortality among the elderly poor. *American Journal of Epidemiology, 119,* 410-423.

4

Religion, the Life Stress Paradigm, and the Study of Depression

CHRISTOPHER G. ELLISON

Introduction

A burgeoning interdisciplinary literature explores the role of social factors in the etiology of depression, distress, and other psychiatric disorders. Over the past decade, mental health researchers in various fields—primarily social epidemiologists, sociologists, psychologists, and gerontologists—have oriented much of their work around what has been termed *the life stress paradigm* (Dohrenwend & Dohrenwend, 1981; Lin & Ensel, 1989). This paradigm directs attention to the role of stressful events and conditions in undermining mental health and increasing the risk of various disorders. Early versions of the life stress paradigm posited a direct link between social stressors and mental and physical health (Selye, 1956). However, more recent research makes it clear that these early versions misspecified the relationships between stress and mental health by omitting critical intervening variables, including social, psychological, and physical resources (Mirowsky & Ross, 1986). Studies conducted within the life stress tradition are typically concerned with the following issues: (1) identifying the deleterious effects of various types of stressful events and conditions on mental health outcomes, (2) specifying the roles of social and psychological resources in mediating and moderating these relationships, and

(3) clarifying the roles of social-structural and institutional factors (e.g., role conflict and role strain) in shaping exposure and vulnerability to stressors and access to the resources that can cushion the impact of these social stressors (Pearlin, 1989).

As this book illustrates, researchers have shown mounting interest in the relationships among religious involvement and mental health, subjective well-being, and related constructs (Ellison, 1991a). Although the results of these studies are not unequivocal, the weight of evidence clearly suggests that aspects of public and private religious involvement facilitate well-being. However, few studies (e.g., Idler & Kasl, 1992) have dealt with clinically recognized psychiatric disorders, and even these have not drawn extensively on the life stress paradigm. Moreover, researchers working within the life stress tradition have given short shrift to the possible role of religious factors in conditioning the levels and effects of stress and resources on mental health outcomes.

This chapter seeks to bridge this gulf by developing a series of arguments that link religious factors with the component items of the life stress paradigm. To maximize continuity with previous empirical studies in the life stress tradition, this discussion centers on depression. However, many of the arguments advanced herein are germane to the study of other disorders as well.

In brief, religious factors may impede depression in the following ways: (1) by reducing the risk of certain major chronic and acute stressors, (2) by providing cognitive and institutional frameworks that make certain stressors seem less threatening to an individual than they might otherwise appear, (3) by generating relatively high levels of objective and subjective social resources, and (4) by enhancing valuable psychological resources, particularly positive self-perceptions. The chapter synthesizes current theory and research in the area of religion and mental health and indicates fruitful directions for future research.

Although this chapter emphasizes ways in which religious factors may reduce the risk of depression and distress, it also describes ways in which public and private religious involvement may actually lead to undesirable mental health consequences, such as through heightening stress and/or reducing access to personal resources. Finally, although the primary focus here is on the indirect links between religious factors and depression, brief attention is also devoted to several ways in which religious involvement may reduce the risk of depression directly.

The Life Stress Paradigm and
the Study of Depression

Stress and Depression

Researchers typically conceptualize stress as any condition that threatens or challenges personal well-being (e.g., George, 1989). The relevant literature identifies at least three distinct types of life stress that are positively related to depression and various other psychiatric disorders. First, *life events* are discrete changes in life circumstances that disrupt routine patterns of behavior or cognitive functioning (Funch & Marshall, 1984; Tausig, 1982). Life events are considered acute (as opposed to chronic) sources of stress. Examples commonly cited in the literature include bereavement, acute illness, job loss, and breakups of marital or close social relationships. Most available information on life events and their consequences pertains to events experienced in the recent past, generally within the past month or year. Given the affective, reactive character of depressive symptoms and disorders, it is reasonable to expect that more recent events may have greater bearing on these outcomes than more distant events. Early discussions of life events often assumed that all major events are stressful because they require adjustment to new and unfamiliar circumstances. However, the weight of current evidence indicates that the degree of stress caused by the same life event varies according to the meaning of that event for the individual.

Second, *chronic stress* refers to long-term conditions that call into question individual well-being. Such conditions include lasting illness or disability, financial deprivation, interpersonal or role strains, and job-related tensions. Although it is the duration of such conditions that distinguishes chronic stressors from acute stressors, Avison and Turner (1988) have cautioned that life events may be more chronic than previous researchers have recognized. Thus the boundaries separating acute and chronic stressors remain somewhat blurred in the research literature.

Third, *daily hassles* are relatively minor yet annoying and frustrating situations encountered in the course of routine activities (DeLongis, Coyne, Dakof, Folkman, & Lazarus, 1982). While hassles constitute ongoing (i.e., not clearly bounded) sources of stress, they are less intense than acute and chronic stressors. Nevertheless, both chronic stressors and daily hassles may be more predictive of depression than life events, although this pattern may partly reflect variations in event recall.

Social Resources and Depression

Although numerous studies document the beneficial effects of social ties on mental and physical health, researchers continue to debate appropriate strategies of conceptualizing and assessing these consequences (Barrera, 1986; Cohen & Wills, 1985). Some investigators have employed objective measures of social contact and integration and/or objective indicators of expressive (e.g., companionship) and instrumental (e.g., goods, services, information) forms of assistance. Other researchers argue that the most useful information regarding social resources and their effects comes from studies that map egocentric networks and attempt to specify their relevant structural characteristics (e.g., density and multiplexity) (Hall & Wellman, 1985). Finally, others contend that perceptions of social ties (e.g., perceived reliability and satisfaction) are more important for the stress process than are objective network features (Thoits, 1985).

Researchers have reported at least three distinct patterns: (1) direct effects of social ties on mental health outcomes, irrespective of stress levels or types; (2) effects of social ties that mediate the impact of stress on such outcomes; and (3) effects of social ties that moderate the deleterious consequences of stress on mental health. In the latter instance, the strongest beneficial effects of subjective support are typically found among persons experiencing high levels of stress. Despite the inevitable inconsistencies across diverse studies, the weight of the evidence to date indicates that perceived support (i.e., perceived reliability of support and satisfaction with network members) has strong positive main effects on mental health, as well as significant stress-buffering effects (Cohen & Wills, 1985; Landerman, George, Campbell, & Blazer, 1990; Wethington & Kessler, 1986).

Psychological Resources and Depression

In addition to social ties, recent research underscores the role of psychological resources in the stress process. The two sets of psychological resources most frequently identified as mediating and/or moderating factors in the relationships between stress and depression are self-esteem, or positive evaluations of one's inherent worth, and personal mastery, or feelings of empowerment and control over one's personal affairs (e.g., Pearlin, Menaghan, Lieberman, & Mullan, 1981; Pearlin & Schooler, 1978). These specific and relatively stable personality traits are of particular interest to researchers in light of prevailing perspectives regarding the social etiology of depression (Levitt, Lubin, & Brooks, 1983; Marsella, Hirschfeld, & Katz, 1987).

First, Beck's (1967) theory of the cognitive triad places self-esteem squarely at center stage as a major factor in the onset of depression. In brief, Beck implicates three major thought patterns in the origin of depression: (1) the worthlessness of the self, (2) the meaninglessness of life, and (3) the hopelessness of the future. This cognitive triad is rooted in and sustained by schemata, or relatively inflexible general principles and enduring assumptions as well as recurrent structural errors in the logical processes of depressed persons. By increasing the likelihood that individuals will develop such negative interpretations of life events, these schemata and logical flaws are thought to increase the risk of depression.

Another influential perspective on depression highlights the role of perceptions that events and circumstances are beyond individual control. These arguments surface in a number of slightly different formulations, including learned helplessness, external locus of control, fatalism, and mastery (see Rosenfield, 1989). Despite their differences, these formulations share an understanding that low personal control is positively related to depression. The perceived inability to affect one's environment may foster feelings of hopelessness and low self-worth, which have been identified as precursors of depression by Beck (1967) and others. Furthermore, the sense that there is little connection between one's actions and their consequences may promote passive and fearful approaches to the social world, leading individuals to adopt passive coping strategies and to discount the usefulness of more active behaviors. In addition, a low sense of personal control may prevent one from learning from previous negative experiences and thus from eliminating behavior with undesirable outcomes (Mirowsky & Ross, 1984). Thus there are sound theoretical and empirical reasons to anticipate that both self-esteem and personal mastery mediate and/or moderate the relationship between stress and depression.

Coping and Depression

Researchers have become increasingly interested in the task of identifying specific strategies that are effective in facilitating adjustment to chronic and acute stressors. According to Lazarus and Launier (1978), coping refers to "efforts, both action-oriented and intrapsychic, to manage (that is, master, tolerate, reduce, minimize) environmental and internal demands, and conflicts among them, which tax or exceed a person's resources" (p. 288). The coping process involves primary and secondary cognitive appraisals of potential stressors and the implementation of response(s) based on those appraisals (Folkman & Lazarus, 1988; Lazarus & Folkman, 1984). In primary appraisals, persons assess the nature of the event or condition and the degree of threat posed to the individual. Such evaluations determine the valence and intensity of emotional reaction to the encounter. In secondary appraisals, persons assess the resources (e.g., social, psychological, informational, and material) available to them and the cognitive and behavioral options for managing the demands of the encounter. Thus investigators are increasingly aware that a similar event or condition may be appraised as a threat by one person and as neutral or a challenge by another.

While the literature contains many typologies of coping behaviors, most researchers in this area distinguish between two types of coping: (1) problem-solving coping, or actions undertaken to change the terms of the person-environment relationship (Folkman & Lazarus, 1988), and (2) palliative coping, or efforts to alter the subjective meaning of an encounter and/or to manage the emotions associated with the encounter or the outcome of the encounter. Although religious factors may also be involved in problem-solving coping, much of the discussion below focuses on the role of religious cognitions in appraisals and in emotion management.

Building on this outline of the life stress paradigm and its component elements, the remainder of this chapter argues that aspects of religious involvement may contribute to individual mental health—and may reduce the risk of depression and other psychiatric disorders—in the following ways: (1) by reducing the risk of exposure to certain stressors and by altering the subjective meanings assigned to potentially stressful events and conditions, (2) by increasing the volume and enhancing the perception of various social resources, (3) by promoting crucial psychological resources, especially positive self-perceptions, and (4) by offering specific cognitive strategies for appraising potential stressors in less threatening terms and for managing the emotions associated with stressors.

Religion, Social Control, and Stress

Embeddedness within religious communities may serve to regulate and constrain the behavior of individual members (Durkheim, 1901/1933,

1897/1951) in ways that facilitate good physical health, positive familial and interpersonal relationships, and ethical work conduct and financial dealings and that generally disincline members from deviant behavioral patterns and lifestyle choices that ultimately would be stress inducing.

Several distinct mechanisms within religious collectivities may regulate these aspects of personal conduct. First, individual religious socialization may result in the internalization of religious norms regarding lifestyle choices and personal conduct. The prospect of violating these deeply held values may induce feelings of psychological and even physical discomfort. This threat of shame may be strongest for persons who are enmeshed within social networks of coreligionists. The religious discourse and ongoing encouragement of coreligionists, along with regular exposure to church teachings, may energize individual religious beliefs and commitment (Cornwall, 1987).

Second, deviant members of religious communities confront the threat of embarrassment, or diminished reputation and loss of social esteem (Grasmick, Bursik, & Cochran, 1991; Weber, 1921/1946, 1905/1958). Members may impose negative sanctions on their coreligionists who fail or refuse to conform to group norms. Churchgoers who depart substantially from accepted standards of lifestyle and moral conduct (e.g., marital indiscretions, frequent carousing) may confront gossip, overt criticism, or even ostracism from their fellows. When instances of such social sanctions become known within the group, they may have the broader effect of deterring others from adopting deviant lifestyles and behaviors. Furthermore, the most egregious deviants may also experience formal pressures from religious institutions, particularly direct interventions by clergy or other religious authorities. In addition, extreme and repeated violations of group norms may evoke formal sanctions from the religious organization including expulsion.

Third, religious collectivities may constitute reference groups for their members. Thus, in contrast to the coercive image of religious groups presented above, as individuals frequently engage in social comparisons as part of the self-definition process (Festinger, 1954), they may voluntarily alter their conduct to make it consistent with that of others they consider important or worthy of emulation. The degree to which religious groups serve as reference groups for a given individual depends on (1) the degree of similarity between the status characteristics of that individual and his or her coreligionists, (2) the degree to which he or she shares core values with coreligionists, (3) the clarity with which the religious group communicates these values, (4) the frequency of sustained interaction between the individual and coreligionists, and (5) the degree to which the individual member considers the religious authorities and coreligionists to be significant others (Bock, Cochran, & Beeghley, 1987; Merton & Rossi, 1968).

Fourth, members of certain religious groups and traditions may confront reduced risk of certain types of potentially stressful events and conditions, yet paradoxically experience them as more devastating than other persons when they do occur. As Pearlin (1989) points out,

> The threat that people experience from the circumstances they face depends to some degree on the values they hold—that is, on what they define as important, desirable, to be cherished. . . . The relationships of social stressors to individual stress may be seen most clearly when we take into account social values that help to shape the meaning of the stressors. (p. 249)

Partly as a consequence of the emphasis placed on certain domains of life experience (e.g., family organization and work) within religious communities, disruptions in those areas may be especially problematic because of (1) the incongruity between objective situations and internalized ideals and (2) feelings of estrangement and inferiority, namely, the religious group.

Finally, it is important to note that religious institutions themselves can engender stress. As "greedy" institutions, certain types of congregations demand substantial investments of time and emotional energy (Kelley, 1972; McGaw & Wright, 1979) in ways that may exacerbate existing role conflicts (e.g., between familial and work obligations) and role strains, or create new ones. In addition, intensive embeddedness within congregational networks may increase the risk that a given individual will become embroiled in conflicts over the affairs of the institution (e.g., leadership disputes and financial administration) as well as personality conflicts with coreligionists. Furthermore, such embeddedness in long-term networks may trap one within certain role identities, limiting the capacity for personal development and self-definition (Mestrovic & Glassner, 1983).

In sum, membership in religious communities may have important (albeit perhaps unintended) consequences for (1) the overall stress levels of their individual members, (2) the likelihood that those persons will experience specific types of social stressors, and (3) the potential interpretation of certain events and conditions as a function of religious values. Below, the evidence is reviewed regarding the impact of religious factors on several prominent stressors. Particular attention is devoted to chronic and acute health conditions, and to marital tension and dissolution. Also briefly discussed is the possible role of religious factors in lowering the risk of several other social sources of stress, including occupational problems, legal difficulties, and intergenerational conflicts.

Chronic and Acute Illness

There is mounting evidence that religious factors influence physical well-being in generally positive ways. Researchers have reported significant denominational variations in incidence of and mortality from various types of cancer, especially those that are linked with lifestyle factors (e.g., alcohol, tobacco, caffeine consumption, and sexual practices). These patterns tend to favor the members of highly proscriptive groups, such as Seventh-Day Adventists and Mormons (Jarvis & Northcott, 1987; Troyer, 1988) and to a lesser extent fundamentalist Protestants (Dwyer, Clarke, & Miller, 1990). In some (but not all) studies, the magnitude of such denominational effects is observed to vary according to level of institutional religious involvement, with more active individuals having especially low cancer rates (e.g., Gardner & Lyon, 1982).

A smaller body of research explores religious differences in a range of additional health outcomes, including hypertension, overall objective and subjective health status, and mortality (see Levin & Vanderpool, 1987, 1989; Idler & Kasl, 1992). To be sure, the results of these diverse studies are not unequivocal. Moreover, much of this work is based on cross-sectional analyses and is lacking appropriate multivariate statistical controls. Nevertheless, there is at least some evidence that regular attendance at religious services has salutary implications for physical well-being, and that affiliation with certain religious groups (e.g., Adventists and Mormons) has protective effects for a wide range of physical disorders.

What factors might account for religious differences in physical health status? First, an impressive array of undesirable health outcomes are caused or exacerbated by the use and/or abuse of alcohol, tobacco, and narcotics, and by certain dietary practices (e.g., Berkman & Breslow, 1983; Wiley & Comacho, 1980). There is mounting evidence that religious norms and practices influence these types of health behaviors. For instance, members of denominations that issue strict behavioral guidelines (e.g., fundamentalist Protestants, Mormons, and Adventists) are much more likely than members of other denominations (e.g., Catholics and liberal Protestants) or nonreligious persons to report abstaining from alcohol entirely (Cochran, Beeghley, & Bock, 1988). In addition, frequency of church attendance and strength of denominational identification are inversely associated with alcohol use among members of these relatively demanding groups, but not among others (Clarke, Beeghley, & Cochran, 1990). Although a substantial proportion of fundamentalist Protestants are teetotalers, several studies indicate that the proportion of heavy or problem drinkers in these groups is often as high as that found in more permissive denominations (e.g., Bock et al., 1987). While there is also limited evidence that the members of these behaviorally strict denominations report lower levels of tobacco consumption than others, the effects (if any) of regular religious attendance and other religious factors on the use of tobacco products remain understudied.

In addition to limiting consumption of alcohol, tobacco, caffeine, and other potentially harmful substances by their members, some religious groups (especially Seventh-Day Adventists) also discourage the consumption of meats and fat products (Troyer, 1988). Adventists also eschew hot spices and highly refined foods (Jarvis & Northcott, 1987). Certain other groups (e.g., Mormons), while not prohibiting meat consumption, emphasize dietary moderation and well-balanced eating habits in general.

Second, while some theological currents downplay the importance of the physical body relative to the soul, there are also themes in the Judeo-Christian tradition that encourage greater attentiveness to physical health (Turner, 1984). For instance, the notion that the physical body is "the temple of God" provides a rationale for the adoption of positive health behaviors and preventive health care. Furthermore, some have extolled the virtues of health as an end in itself, as a state that facilitates the full enjoyment of God's gifts. On the other hand, a long tradition of religious thought underscores the importance of physical well-being as a means to other ends. In particular, healthy individuals are better able to remain active in the service of God and others (Ott, 1991). Physical health permits individuals to discharge their moral responsibilities toward others, including providing for the material and emotional welfare of their families, and it allows persons to live in dignity without fear of being dependent on or burdensome to others. In addition, a concern for physical health in some quarters may stem from more basic views regarding the moral superiority of moderation in all things. Third, on a more speculative note, there may also be a general link between public religious involvement and some health behaviors. That is, churchgoers may be more likely on average to engage in relatively risk-free lifestyles (Mechanic, 1990). These patterns tend to involve regularity in the timing of meals and the composition of diet (McIntosh & Shifflett, 1984), sleep, and exercise. In addition, these lifestyles are also characterized by relatively conservative sexual practices and infrequent carousing. While these patterns may be especially compatible with the social expectations and religious teachings of more conservative religious denominations, one suspects that such lifestyles prevail within most mainstream religious groups as well.

Marital Tension and Dissolution

Numerous researchers have called attention to denominational variations in attitudes toward marriage and divorce, and to parallel differences in rates of marital dissolution (e.g., Levinger, 1965). These various ideological and institutional disincentives regarding marital disruption and dissolution are especially striking among Catholics, fundamentalist Protestants, and Mormons (Heaton, 1988; Heaton & Goodman, 1985; McCarthy, 1979). Furthermore, religious factors are important predictors of marital quality as well as marital stability. A growing body of research indicates that marital happiness and satisfaction are higher (Heaton, 1984) and divorce is less likely (Chi & Houseknecht, 1983; Heaton, Albrecht, & Martin, 1985) when marriages are religiously homogeneous—that is, when marital partners hold the same denominational preference. Moreover, the unfavorable consequences of denominational heterogamy for marital quality and durability appear to vary systematically according to the degree of theological distance separating the respective denominations of the marital partners (Ortega, Whitt, & Williams, 1988). There is also evidence that marriages in which spouses have comparable attendance patterns are somewhat happier and more stable than others (Heaton & Pratt, 1990).

Why are these aspects of religious homogamy positively associated with marital quality? First, religious orientations influence child rearing practices, leisure activity, choice of friends and associates, gender roles and household division of labor, and numerous other aspects of family life. Second, marital partners with common religious orientations and attendance patterns may also enjoy more integrated and more religiously similar social networks of relatives and friends. This may reinforce the family lifestyle choices made by marital partners by providing relatively homogeneous input and feedback, and by offering consensual opinions concerning strategies for resolving marital conflicts (Heaton & Pratt, 1990).

In addition to the religious homogamy of couples, the religiosity of individuals also is positively related to perceptions of marital quality (Filsinger & Wilson, 1984; Hansen, 1981, 1987; Wilson & Filsinger, 1986). Embeddedness within religious communities—along with frequent personal devotional activity—may reinforce beliefs in the sanctity of marriage as an institution and the essential validity and importance of efforts to fulfill family roles. Moreover, through public and private religious activities, marital partners may cultivate a sense of purpose and values centered on loving and caring (Scanzoni & Arnett, 1987) and on the needs and welfare of others (Larson & Goltz, 1989; Schumm, 1985).

Other Social Stressors

Although empirical evidence is relatively thin, there are sound reasons to anticipate that aspects of religious involvement may reduce the risk of several additional types of social stressors, especially work-related problems, legal troubles, and intergenerational conflicts. While some job-related stressors are clearly beyond the control of the individual worker (e.g., undesirable or unsafe working conditions, abusive supervisors, and layoffs), it is reasonable to suspect that persons who are (or are perceived to be) honest, diligent employees are at lower risk of termination and job-related conflicts than other persons. First, individuals who are actively involved in religious communities—especially conservative groups—may believe that their occupation holds special significance as a "calling." They may also tend to embrace the view that personal morality and spiritual fitness require a type of "inner-worldly asceticism": honesty, thrift, sobriety, acceptance of authority in the workplace, and a fair day's work for a fair day's pay. Second, some jobs offer opportunities to serve God by serving the general public or particular groups in need, or to bear witness to others regarding matters of religious doctrine or personal faith—and some religious individuals may select jobs that maximize these opportunities (e.g., Ammerman, 1987; Wilson & Clow, 1981). Third, given the substantial prestige attached to religious institutions in some quarters, employers and coworkers may make certain assumptions—whether warranted or not—about the moral character of those persons who are known to be religious and may, therefore, attribute desirable qualities to those individuals. For any or all of these reasons, individuals who exhibit strong public commitment to religious activities may experience fewer difficulties on the job than those persons who do not. Paradoxically, however, these (sub)cultural values emphasizing the intrinsic significance of work experiences or provider roles may make the effects of job loss or other job-related problems more devastating for such persons, especially male breadwinners.

Furthermore, it appears that aspects of religious involvement are inversely associated with actual and hypothetical adult deviance as well (Grasmick, Bursik, & Cochran, 1991; Grasmick, Kinsey, & Cochran, 1991; Tittle & Welch, 1983), suggesting that religious persons, particularly Mormons and conservative Protestants, may be especially unlikely to experience criminal proceedings and other legal disputes. To the extent that general statements can be made at this point, it appears that religion's constraining effects on adult deviance are most evident when norms concerning the given form of deviance (e.g., tax cheating) are clearly communicated by the religious group, and when religious norms diverge from those endorsed by mass culture or other social institutions. The understudied area of religion and crime promises to receive further attention from researchers.

In addition, in many households religious involvement may reduce the risk of intergenerational conflict, especially problems involving parent-child relations. The discourse and practices of some religious denominations—notably Mormon and conservative Protestant traditions—underscore the centrality of nuclear family life and the significance of parenting. These groups offer hierarchical blueprints for family organization, outlining the appropriate roles and behaviors of family members in considerable detail (Ellison & Sherkat, 1993, in press; Heaton, 1988; McNamara, 1985).

Moreover, while the literature on religiosity and adolescent deviance has been characterized by a morass of discrepant findings (Stark, 1984; Tittle & Welch, 1983), most recent studies have reported inverse associations between religious involvement and deviant behaviors or inclinations (e.g., Cochran & Akers, 1989; Sloane & Potvin, 1986). Specific deviant activities considered in these studies include alcohol and drug use/abuse, petty criminal activities (e.g., theft and vandalism), and premarital sexual license (e.g., Beck, Cole, & Hammond, 1991; Studer & Thornton, 1987).

In sum, religious involvement may enhance mental health by lowering the risk of several specific types of social stressors: (1) chronic and acute health problems, (2) marital discord and dissolution, (3) occupational conflicts, (4) legal difficulties, and (5) parent-child conflicts. Thus individuals who are embedded within religious networks (particularly in more conservative groups) as well as those who are guided by internalized religious values (products of institutional socialization processes) may encounter lower overall levels of stress than their less religious counterparts (Ellison, 1992a).

Directions for Future Research

These arguments regarding possible links between religious factors and social stressors suggest promising directions for future data collection and analysis. For instance, although this section has elaborated a number of promising hypotheses, the precise religious mechanisms promoting healthy lifestyles await clarification. At a minimum, the adjudication of these claims requires the cumulation of the following types of data: (1) various health behaviors, including alcohol and tobacco consumption, sleep and relaxation, exercise, dietary practices, and other risk-taking activities; (2) perceptions of behavioral and lifestyle norms germane to health within religious institutions and networks; and (3) projections of embarrassment (i.e., unfavorable gossip and/or ostracism) and shame (i.e., feelings of guilt or discomfort) resulting from prospective violations of these norms.

In addition, while the weight of empirical evidence suggests that various religious factors reduce the risk of marital disharmony and dissolution, a long tradition of theory and research contends that these observed associations are artifacts of response set bias, due to the tendencies of religious persons to idealize spousal traits and marital quality (see Edmonds, 1967; Ellis, 1948). The evidence bearing directly on this marital conventionalization hypothesis has been mixed to date (Edmonds, Withers, & DiBatista, 1972; Filsinger & Wilson, 1984; Wilson & Filsinger, 1986), with studies typically suffering from serious limitations such as reliance on small, unrepresentative samples. In addition, some researchers maintain that idealization of spousal traits may in fact constitute a positive strategy for enhancing the quality of intimate relationships (Hansen, 1981). These issues deserve closer scrutiny in future research.

As indicated above, the relationships between religious factors and social stressors are woefully understudied. Future research should also explore the possible impact of denominational background and affiliation, religious participation, and theological orientations on the following outcomes of interest: (1) employment status and the risk of job termination, (2) job-related values that may bear on employability and work habits (e.g., the centrality of work for self-image, the relative importance of intrinsic versus extrinsic rewards, attitudes toward discipline, personal ethical standards), (3) employer perceptions of religious and nonreligious workers, (4) attitudes toward institutional authorities (e.g., employers and supervisors, police and courts, government agencies), and (5) projections of embarrassment and shame at the prospect of being terminated, encountering legal difficulties, and/or experiencing other types of stressful circumstances.

Religious Involvement and Social Resources

Although several reviews of the social support literature have urged researchers to focus on the possible institutional bases of support networks and perceived support (e.g., House, Umberson, & Landis, 1988), to date there have been few systematic explorations of this type. In particular, sociological topics such as the distribution of objective and perceived social support in community populations or the role of social structures and institutions in facilitating or impeding the development of supportive social ties have received little attention.

Institutional religious involvement may enhance social support in several ways. First, individuals who are embedded within religious communities may enjoy larger and denser social networks than their nonreligious counterparts. Second, they may receive more social support (i.e., tangible aid and socioemotional support) than other persons. Third, they may perceive their support networks as more reliable and more satisfactory than other persons (Ellison, 1991b).

Network Size, Density, and Receipt of Social Support

Involvement in religious groups may contribute to larger social networks and more frequent interactions with network members, who may be actual or potential sources of help. A long tradition of research in social psychology indicates that (1) the more people interact, the more they are likely to gain affective closeness (Festinger, 1950; Sherif,

White, & Harvey, 1955) and (2) friendships develop most readily between persons who share a core set of interests and values (Kelley, 1979; Verbrugge, 1977). Like other social institutions, religious groups are network driven (Cornwall, 1987, 1989). Religious services and other church-based activities offer regular opportunities for social intercourse between persons with common religious beliefs. These persons may also hold common social and political values as well (e.g., Wald, Owen, & Hill, 1990). In addition, participation in church-related activities brings together individuals with similar status characteristics, such as race, social class, lifestyle, and educational background. Given the relative ideological and status homogeneity (and often residential propinquity) of their members, religious institutions offer fertile ground for the initiation of friendships, which may be cultivated more extensively in secular social contexts.

Public religious participation may also help individuals to enlarge and extend their social networks in other ways. Through these institutional contacts, individuals may become integrated into wider, more diffuse social networks, reaching beyond the confines of their particular congregation (McIntosh & Alston, 1982). This may occur informally, as individuals bring their coreligionists into casual social contact with nonmembers, or as coreligionists exchange information about local voluntary associations and social activities. Furthermore, because of their congregational ties and activities, some individuals may be seen as public-spirited and morally upright. If so, they may be especially attractive recruits for nonreligious civic commitments.

In addition to experiencing more frequent contacts with social network members, churchgoers may actually receive more social support on average than persons who are not involved in religious groups. Much of this help may be provided informally by other congregational members, and it may include socioemotional support (companionship and confiding), instrumental aid (money, goods, and services), and informational assistance (referrals to external agencies or support groups) (Maton, 1989; Ortega, Crutchfield, & Rushing, 1983; Taylor & Chatters, 1988). Furthermore, many religious institutions sustain formal programs aimed at helping victims of acute stress, such as serious illness, bereavement, and unemployment as well as certain others needing special consideration, including the poor, elderly, and infirm (Haber, 1984; Steinitz, 1981). Such efforts can involve various types of assistance, from organized service provision to pastoral counseling and visitations by staff members (Chalfant et al., 1990; Eng, Hatch, & Callan, 1985).

The Perceived Reliability of Support Networks

This section has suggested that religious institutions may augment objective features of social support networks. Religious participation may also enhance perceptions of network reliability. Unlike many types of support networks, church-based exchange relations are ongoing. Given that personal ties to religious organizations often endure for a number of years, churches can thus provide an institutional context for the development of support convoys, or accumulations of mutually supportive (or potentially supportive) social relationships over the life course (Kahn & Antonucci, 1980). Individuals who provide support to others are aware that they build up social credits, which are likely to be honored in the future. Thus the positive perceptions of support networks and transactions among churchgoers may reflect realistic expectations for future support from coreligionists, based on shared norms of mutual obligation and reciprocity.

It is also possible that churchgoers' confidence about the reliability of their networks may simply reflect realistic assessments of the personal character of their coreligionists. Although the experimental evidence is less encouraging (see Batson & Ventis, 1982, pp. 281-289), survey studies indicate that persons who report praying frequently and those who perceive an active God working in their lives offer more altruistic responses than their less religious counterparts in a wide range of hypothetical situations (Morgan, 1983; Piazza & Glock, 1979). Although it is tempting to attribute these response patterns to the social desirability motives of religious individuals, interviewers also tend to rate religious respondents as friendlier, more cooperative, and more open interviewees than the less religious (Ellison, 1992b; Morgan, 1983).

Collective participation in religious rituals may also build interpersonal trust and feelings of mutuality and, therefore, bolster perceptions of network reliability. Research indicates that the more important that collective events are to participants, the greater the community bond (McMillan & Chavis, 1986). Regular attendance at collective worship services implies engagement in various rituals and activities to which participants accord special significance (Johnson & Mullins, 1990). In a sense, these events define the group. Practices such as revivals and homecomings may facilitate bonding among group members by commemorating the collective past and by recalling the group to a shared sense of meaning and purpose.

Satisfaction With Social Support

In addition to enjoying (or believing that they enjoy) more reliable support networks than their less religious counterparts, regular participants in public religious activities also may express relatively high levels of satisfaction with the social support they do receive. There are several distinct rationales for this expectation. First, supportive exchanges within religious settings may be characterized by bidirectionality and symmetry (Maton, 1987). Participants in these types of exchange relations tend to view these experiences as more positive and beneficial than those persons who are involved in unidirectional and/or asymmetrical patterns of exchange.

Second, research on social support processes suggests that relationships among persons with common status characteristics yield greater psychological benefits, on average, than those ties among individuals of disparate backgrounds (Lin, Woelfel, & Light, 1985). Recall the earlier observation that religious communities are relatively homogeneous in terms of many of these status characteristics. It is possible that churchgoers are more satisfied with the support they receive simply because it is provided by people of similar race, sex, age, educational background, and other shared social attributes.

Third, support from coreligionists may be especially beneficial by virtue of its congruence with the values and expectations of the recipient. There is ample evidence that individuals who share beliefs about matters of ultimate concern also hold compatible views about a wide range of additional issues. This consideration is especially important, given that notions of what constitutes supportive behavior harbored by providers and recipients can sometimes diverge sharply and attempts at supportive conduct may actually have unintended destructive consequences (Wortman & Lehman, 1985). Efforts at support may be especially valuable when both providers and recipients share similar cultural beliefs regarding the practices and meanings of helping behavior (see Jacobson, 1987). Empathy and caring are integral to the rhetoric and rationale of religious congregations and may, therefore, provide the basis of a common discourse regarding interpersonal support. Thus churchgoers may derive a greater sense of affirmation and comfort from their coreligionists than from others, because coreligionists may assist them in placing life experiences within broader contexts of meaning (e.g., "they know just what to say").

In sum, religious involvement may contribute to individual mental health indirectly, by enhancing social network size and density, received social support, perceived reliability of support networks, and satisfaction with social relationships and support. Because previous discussions have paid little attention to the distinctive institutional milieus in which supportive social ties are formed, cultivated, and sustained, investigation of these indirect influences of religious involvement on mental health could fill a substantial gap in the research literature.

Directions for Future Research

While many of these arguments regarding religious factors and social ties are intuitively plausible, the available empirical evidence bearing on these claims is quite limited. Does public religious involvement actually promote the development of friendships and other voluntary social pursuits? Future research should address this issue by collecting egocentric network data (Burt, 1984; Marsden, 1990) on social ties, along with information on various voluntary social and civic activities (e.g., clubs and charity work). It is important to understand the histories of these social relationships, memberships, and other commitments. How did a given individual meet his or her closest friends? Who introduced them, and where and how did they cultivate a relationship? This kind of information could also shed light on the thorny issue of causal direction. To clarify the role of religious groups in network building, it will be necessary to take into account the possibility that individuals are frequently recruited into religious groups through other prior community activities and network ties (e.g., Stark & Bainbridge, 1980).

In addition, multiple name generators should perhaps be used to elicit information on various types of support and their providers (Barrera, 1986; Tardy, 1985). Information is also needed concerning specific types of support provided by collectivities (e.g., formal church groups and neighborhood groups). These data are essential for (1) gauging the role of religious institutions and coreligionists in the development of friendships and in the circulation of information about opportunities to join groups and (2) comparing the importance of religious communities for network construction and support provision with that of other institutional settings, such as the workplace (House, 1981).

One also anticipates that members of religious communities also will express greater satisfaction with support from coreligionists than with attempted support by others. This empirical pattern may reflect shared socioreligious meanings regarding certain types of stressors and/or supportive behaviors. If this is the case, one might anticipate that the theological distance between support providers and recipients also is inversely associated with perceived support (in terms of satisfaction and perceived reliability). In addition, the members of religious communities may perceive their coreligionists as more reliable network members than others. This pattern may reflect the role of religious institutions as communities of reciprocity and mutual obligation, by virtue of the prominence of bidirectional support patterns and the cultivation of support convoys. On the other hand, as suggested above, such perceptions may also stem from status homophily. Future research could contribute greatly to our understanding of social support processes by adjudicating these contending arguments.

Finally, researchers working in this area must consider the role of personality variables, which may have the following consequences for support processes rooted in religious institutions and cognitions: (1) impeding the initial cultivation of social contacts (e.g., shyness), (2) undermining the development of stable, intimate social ties (e.g., hostility, self-centeredness), (3) disinclining individuals from attempting to mobilize social support in stressful circumstances (e.g., lack of faith in the efficacy of support processes), and (4) negatively coloring individuals' evaluations of the support they actually do receive and the interpersonal relationships they do sustain (e.g., neuroticism) (Eckenrode, 1983; Hansson, Jones, & Carpenter, 1984; Henderson, Byrne, & Duncan-Jones, 1981).

Religious Factors and Self-Perceptions

The theoretical and empirical links between religious involvement and self-perceptions have long been the focus of debate. Social psychologists have investigated these associations intermittently for at least four decades, with few consistent results (Bergin, 1983). At first glance, these studies would appear to offer little incentive for further inquiry. However, this literature has been characterized by the following serious deficiencies that threaten the reliability of these findings: (1) an atheoretical approach; (2) use of small, unrepresentative samples, providing findings of dubious generalizability; and (3) frequent failure to use rigorous multivariate strategies or to hold constant the confounding effects of other relevant factors. This section considers several ways in which religious factors, properly studied, may be found to enhance or undermine self-esteem, personal efficacy, and related psychological resources.

Theological Orientations

A venerable tradition of psychological literature contends that Christian theology undermines self-esteem among the faithful. Traditional notions of sin come in for particularly harsh denunciation for promoting feelings of guilt and self-doubt (Branden, 1969, 1983; Ellis, 1962, 1980). First, labeling behaviors as sinful may have the effect of stigmatizing the total person as a "sinner." This practice may divert energy and attention from the task of altering inappropriate behaviors. Second, the notion of sin invites negative judgments of individuals for misbehaviors that may actually have complex determinants. According to critics, the preoccupation with moral blame and retributive punishment obscures the need and reduces the ability to identify and alter extraindividual causes of inappropriate behavior, including situational and structural factors.

Such criticisms have elicited several rejoinders. Some commentators, particularly conservative Protestants, contend that secular psychological notions of the self are problematic (Kilpatrick, 1983; Vitz, 1977). They claim that traditional ideas of sin are (1) psychologically beneficial, because they link matters of ultimate concern with absolute standards of personal moral conduct, and (2) socially functional, to the extent that they discourage selfishness and sensitize individuals to the needs and well-being of others. Others propose recasting beliefs regarding human sin in ways that are more congruent with prevailing psychological insights (Schuller, 1982). Predictably, such reformulations are seen as pernicious invitations to self-worship by more conservative Christians (e.g., Adams, 1986). A third group of religious commentators maintains that antireligious critics (and perhaps some religious individuals as well) have simply misconstrued biblical conceptualizations of sin, ignoring the fact that beliefs about sin and guilt are often framed by a belief in divine grace (Hoekema, 1983; Watson, Morris, & Hood, 1988).

It also is noteworthy that some claim that conventional measures of self-esteem and personal mastery are biased against orthodox Christians (Gartner, 1983). In this view, the questionnaire items most frequently used to measure self-perceptions require subjects to disclaim their humility and belief in sin in order to exhibit high self-esteem and to reject divine control over their lives in order to exhibit a sense of mastery. Thus some commentators argue that these crucial ideas require reconceptualization and new measurement strategies to tap the self-concepts of conservative Christians adequately.

In addition to making claims about the implications of religiosity for self-esteem, antireligious critics also argue that religious worldviews—especially those seen as dogmatic and absolutist—serve as psychological crutches. By teaching adherents to rely on an external, omnipotent deity as the sole source of truth and comfort, traditional religious institutions and beliefs are thought to undermine the sense of personal control over one's affairs and divert energy from more constructive strategies of problem solving. Moreover, some themes in orthodox Christian thought (e.g., a preoccupation with the afterlife as a source of comfort and reward) may deemphasize or discourage other types of worldly accomplishments (e.g., economic gain and social mobility), which might otherwise build a sense of personal efficacy.

Research findings bearing on these issues are meager and discrepant. Furthermore, while theological conservatives are especially likely to attribute some important life events to God, the precise relationship between attributional tendencies (e.g., "God control") and more general orientations of passivity or external locus of control defy easy summary (e.g., Ritzema & Young, 1983), and they may well vary across specific loci of control domains. Finally, some have suggested that variations in loci of control may reflect the lingering influence of different theological traditions, such as Calvinist and Wesleyan thought (Levin & Schiller, 1986; Williams, 1990). Nonetheless, despite their potential importance for mental and physical health, the links between theology and self-perceptions have received only minimal exploration.

Divine Relations

In a seminal discussion of personal religiosity and well-being, Pollner (1989) noted that individuals may construct ties with a divine "other" much as they build their concrete social relationships (see Poloma & Gallup, 1991). A divine personification may be experienced through identification with various figures portrayed in sacred texts and other religious media (Sunden, 1965; Wikstrom, 1987). By identifying with these figures, individuals may come to define their own life circumstances in terms of a biblical figure's plight, and then begin to interpret their situations from the point of view of the "God-role" (i.e., what God would want and/or expect of them).

How might these processes of divine role-taking influence self-esteem and/or feelings of mastery? Pollner (1989) suggests two such ways. First, he suggests that individuals may gain a sense of personal importance and control through vicarious identification with a high-status other with truly cosmic standing, whose wisdom and power outstrip those of all other entities. Thus, in addition to enhancing feelings of self-worth, these perceived divine relations may bolster confidence that one's daily affairs and problems are manageable. Second, a long tradition of theory and research holds that an individual's self-perceptions are products of reflected appraisals—that is, how that person believes others perceive him or her (Rosenberg, 1981). A divine other can be said to occupy a position within the cognitive social network of the individual, to be engaged interactively in a quest for solace and guidance (Pargament et al., 1990). To the extent that each individual is special as a "child of God" (McDowell, 1978), he or she is imbued with enduring significance beyond physical self and life (Capps, 1985). Furthermore, God is believed to have unconditional positive regard for each individual, and to have cared enough for his creation to provide for its redemption from fallenness. Such beliefs lead one to expect that many religious persons—particularly those with orthodox Christian beliefs—may enjoy relatively high levels of self-esteem and/or personal mastery (Ellison, 1993; Krause & Tran, 1989).

Public Religious Participation

In addition to theological orientations and divine relations, involvement in public religious activities may also enhance feelings of self-esteem and personal mastery. As I have suggested above, churches provide institutional settings in which individuals with similar status characteristics, religious beliefs, and worldviews interact regularly with like-minded others. These interactions are likely to reinforce basic role identities and role expectations, which are particularly important in the development of positive self-perceptions (Thoits, 1985). Through informal social contacts—as well as through sermons, Sunday school lessons, and other teachings—these persons may gain affirmation that their personal conduct in regard to daily events, experiences, and community affairs is reasonable and appropriate. Although they may not be perfect, many regular churchgoers can see themselves as "good" spouses, parents, citizens, neighbors, and so forth. Moreover, certain types of religious communities may provide an interpersonal context in which members are evaluated—and hence come to evaluate themselves—on the basis of distinctive sets of criteria. These are not the material, educational, or occupational achievements that are often the foundation of social comparisons. Rather these alternative criteria may include the following: (1) their inherent individuality, (2) their sociability and service to others in need and to the community at large, (3) specific skills and abilities that are especially valued in connection with church-related activities (e.g., singing), and (4) personal spiritual qualities, such as wisdom, morality, and equanimity (Ellison, 1993).

Somewhat paradoxically, one suspects that regular churchgoers may be aided in cultivating positive self-images by the efforts of many religious groups to label certain patterns of conduct as sinful (i.e., those practiced by out groups) and others as righteous. This tendency—virtually universal among religious groups, but possibly most evident in conservative groups—may facilitate downward social comparisons (Wills, 1981). Active participants in religious communities may derive an elevated sense of their own morality and self-worth by denigrating (collectively and individually) the lifestyles and beliefs of others. This idea, while intuitively plausible, has been largely overlooked by researchers.

This section of the chapter has argued that, in addition to reducing stress levels and increasing social resources, religious beliefs and practices may enhance individual mental health indirectly by bolstering individual psychological resources, particularly self-esteem and personal mastery. In sharp contrast to the received wisdom in this area, certain orthodox theological convictions may promote positive self-evaluations. Furthermore, individuals may gain feelings of self-esteem and mastery as a result of private devotional activities (e.g., prayer and meditation) by establishing and sustaining a personal relationship with a (perceived) divine other. Finally, religious communities may augment the psychological resources of their individual members by fostering positive reflected appraisals and by affirming crucial role identities.

Directions for Future Research

Although this section has suggested a number of ways in which religious factors may shape individual self-perceptions, empirical evidence in this area is quite limited. Several topics warrant further examination. First, it is critical to resolve debates over the role of theological orientations, particularly doctrinal beliefs about the nature of sin and divine forgiveness, in shaping self-perceptions. Although many recent studies have advanced our ability to measure certain of these beliefs, researchers need more information on the links between (1) religious background and socialization; (2) attitudes toward sin, human nature, and the nature of God; (3) beliefs in (and the experience of) divine grace; and (4) attitudes toward the self, using larger community or population samples. Such a research program is crucial for verifying or dismissing the claims of antireligious critics (e.g., Branden, 1983; Ellis, 1962), but it also may shed light on hypotheses regarding the consequences of broader theological traditions for personal mastery and internal locus of control (Levin & Schiller, 1986).

Second, additional research is needed into the ways in which individuals experience rituals, sermons, and other aspects of collective worship as affirming and validating. Beneficial effects of church involvement on self-regard may be due to the distinctively supportive social resources provided by church communities. Several ethnographies have reported that participation in ecstatic worship services, characterized by high levels of emotional release and disclosure, also seems to heighten the sense of self-worth (Gritzmacher, Bolton, & Dana, 1988).

Religiosity and
the Practice of Coping

Until recently, studies of coping strategies and their outcomes typically ignored religious coping. This now appears to have been more than a trivial oversight. Religious factors may be primarily relevant in the cognitive appraisal of stressors and in the subsequent regulation of emotions associated with those stressors. However, there are few existing data on the ways in which religious cognitions and practices are fashioned into stress-managing patterns. This section discusses issues germane to the study of religious coping.

Attributions

One important aspect of stressor appraisal involves attributions of responsibility or control for a given event or condition. An emerging literature on religious attributions suggests that, contrary to conventional psychological wisdom, individuals may reduce worry or self-blame, and thereby enhance their well-being, by abrogating responsibility for and control over particularly difficult or insoluble conditions to a divine other (Spilka, Shaver, & Kirkpatrick, 1985). Despite the methodological limitations of studies in this area, several consistent findings are noteworthy. In general, with the exception of medical conditions, positive events are more likely than negative events to be the subject of religious attributions. Furthermore, personal events are more likely to be attributed to divine influence than impersonal events. Regardless of event valence, medical conditions are especially likely to elicit religious attributions (Pargament & Hahn, 1986; Spilka & Schmidt, 1983). Conditions (even serious ones) for which plausible, worldly explanations exist are unlikely to result in religious attributions (e.g., Kroll-Smith & Couch, 1987). Thus individuals are less likely to invoke religion to account for economic matters than to explain medical stressors, and they are particularly disinclined to attribute interpersonal problems to divine forces (Spilka & Schmidt, 1983). Fundamentalist Protestants and persons who express high personal religiosity are particularly prone to engage in religious attributions (Gorsuch & Smith, 1983).

Event Specificity

Available evidence suggests that certain life events and chronic conditions are particularly likely to elicit religious coping responses, including illnesses and physical disabilities (Jenkins & Pargament, 1988; Pargament & Hahn, 1986); chronic pain (Kotarba, 1983); bereavement (Mattlin, Wethington, & Kessler, 1990; Rosik, 1989), especially untimely bereavement (Cook & Wimberley, 1983); serious accidents (Bulman & Wortman, 1977); and other loss events (Carver, Schreiber, & Weintraub, 1989; McCrae & Costa, 1986; Mattlin et al., 1990). Furthermore, Mattlin and colleagues (1990) show that religious coping efforts are strongly associated with lower levels of both anxiety and depression in the context of loss events (principally bereavements) but not in the context of other types of acute and chronic stressors.

Why should religious coping be particularly likely and effective in response to these specific stressors? The perceived and actual effectiveness of a given coping behavior often depends on the possibilities for altering problematic conditions. Bereavement admits of no active coping response, and illness is only somewhat amenable to such coping strategies (e.g., following treatment regimens). At one level, then, it is not surprising that emotion-focused coping strategies like religious devotion are more helpful than alternative coping efforts in such situations.

In addition, however, religion offers a template for the ordering and interpretation of human events. There is mounting evidence that persons who enjoy a greater sense of coherence and order in their lives also have better psychological and physical well-being (Antonovsky, 1987). One consequence of the existential certainty afforded by religious beliefs is that, in the context of strong beliefs regarding matters of ultimate concern, seemingly routine personal affairs and major life traumas alike may take on particular meaning and significance (Ellison, 1991a; Foley, 1988). As Berger (1967, pp. 42-44) points out, the legitimating function of religion may be especially evident under conditions that call into question basic assumptions of individual or collective existence—or even of existence itself. Bereavement, major illness, and serious accidents exemplify such conditions.

Moreover, some observers argue that individuals continually struggle to maintain the perception of a "just" world, a world in which good fortune comes to good people and bad people get what they deserve (see Lerner, 1980). There is at least some evidence that just-world orientations are inversely related to depression (Ritter, Benson, & Snyder, 1990). The kinds of events and situations identified above—serious illnesses, unyielding pain, deaths (especially sudden deaths), major accidents—often violate such assumptions. By reframing these events in broadly religious terms, individuals may be able to manage their emotional consequences while still salvaging their belief in a just world. It is noteworthy that persons professing high levels of personal religiosity and those reporting fundamentalist affiliations are particularly likely to entertain just-world orientations (see Rubin & Peplau, 1975).

One other way in which religious practices facilitate palliative coping may have little to do with the actual content of those practices: Church-related activities and/or prayer and scriptural studies may simply divert attention from specific sources of worry or concern. One suspects that the effectiveness of this diversionary role depends on the relative malleability of the stressor.

Religious Role Taking

The role-taking processes discussed above also may influence the appraisal and emotion-regulating aspects of coping. In brief, a divine personification may be experienced through the identification with various figures portrayed in religious texts (Pollner, 1989; Wikstrom, 1987). Individuals may resolve problematic situations more easily by defining them in terms of a biblical figure's plight and by considering their own personal circumstances from the vantage point of the "God role." To date, however, most concrete discussions of such role-taking processes appear in case studies of the spiritual development of various historical figures (Capps, 1982; Sunden, 1990). Therefore, while there is ample evidence that individuals find religious endeavors to be sources of strength in difficult times, there is little systematic information about the ways in which individuals draw on scriptures and devotional practices to confront specific stressors (Foley, 1988).

Additional Considerations

One promising direction in the literature on religious coping has been enriched by the recent work of Pargament and colleagues (1988), who have identified three broad styles of religious coping among church members. First, deferential religious copers cede control over problematic situations to a divine other, who then becomes a psychological crutch. This style of coping bears a striking resemblance to the type criticized by several generations of psychologists. In contrast, collaborative religious copers perceive themselves as being actively engaged in dynamic partnerships with a divine other. Finally, self-directed religious copers employ religious cognitions and activities only sparingly in response to stressors. These three distinct religious coping styles are associated with sharply divergent profiles of psychological functioning; both collaborative and self-directed copers have greater self-esteem and higher scores on the MMPI and other personality measures than deferential religious copers. Subsequent analyses also suggest that collaborative religious coping buffers the negative effects of high levels of stress on affective well-being (Pargament et al., 1990).

This discussion has emphasized the role of religious factors in palliative coping, at the expense of problem-focused coping. However, pastoral counseling continues to play an important role in the coping efforts of many individuals (e.g., Chalfant et al., 1990). Religious institutions also serve as channels of information about active coping options, and churches also may refer members in need to appropriate government agencies and relevant private organizations (e.g., self-help groups) and individuals (e.g., therapists). Furthermore, some have argued that stressor reappraisals—perhaps including religious cognitions—may stimulate new efforts at problem solving by making individuals aware of behavioral options that were not initially apparent (Taylor,

1983). In addition, religious cognitions, including moral values, may play a less obvious role in shaping problem-focused coping strategies, by suggesting new priorities and options while precluding other potential means of altering stressful environmental conditions. These specific issues deserve greater attention from researchers.

Directions for Future Research

Several directions for further research on religious coping appear particularly worthwhile. First, although religious role taking may seem to be a highly individual, even idiosyncratic, cognitive project, some observers have suggested the institutional roots of these processes. They maintain that different theological traditions emphasize divergent themes, images of God, biblical passages and parables, and so forth (Holm, 1987). While this is almost certainly the case, there is little systematic evidence on precisely which themes are highlighted in various traditions (see Ebaugh, Richman, & Chafetz, 1984). More research is needed to ascertain how variations in religious socialization (both in childhood and adulthood) may yield divergent sets of coping resources and to indicate how and whether those differences are linked with more or less favorable stress management patterns and mental health outcomes.

Second, although event character and context influence the adoption of coping strategies, it is clear that social location also conditions both resources and behaviors (e.g., Pearlin, 1989). To date, surprisingly little is known about the impact of location in various dimensions of the stratification system on coping patterns. One intriguing, albeit speculative, line of investigation involves the potential relationships between one's occupational life world (particularly occupational self-direction) and coping repertoires.

Third, although the body of evidence concerning religious attributions is growing, there are fundamental methodological limitations to these studies. For the most part, these studies rely on small, unrepresentative samples of convenience, typically controlling for the confounding effects of age, education, and theological influences on attributional patterns by, for example, comparing college students at a state university with those at a fundamentalist Bible college. Only when such exploratory efforts are supplanted by more systematic studies—e.g., by gathering data on larger, representative population samples—will we learn more about theological and other differences in religious attributions.

Fourth, researchers have long been aware that coping implies a potentially lengthy temporal process. However, we have little information on the ways in which religious cognitions, practices, and networks are differently relevant at various stages of this process (Jacobson, 1986). This is an urgent priority for further study. Given the substantial gaps in our understanding, researchers might profitably begin with in-depth interviews of victims of specific stressors at various points during their coping, before moving on to more systematic quantitative approaches.

Finally, there has been surprisingly little attention paid to the role of specific doctrinal tenets in coping with various stressors. Wuthnow, Christiano, and Kuzlowski (1980) have hypothesized that belief in an afterlife may mitigate the negative effects of bereavement-related stress and that an image of the afterlife as a time of reunion with loved ones may be especially helpful to the bereaved. To date, there has been no empirical test of these hypotheses. In addition, while some religious ideologies may encourage attention to physical well-being (as discussed earlier), the deemphasis of the body relative to the soul remains a prominent theme in Christian theology. There is some evidence that this orientation may ameliorate the negative psychosocial consequences of various physical disabilities and related deficits, including chronic illness and unattractiveness (Ellison, 1993; Idler & Kasl, 1992). Certain beliefs and practices that are denomination specific might be particularly valuable in dealing with stress. For instance, Catholic views on the intercession of the saints and last rites might comfort the dying or bereaved. However, the significance, if any, of such doctrinal variations for the study of affective well-being and mental health remains unexplored.

Contextualizing the Study of Religion and Mental Health

To date, research on religion and mental health has drawn on two parallel methodological traditions. One tradition hews closely to Durkheim's (1897/1951) original *ecological* strategy, relating the spatial distribution of religious denominations, church membership, and other indicators of collective religious involvement to aggregate rates of suicide and other indicators of social pathology (Breault, 1986; Pescosolido, 1990; Pescosolido & Georgianna, 1989). Research in this vein typically uses data gathered at the SMSA, county, or state levels. A second line of research explores the effects of public religious participation, private religious devotion, and other aspects of religious ideology and practice on *individual* mental health outcomes (e.g., Ellison, 1991a). These studies are far more common and usually involve the analysis of secondary data from large surveys.

Although scholarly understanding has benefited from both types of investigations, it is feasible and desirable to bridge the gap between the aggregate and individual levels of analysis. Individual mental health outcomes should be understood as the likely products of a complex web of individual and supraindividual factors and processes. Although both types of studies often make assumptions about institutional-level processes, these factors remain largely unexplored. Nevertheless, various institutional properties and organizational cultures of congregations may have important implications for the social and psychological resources of members as well as their levels of stress.

First, congregational structure merits greater attention from researchers. For instance, one suspects that the relationships between individual church involvement and social resources are conditioned by the proportion of members who share broadly similar status characteristics (i.e., race, educational attainment, occupational background, household incomes, age). In addition, individuals may enjoy more opportunities to cultivate fresh social contacts in large and rapidly growing congregations, which can support a wider range of groups and organized activities, than in small and/or stagnant ones (Olson, 1989).

Second, Pargament, Silverman, Johnson, Echemendia, and Snyder (1983) have identified several dimensions of congregational climates that may be psychologically salient for members. These dimensions include autonomy, sense of community, activity levels (in terms of programs and groups), social concern, openness to change, order and clarity of goals, and average intrinsic and extrinsic religiosity. Pargament and colleagues also present tentative evidence that these climates are related to nontrivial variations in the psychosocial competence and psychological resources (e.g., self-esteem) of individual members, although questions concerning the causal direction of these associations persist.

These aspects of organizational culture may also influence the stress levels of individual members. For instance, variations in the perceived intrinsic and extrinsic religious orientations of congregants as well as variations in the order and clarity of collective goals may increase or reduce the capacity of congregations to promote ideational and behavioral conformity and to bring informal or formal sanctions to bear on deviant members (Welch, Tittle, & Petee, 1991). In sum, while research on this topic remains in its early stages, further empirical exploration of these organizational cultures within religious institutions seems to be a promising direction.

Third, congregational identities, or shared perceptions of members and elites about themselves, their congregation, and its mission, also may have implications for the social and psychological resources of members. Based on interviews with clergy, staff, and influential laity in a national sample of Presbyterian congregations, Carroll and Roozen (1990) develop an identity typology. They find several clusters of congregations, which also differ notably in various structural features: average size, patterns of growth and decline, racial composition and average socioeconomic status of membership, and prevalence and types of serious interpersonal conflicts. In addition, they also find signs that certain types of congregational identities may partly be responses to broader aspects of community structure and change.

These points underscore the potential value of collecting data at multiple levels (i.e., institutional and individual) and analyzing the effects of institutional contexts on individual outcomes. A variety of multilevel estimation procedures are now available for use in conjunction with such a research program (e.g., Entwistle, Casterline, & Sayed, 1989), and alternative sampling strategies are available for accomplishing these objectives. Samples can be drawn of congregations, through collecting information from clergy and staff members about the types of institutional factors discussed above, and then sampling individuals from congregational membership rolls (Leege & Welch, 1989). Alternatively, "hypernetwork" strategies would begin at the individual level to build an egocentric data file on institutions (McPherson, 1982; Parcel, Kaufman, & Jolly, 1991). Depending on the precise objectives of a given research program and the resources available for discharging those objectives, each sampling strategy may facilitate the consideration of contextual and multilevel religious effects. In addition to congregational factors, future research might profitably investigate whether the impact of religious variables on stress, resources, and outcomes varies according to broader community-level factors. Three speculative examples illustrate this point.

First, although levels of public religious involvement may be quite high in rural areas, religious institutions may be relatively more important sources of social ties and support in urban and/or suburban areas

(House, Umberson, & Landis, 1988). This may be the case because the fabric of rural life provides more opportunities for routine friendliness and chance interpersonal encounters that affirm personal role identities, whereas the diversity of values and backgrounds in urban contexts may make durable, affirming ties more dependent on planned encounters within institutional settings like churches or synagogues (Ellison, 1991b).

Second, the larger average population of voluntary associations in urban settings, compared with rural locales, may reduce the effectiveness of religious groups as social control institutions—with clear implications for the risk of certain stressors—because urbanites have many other organizational and lifestyle options in contrast to their rural counterparts.

Third, and more generally, while certain religious values or practices may enhance individual self-perceptions, these beneficial effects may be magnified in spatial settings with high concentrations of coreligionists. In such areas, one is more likely to encounter by chance strangers who share religious worldviews and, consequently, other social and political values; thus these encounters are more likely to be experienced as affirming. Spatial concentrations of coreligionists also enhance the odds that social contacts and friends cultivated outside congregational networks will share, at least broadly, religious and social values (Pescosolido, 1990). Moreover, Stark (1984) and others have suggested that the constraining effects of religious values and institutions on individuals are most evident in spatial units heavily populated by coreligionists. These are intriguing and worthwhile issues that can be addressed only by linking data on individual religiosity, stress, resources, and outcomes with community-level data on church membership rates and denominational concentrations. Fortunately, current data of this type are becoming widely available (Bradley, Green, Jones, Lynn, & McNeil, 1992).

Summary and Concluding Remarks

This chapter has reviewed various observed and hypothesized links between aspects of religious involvement and components of the life stress paradigm, including stress, social resources, psychological resources, and more specific coping strategies and mechanisms. The focus has been to summarize and synthesize relevant research from diverse sources and disciplines, and to identify promising avenues for further research on the affective consequences of the religious life.

To summarize, there are ample theoretical and empirical reasons to expect that certain aspects of religious involvement—particularly high levels of institutional participation, and involvement in certain conservative denominations—reduce the risk of a number of major social stressors. The evidence is most compelling in relation to physical health and marital relations, and at least suggestive in regard to work experiences, legal difficulties, and intergenerational relationships. In addition, there is mounting evidence that religious communities facilitate the cultivation of comparatively dense social networks and the exchange of tangible and socioemotional support in times of need. There is also some evidence that members of religious communities perceive their social networks as more reliable and satisfying than other persons. Furthermore, religious beliefs and practices contribute to positive self-perceptions, especially feelings of self-esteem and personal mastery. Finally, religion is perceived by many adults as an important source of strength in stressful circumstances, and a growing body of research has explored the richness and diversity of religious coping strategies.

The bulk of this discussion has turned on the indirect effects of religious factors on mental health outcomes. In these concluding observations, it is appropriate to call attention to at least three direct relationships that merit careful scrutiny in future research. First, while religious values and practices may be especially beneficial to persons encountering high levels of stress, strong religious plausibility structures may also imbue daily affairs and seemingly trivial events with new meaning, significance, and coherence (Berger, 1967; Ellison, 1991a).

Second, participation in certain types of collective worship services may promote euphoria, while reducing feelings of depression and anxiety (Gritzmacher et al., 1988). This is especially the case in regard to ecstatic services that are geared to the release of tensions and the articulation and management of grief and sorrow. At present, there is supportive evidence primarily from case studies of Pentecostals and similar groups. Findings also suggest that such services are particularly popular among African-Americans, as manifest in the distinctive styles of preaching, musical accompaniment, and free-form collective participation that characterize certain black churches (Gilkes, 1980; Griffith, Young, & Smith, 1984).

Third, some observers have suggested a physiological explanation for the effect of devotional activities such as meditative prayer on psychological well-being. Meditation and related techniques lower levels of somatic arousal, bringing on neurological changes and altering affective states (Holmes, 1984; Woolfolk, 1975). To be sure, much of the supportive evidence has been generated via laboratory experiments, and its generalizability to real-world conditions remains open to question. Nevertheless, such physiological arguments offer a promising area for future research, and they may eventually clarify the links between prayer and mental health (see Poloma & Gallup, 1991).

The continuing vibrancy and ubiquity of religious life, which confounds the assumptions of earlier generations of social thinkers (see Hadden, 1987), may hold a variety of consequences for individual affective states and mental health. It is unfortunate that investigators of the social etiology of depression and other affective disorders and particularly those researchers working within the life stress paradigm have largley neglected the implications of religious factors. It is hoped that this chapter will serve to encourage the work of scholars and other interested professionals in these areas.

References

Adams, J. E. (1986). *The biblical view of self-esteem, self-love, and self-image.* Eugene, OR: Harvest House.

Ammerman, N. T. (1987). *Bible believers.* New Brunswick, NJ: Rutgers University Press.

Antonovsky, A. (1987). *Unravelling the mystery of health.* San Francisco: Jossey-Bass.

Avison, W. R., & Turner, R. J. (1988). Stressful life events and depressive symptoms: Disaggregating the effects of acute stressors and chronic strains. *Journal of Health and Social Behavior, 29,* 253-264.

Barrera, M. (1986). Distinctions between social support concepts, measures, and models. *American Journal of Community Psychology, 14,* 413-445.

Batson, C. D., & Ventis, W. L. (1982). *The religious experience.* New York: Oxford University Press.

Beck, A. T. (1967). *Depression: Causes and treatment.* Philadelphia: University of Pennsylvania Press.

Beck, S. H., Cole B. S., & Hammond, J. A. (1991). Religious heritage and premarital sex: Evidence from a national sample of young adults. *Journal for the Scientific Study of Religion, 30,* 173-180.

Berger, P. L. (1967). *The sacred canopy.* Garden City, NY: Doubleday.

Bergin, A. E. (1983). Religiosity and mental health: A critical reevaluation and meta-analysis. *Professional Psychology: Research and Practice, 14,* 170-184.

Berkman, L. F., & Breslow, L. (1983). *Health and ways of living: The Alameda County Study.* New York: Oxford University Press.

Bock, E. W., Cochran, J. K., & Beeghley, L. (1987). Moral messages: The relative influence of denomination on the religiosity-alcohol relationship. *Sociological Quarterly, 28,* 86-105.

Bradley, M. B., Green, N. M., Jones, D. E., Lynn, M., & McNeil, L. (1992). *Churches and church membership in the United States: 1990.* Atlanta: Glenmary Research Institute.

Branden, N. (1969). *The psychology of self-esteem.* New York: Bantam.

Branden, N. (1983). *Honoring the self.* New York: Bantam.

Breault, K. D. (1986). Suicide in America: A test of Durkheim's theory of religious and family integration, 1933-1980. *American Journal of Sociology, 92,* 628-656.

Bulman, R. J., & Wortman, C. B. (1977). Attributions of blame and coping in the "real world": Severe accident victims react to their lot. *Journal of Personality and Social Psychology, 35,* 351-361.

Burt, R. S. (1984). Network items and the General Social Survey. *Social Networks, 6,* 293-339.

Capps, D. (1982). Sunden's role-taking theory: The case of John Henry Newman and his mentors. *Journal for the Scientific Study of Religion, 21,* 58-70.

Capps, D. (1985). Religion and psychological well-being. In P. E. Hammond (Ed.), *The sacred in a secular age: Toward revision in the scientific study of religion* (pp. 237-256). Berkeley: University of California Press.

Carroll, J. W., & Roozen, D. A. (1990). Congregational identities in the Presbyterian Church. *Review of Religious Research, 31,* 351-369.

Carver, C. S., Schreiber, M. F., & Weintraub, J. K. (1989). Assessing coping strategies: A theoretically based approach. *Journal of Personality and Social Psychology, 56,* 267-283.

Chalfant, H. P., Heller, P. L., Roberts, A., Briones, D., Aguirre-Hochbaum, S., & Farr, W. (1990). The clergy as a resource for those encountering psychological distress. *Review of Religious Research, 31,* 305-313.

Chi, S. P., & Houseknecht, S. K. (1983). Protestant fundamentalism and marital success: A comparative approach. *Sociology and Social Research, 69,* 351-375.

Clarke, L., Beeghley, L., & Cochran, J. K. (1990). Religiosity, social class, and alcohol use: An application of reference group theory. *Sociological Perspectives, 33,* 201-218.

Cochran, J. K., & Akers, R. (1989). Beyond hellfire: An exploration of the variable effects of religiosity on adolescent marijuana and alcohol use. *Journal of Research in Crime and Delinquency, 26,* 198-225.

Cochran, J. K., Beeghley, L., & Bock, E. W. (1988). Religiosity and alcohol behavior: An exploration of reference group theory. *Sociological Forum, 3,* 256-276.

Cohen, S., & Wills, T. A. (1985). Stress, social support, and the buffering hypothesis. *Psychological Bulletin, 98,* 310-357.

Cook, J. A., & Wimberly, D. (1983). If I should die before I wake: Religious commitment and adjustment to the death of a child. *Journal for the Scientific Study of Religion, 22,* 222-238.

Cornwall, M. (1987). The social bases of religion: A study of the factors influencing religious beliefs and commitment. *Review of Religious Research, 29,* 44-56.

Cornwall, M. (1989). The determinants of religious behavior: A theoretical model and empirical test. *Social Forces, 68,* 572-592.

DeLongis, A., Coyne, J., Dakof, G., Folkman, S., & Lazarus, R. S. (1982). Relationship of daily hassles, uplifts, and major life events to health status. *Health Psychology, 1,* 119-136.

Dohrenwend, B. S., & Dohrenwend, B. P. (1981). Life stress and illness: Formulation of the issues. In B. S. Dohrenwend & B. P. Dohrenwend (Eds.), *Stressful life events and their contexts* (pp. 1-27). New York: Prodist.

Durkheim, E. (1933). *The division of labor in society.* New York: Free Press. (Original work published 1901)

Durkheim, E. (1951). *Suicide.* New York: Free Press. (Original work published 1897)

Dwyer, J. W., Clarke, L. L., & Miller, M. K. (1990). The effect of religious concentration and affiliation on county cancer mortality rates. *Journal of Health and Social Behavior, 31,* 185-202.

Ebaugh, H., Richman, K., & Chafetz, J. (1984). Life crises among the religiously committed: Do sectarian differences matter? *Journal for the Scientific Study of Religion, 23,* 19-31.

Eckenrode, J. (1983). The mobilization of social supports: Some individual constraints. *American Journal of Community Psychology, 11,* 509-528.

Edmonds, V. H. (1967). Marital conventionalization: Definition and measurement. *Journal of Marriage and the Family, 29,* 681-688.

Edmonds, V. H., Withers, G., & DiBatista, B. (1972). Adjustment, conservatism, and marital conventionalization. *Journal of Marriage and the Family, 34,* 96-103.

Ellis, A. (1948). The value of marriage prediction tests. *American Sociological Review, 13,* 710-718.

Ellis, A. (1962). *Reason and emotion in psychotherapy.* Secaucus, NJ: Lyle Stuart.

Ellis, A. (1980). Psychotherapy and aesthetic values: A response to A. E. Bergin's "Psychotheraphy and Religious Values." *Journal of Consulting and Clinical Psychology, 48,* 635-639.

Ellison, C. G. (1991a). Religious involvement and subjective well-being. *Journal of Health and Social Behavior, 32,* 80-99.

Ellison, C. G. (1991b). *Bringing religion back in: The life stress paradigm and the sociological study of depression.* Doctoral dissertation, Duke University, Durham, NC.

Ellison, C. G. (1992a). *Religious involvement and the incidence of stressful life events among black Americans.* Unpublished manuscript, University of Texas at Austin.

Ellison, C. G. (1992b). Are religious people nice people?: Evidence from the National Survey of Black Americans. *Social Forces, 71,* 411-430.

Ellison, C. G. (1993). Religious involvement and self-perception among black Americans. *Social Forces, 71,* 1027-1055.

Ellison, C. G., & Sherkat, D. E. (1993). Conservative Protestantism and support for corporal punishment. *American Sociological Review, 58,* 131-144.

Ellison, C. G., & Sherkat, D. E. (in press). Obedience and autonomy: Religion and parental values reconsidered. *Journal for the Scientific Study of Religion.*

Eng, E., Hatch, J., & Callan, A. (1985). Institutionalizing social support through the church and into the community. *Health Education Quarterly, 12,* 81-92.

Entwistle, B., Casterline, J. B., & Sayed, H. (1989). Villages as contexts for contraceptive behavior in rural Egypt. *American Sociological Review, 54,* 1019-1034.

Festinger, L. (1950). Laboratory experiments: The role of group belongingness. In J. G. Miller (Ed.), *Experiments in social process* (pp. 31-46). New York; McGraw-Hill.

Festinger, L. (1954). A theory of social comparison processes. *Human Relations, 7,* 117-140.

Filsinger, E. E., & Wilson, M. R. (1984). Religiosity, socioeconomic rewards, and family development: Predictors of marital adjustment. *Journal of Marriage and the Family, 46,* 663-670.

Foley, D. P. (1988). Eleven interpretations of personal suffering. *Journal of Religion and Health, 27,* 321-328.

Folkman, S., & Lazarus, R. S. (1988). The relationship between coping and emotion: Implications for theory and research. *Social Science and Medicine, 26,* 309-317.

Funch, D. P., & Marshall, J. R. (1984). Measuring life stress: Factors affecting fall-off in the reporting of life events. *Journal of Health and Social Behavior, 25,* 453-464.

Gardner, J. W., & Lyon, J. L. (1982). Cancer in Utah Mormon men by lay priesthood level. *American Journal of Epidemiology, 116,* 243-257.

Gartner, J. D. (1983). Self-esteem tests: Assumptions and values. In C. W. Ellison (Ed.), *Your better self: Christianity, psychology, and self-esteem* (pp. 98-110). San Francisco: Harper & Row.

George, L. K. (1989). Social and economic factors. In E. W. Busse & D. G. Blazer (Eds.), *Geriatric psychiatry.* Washington, DC: American Psychiatric Press.

Gilkes, C. (1980). The black church as a therapeutic community: Suggested areas for research into the black religious experience. *Journal of the Interdenominational Theological Center, 8,* 29-44.

Gorsuch, R. L., & Smith, C. S. (1983). Attributions of responsibility to God: An interaction of religious beliefs and outcomes. *Journal for the Scientific Study of Religion, 22,* 340-352.

Grasmick, H. G., Bursik, R. J., & Cochran, J. K. (1991). "Render unto Caesar what is Caesar's": Religiosity and taxpayers' inclinations to cheat. *Sociological Quarterly, 32,* 251-266.

Grasmick, H. G., Kinsey, K., & Cochran, J. K. (1991). Denomination, religiosity, and compliance with the law: A study of adults. *Journal for the Scientific Study of Religion, 30,* 99-107.

Griffith, E. E. H., Young, J. L., & Smith, D. L. (1984). An analysis of the therapeutic elements in a black church service. *Hospital and Community Psychiatry, 35,* 464-469.

Gritzmacher, S. A., Bolton, B., & Dana, R. H. (1988). Psychological characteristics of Pentecostals: A literature review and psychodynamic synthesis. *Journal of Psychology and Theology, 16,* 233-245.

Haber, D. J. (1984). Church-based programs for black care givers of non-institutionalized elders. *Journal of Gerontological Social Work, 7*(4), 43-56.

Hadden, J. (1987). Desacralizing secularization theory. *Social Forces, 65,* 587-611.

Hall, A., & Wellman, B. (1985). Social networks and social support. In S. Cohen & S. L. Syme (Eds.), *Social support and health* (pp. 23-41). New York: Academic Press.

Hansen, G. L. (1981). Marital adjustment and conventionalization: A reexamination. *Journal of Marriage and the Family, 43,* 855-863.

Hansen, G. L. (1987). The effect of religiosity on factors predicting marital adjustment. *Social Psychology Quarterly, 50,* 264-269.

Hansson, R. O., Jones, W. H., & Carpenter, B. N. (1984). Relational competence and social support. In P. Shaver (Ed.), *Review of personality and social psychology* (Vol. 5, pp. 265-288). Beverly Hills: Sage.

Heaton, T. B. (1984). Religious homogamy and marital satisfaction reconsidered. *Journal of Marriage and the Family, 46,* 729-733.

Heaton, T. B. (1988). Four c's of the Mormon family: Chastity, conjugality, children, and chauvinism. In D. L. Thomas (Ed.), *The religion and family connection: Social science perspectives* (pp. 107-124). Provo, UT: Brigham Young University Religious Studies Center.

Heaton, T. B., Albrecht, S. L., & Martin, T. K. (1985). The timing of divorce. *Journal of Marriage and the Family, 47,* 631-639.

Heaton, T. B., & Goodman, K. L. (1985). Religion and family formation. *Review of Religious Research, 26,* 343-359.

Heaton, T. B., & Pratt, E. L. (1990). The effects of religious homogamy on marital satisfaction and stability. *Journal of Family Issues, 11,* 191-207.

Henderson, A. S., Byrne, D. B., & Duncan-Jones, P. (1981). *Neurosis and the social environment.* Sydney, Australia: Academic Press.

Hoekema, A. A. (1983). The Christian self-image: A Reformed perspective. In C. W. Ellison (Ed.), *Your better self: Christianity, psychology, and self-esteem* (pp. 23-36). San Francisco: Harper & Row.

Holm, N. G. (1987). Sunden's role theory and glossolalia. *Journal for the Scientific Study of Religion, 26,* 383-389.

Holmes, D. S. (1984). Meditation and somatic arousal reduction: A review of the experimental evidence. *American Psychologist, 39,* 1-10.

House, J. S. (1981). *Work, stress, and social support.* Reading, MA: Addison-Wesley.

House, J. S., Umberson, D., & Landis, K. R. (1988). Structures and processes of social support. *Annual Review of Sociology, 14,* 293-318.

Idler, E. L., & Kasl, S. V. (1992). Religion, disability, depression, and the timing of death. *American Journal of Sociology, 97,* 1052-1079.

Jacobson, D. E. (1986). Types and timing of social support. *Journal of Health and Social Behavior, 27,* 250-264.

Jacobson, D. E. (1987). The cultural context of social support and social networks. *Medical Anthropology Quarterly, 1,* 42-67.

Jarvis, G. K., & Northcott, H. C. (1987). Religion and differences in morbidity and mortality. *Social Science and Medicine, 25,* 813-824.

Jenkins, R. A., & Pargament, K. I. (1988). Cognitive appraisals in cancer patients. *Social Science and Medicine, 26,* 625-633.

Johnson, M. A., & Mullins, P. (1990). Moral communities: Religious and secular. *Journal of Community Psychology, 18,* 153-166.

Kahn, R. L., & Antonucci, T. (1980). Convoys over the life course: Attachment, roles, and social support. In P. B. Baltes & O. Brim (Eds.), *Life-span development and behavior* (Vol. 3, pp. 254-286). Lexington, MA: D. C. Heath.

Kelley, D. M. (1972). *Why conservative churches are growing.* New York: Harper & Row.

Kelley, H. H. (1979). *Personal relationships.* Hillsdale, NJ: Lawrence Erlbaum.

Kilpatrick, W. K. (1983). *Psychological seduction.* Nashville: Thomas Nelson.

Kotarba, J. A. (1983). Perceptions of death, belief systems, and the process of coping with chronic pain. *Social Science and Medicine, 17,* 683-691.

Krause, N., & Tran, T. V. (1989). Stress and religious involvement among older blacks. *Journal of Gerontology: Social Sciences, 44,* S4-S13.

Kroll-Smith, J. S., & Couch, S. R. (1987). A chronic technical disaster and the irrelevance of religious meaning: The case of Centralia, Pennsylvania. *Journal for the Scientific Study of Religion, 26,* 25-37.

Landerman, R., George, L. K., Campbell, R. T., & Blazer, D. G. (1990). Alternative models of the stress buffering hypothesis. *American Journal of Community Psychology, 17,* 625-642.

Larson, L. E., & Goltz, J. W. (1989). Religious participation and marital commitment. *Review of Religious Research, 30,* 387-400.

Lazarus, R. S., & Folkman, S. (1984). *Stress, appraisal, and coping.* New York: Springer.

Lazarus, R. S., & Launier, R. (1978). Stress-related transactions between person and environment. In L. Pervin and M. Lewis (Eds.), *Perspectives in interactional psychology* (pp. 287-327). New York: Plenum.

Leege, D. C., & Welch, M. R. (1989). Catholics in context: Theoretical and methodological issues in studying American Catholic parishes. *Review of Religious Research, 31,* 132-148.

Lerner, M. J. (1980). *The belief in a just world: A fundamental delusion.* New York: Plenum.

Levin, J. S., & Schiller, P. L. (1986). Religion and the Multidimensional Health Locus of Control Scales. *Psychological Reports, 59,* 26.

Levin, J. S., & Vanderpool, H. Y. (1987). Is frequent religious attendance *really* conducive to better health?: Toward an epidemiology of religion. *Social Science and Medicine, 24,* 589-600.

Levin, J. S., & Vanderpool, H. Y. (1989). Is religion therapeutically significant for hypertension? *Social Science and Medicine, 29,* 69-78.

Levinger, G. (1965). Marital cohesiveness and dissolution: An integrative review. *Journal of Marriage and the Family, 27,* 19-28.

Levitt, E. E., Lubin, B., & Brooks, J. M. (1983). *Depression: Concepts, controversies, and some new facts.* Hillsdale, NJ: Lawrence Erlbaum.

Lin, N., and Ensel, W. M. (1989). Life stress and health: Stressors and resources. *American Sociological Review, 54,* 382-399.

Lin, N., Woelfel, M. W., & Light, S. C. (1985). The buffering effect of social support subsequent to an important life event. *Journal of Health and Social Behavior, 26,* 247-263.

Marsden, P. V. (1990). Network data and measurement. *Annual Review of Sociology, 16,* 435-463.

Marsella, A. J., Hirschfeld, R. M. A., & Katz, M. M. (Eds.). (1987). *The measurement of depression.* New York: Guilford.

Maton, K. I. (1987). Patterns and psychological correlates of material support within a religious setting: The bidirectional support hypothesis. *American Journal of Community Psychology, 15,* 185-207.

Maton, K. I. (1989). Community settings as buffers of life stress?: Highly supportive churches, mutual help groups, and senior centers. *American Journal of Community Psychology, 17,* 203-232.

Mattlin, J. A., Wethington, E., & Kessler, R. C. (1990). Situational determinants of coping and coping effectiveness. *Journal of Health and Social Behavior, 31,* 103-122.

McCarthy, J. (1979). Religious commitment, affiliation, and marriage dissolution. In R. Wuthnow (Ed.), *The religious dimension: New directions in quantitative research* (pp. 179-198). New York: Academic Press.

McCrae, R. R., & Costa, P. T. (1986). Personality, coping, and effectiveness in an adult sample. *Journal of Personality and Social Psychology, 54,* 385-405.

McDowell, J. (1978). *Building your self-image.* Wheaton, IL: Tyndale House.

McGaw, D. B., & Wright, E. (1979). *A tale of two congregations: Commitment and social structure in a charismatic and mainline congregation.* Hartford, CT: Hartford Seminary Foundation.

McIntosh, W. A., & Alston, J. P. (1982). Lenski revisited: The linkage role of religion in primary and secondary groups. *American Journal of Sociology, 87,* 852-882.

McIntosh, W. A., & Shifflett, P. A. (1984). Dietary behavior, dietary adequacy, and religious social support: An exploratory study. *Review of Religious Research, 26,* 158-175.

McMillan, D. W., & Chavis, D. M. (1986). Sense of community: A definition and theory. *Journal of Community Psychology, 14,* 6-23.

McNamara, P. H. (1985). The New Christian Right's view of the family and its social science critics: A study in differing presuppositions. *Journal of Marriage and the Family, 47,* 449-458.

McPherson, J. M. (1982). Hypernetwork sampling: Duality and differentiation among voluntary associations. *Social Networks, 3,* 225-249.

Mechanic, D. (1990, January-February). Promoting health. *Society,* pp. 16-22.

Merton, R. K., & Rossi, A. S. (1968). Contributions to the theory of reference group behavior. In R. K. Merton (Ed.), *Social theory and social structure* (pp. 279-334). New York: Free Press.

Mestrovic, S., & Glassner, B. (1983). A Durkheimian hypothesis on stress. *Social Science and Medicine, 17,* 1315-1327.

Mirowsky, J., & Ross, C. E. (1984). Mexican culture and its emotional contradictions. *Journal of Health and Social Behavior, 25,* 2-13.

Mirowsky, J., & Ross, C. E. (1986). Social patterns of distress. *Annual Review of Sociology, 12,* 23-45.

Morgan, S. P. (1983). A research note on religion and morality: Are religious people nice people? *Social Forces, 61,* 683-692.

Olson, D. V. A. (1989). Church friendships: Boon or barrier to church growth? *Journal for the Scientific Study of Religion, 28,* 432-447.

Ortega, S. T., Crutchfield, R. D., & Rushing, W. A. (1983). Race differences in elderly personal well-being: Friendship, family, and church. *Research on Aging, 4,* 101-117.

Ortega, S. T., Whitt, H. P., & Williams, J. A. (1988). Religious homogamy and marital happiness. *Journal of Family Issues, 9,* 224-239.

Ott, P. W. (1991). John Wesley on health as wholeness. *Journal of Religion and Health, 30,* 43-58.

Parcel, T. L., Kaufman, R. L., & Jolly, L. (1991). Going up the ladder: Multiplicity sampling to create linked macro-micro organizational samples. In P. V. Marsden (Ed.), *Sociological methodology 1991* (pp. 43-78). San Francisco: Jossey-Bass.

Pargament, K. I., Ensing, D. S., Falgout, K., Olsen, H., Reilly, B., Van Haitsma, K., & Warren, R. (1990). God help me: I. Religious coping efforts as predictors of the outcomes to significant negative life events. *American Journal of Community Psychology, 18,* 793-824.

Pargament, K. I., & Hahn, J. (1986). God and the just world: Causal and coping attributions to God in health situations. *Journal for the Scientific Study of Religion, 25,* 193-207.

Pargament, K. I., Kennell, J., Hathaway, W., Grevengoed, N., Newman, J., & Jones, W. (1988). Religion and the problem-solving process: Three styles of religious coping. *Journal for the Scientific Study of Religion, 27,* 90-104.

Pargament, K. I., Silverman, W., Johnson, S., Echemendia, R., & Snyder, S. (1983). The psychosocial climate of religious congregations. *American Journal of Community Psychology, 11,* 351-383.

Pearlin, L. I. (1989). The sociological study of stress. *Journal of Health and Social Behavior, 30,* 241-257.

Pearlin, L. I., Menaghan, E. G., Lieberman, M. A., & Mullan, J. T. (1981). The stress process. *Journal of Health and Social Behavior, 22*, 337-356.

Pearlin, L. I., & Schooler, C. (1978). The structure of coping. *Journal of Health and Social Behavior, 19*, 2-21.

Pescosolido, B. (1990). The social context of religious integration and suicide: Pursuing the network explanation. *Sociological Quarterly, 31*, 337-357.

Pescosolido, B., & Georgianna, S. (1989). Durkheim, suicide, and religion: Toward a network theory of suicide. *American Sociological Review, 54*, 33-48.

Piazza, T., & Glock, C. Y. (1979). Images of God and their social meanings. In R. Wuthnow (Ed.), *The religious dimension: New directions in quantitative research* (pp. 69-92). New York: Academic.

Pollner, M. (1989). Divine relations, social relations, and well-being. *Journal of Health and Social Behavior, 30*, 92-104.

Poloma, M. M., & Gallup, G. (1991). *Varieties of prayer: A survey report*. Philadelphia: Trinity Press International.

Ritter, C., Benson, D. E., & Snyder, C. (1990). Belief in a just world and depression. *Sociological Perspectives, 33*, 235-252.

Ritzema, R. J., & Young, C. (1983). Causal schemata and the attribution of supernatural causality. *Journal of Psychology and Theology, 11*, 36-43.

Rosenberg, M. (1981). The self-concept: Social product and social force. In M. Rosenberg & R. Turner (Eds.), *Social psychology: Sociological perspectives* (pp. 593-624). New York: Basic Books.

Rosenfield, S. (1989). The effects of women's employment: Personal control and sex differences in mental health. *Journal of Health and Social Behavior, 31*, 77-91.

Rosik, C. H. (1989). The impact of religious orientation on conjugal bereavement among older adults. *International Journal of Aging and Human Development, 28*, 251-261.

Rubin, Z., & Peplau, L. A. (1975). Who believes in a just world? *Journal of Social Issues, 31*(3), 65-89.

Scanzoni, J., & Arnett, C. (1987). Enlarging the understanding of marital commitment via religious devoutness, gender role preferences, and locus of marital control. *Journal of Family Issues, 8*, 136-156.

Schuller, R. (1982). *Self-esteem: The new reformation*. Waco, TX: Word Books.

Schumm, W. R. (1985). Beyond relationship characteristics of strong families: Constructing a model of family strengths. *Family Perspective, 19*, 1-9.

Selye, H. (1956). *The stress of life*. New York: McGraw-Hill.

Sherif, M., White, B. J., & Harvey, O. J. (1955). Status in experimentally produced groups. *American Journal of Sociology, 60*, 370-379.

Sloane, D. M., & Potvin, R. H. (1986). Religion and delinquency: Cutting through the maze. *Social Forces, 65*, 87-105.

Spilka, B., & Schmidt, G. (1983). General attribution theory for the psychology of religion: The influence of event-character on attributions to God. *Journal for the Scientific Study of Religion, 22*, 326-339.

Spilka, B., Shaver, P., & Kirkpatrick, L. A. (1985). A general attribution theory for the psychology of religion. *Journal for the Scientific Study of Religion, 24*, 1-20.

Stark, R. (1984). Religion and conformity: Reaffirming a sociology of religion. *Sociological Analysis, 45*, 273-282.

Stark, R., & Bainbridge, W. S. (1980). Networks of faith: Interpersonal bonds and recruitment to cults and sects. *American Journal of Sociology, 85*, 1376-1395.

Steinitz, L. Y. (1981). The local church as social support for the elderly. *Journal of Gerontological Social Work, 4*(2), 43-54.

Studer, M., & Thornton, A. (1987). Adolescent religiosity and contraceptive usage. *Journal of Marriage and the Family, 49,* 117-128.

Sunden, H. (1965). What is the next step to be taken in the study of religious life? *Harvard Theological Review, 58,* 445-451.

Sunden, H. (1990). Augustine at Cassiciacum: Hearing the words of another. In D. Capps and J. E. Dittes (Eds.), *The hunger of the heart: Reflections on the confessions of Augustine* (Society for the Scientific Study of Religion Monograph Series). West Lafeyette, IN: Society for the Scientific Study of Religion.

Tardy, C. H. (1985). Social support measurement. *American Journal of Community Psychology, 13,* 187-202.

Tausig, M. (1982). Measuring life events. *Journal of Health and Social Behavior, 23,* 52-64.

Taylor, R. J., & Chatters, L. M. (1988). Church members as a source of informal social support. *Review of Religious Research, 30,* 193-202.

Taylor, S. (1983). Adjusting to threatening events: A theory of cognitive adaptation. *American Psychologist, 28,* 1161-1173.

Thoits, P. A. (1985). Social support and psychological well-being: Theoretical possibilities. In I. G. Sarason & B. R. Sarason (Eds.), *Social support: Theory, research, and applications* (pp. 51-72). Dordrecht: Martinus Nijhoff.

Tittle, C. R., & Welch, M. R. (1983). Religiosity and deviance: Toward a contingency theory of constraining effects. *Social Forces, 61,* 653-682.

Troyer, H. (1988). Review of cancer among four religious sects: Evidence that life-styles are distinctive sets of risk factors. *Social Science and Medicine, 26,* 1007-1017.

Turner, B. S. (1984). *The body and society: Explorations in social theory.* London: Basil Blackwell.

Verbrugge, L. M. (1977). The structure of adult friendship choices. *Social Forces, 56,* 576-597.

Vitz, P. C. (1977). *Psychology as religion: The cult of self-worship.* Grand Rapids, MI: Eerdmans.

Wald, K. D., Owen, D. E., & Hill, S. S. (1990). Political cohesion in churches. *Journal of Politics, 52,* 197-215.

Watson, P. J., Morris, R. J., & Hood, R. W. (1988). Sin and self-functioning. Part I: Grace, guilt, and self-consciousness. *Journal of Psychology and Theology, 16,* 254-269.

Weber, M. (1946). The Protestant sects and the spirit of capitalism. In H. Gerth & C. W. Mills (Eds.), *From Max Weber: Essays in sociology* (pp. 302-322). New York: Free Press. (Original work published 1921)

Weber, M. (1958). *The Protestant ethic and the spirit of capitalism.* New York: Charles Scribner's Sons. (Original work published 1905)

Welch, M. R., Tittle, C. R., & Petee, T. (1991). Religion and deviance among adult Catholics: A test of the "moral communities" hypothesis. *Journal for the Scientific Study of Religion, 30,* 159-172.

Wethington, E., & Kessler, R. C. (1986). Perceived support, received support, and adjustment to stressful life events. *Journal of Health and Social Behavior, 27,* 78-89.

Wikstrom, O. (1987). Attribution, roles, and religion: A theoretical analysis of Sunden's role theory and attributional approach to religious experience. *Journal for the Scientific Study of Religion, 26,* 390-400.

Wiley, J. A., & Comacho, T. C. (1980). Life-style and future health: Evidence from the Alameda County Study. *Preventive Medicine, 9,* 1-21.

Williams, R. (1990). *A Protestant legacy: Attitudes to death and illness among older Aberdonians.* Oxford: Clarendon.

Wills, T. A. (1981). Downward comparison principles in social psychology. *Psychological Bulletin, 90,* 245-271.

Wilson, J., & Clow, H. K. (1981). Themes of power and control in a Pentecostal assembly. *Journal for the Scientific Study of Religion, 20,* 241-250.

Wilson, M. R., & Filsinger, E. E. (1986). Religiosity and marital adjustment: Multidimensional interrelationships. *Journal of Marriage and the Family, 48,* 147-151.

Woolfolk, R. L. (1975). Psychophysiological correlates of meditation. *Archives of General Psychiatry, 32,* 1326-1333.

Wortman, C. B., & Lehman, D. R. (1985). Reactions to victims of life crises: Support attempts that fail. In I. G. Sarason & B. R. Sarason (Eds.), *Social support: Theory, research, and applications* (pp. 463-489). Boston: Martinus Nijhoff.

Wuthnow, R., Christiano, K., & Kuzlowski, J. (1980). Religion and bereavement: A conceptual framework. *Journal for the Scientific Study of Religion, 19,* 408-422.

PART II

Methodological Frontiers

5

The Measurement of Religion in Epidemiologic Studies

Problems and Prospects

DAVID R. WILLIAMS

Background

Within the last decade there has been a spate of reviews on the role of religion in physical and mental health (see Chapter 7 in this volume). However, it would be a mistake to perceive this interest as new, because a role for religion in health was explicit in the writings of several of the early social scientists. James (1902) distinguished healthy-minded religion from religion of the sick soul. The provision of social integration and meaning systems that Durkheim (1897/1951) and Weber (1964), respectively, attributed to religion have clear health consequences. Marx and Freud had decidedly uncharitable views of religion, but even they conceded that religion may have certain salutogenic effects. In the celebrated passage in which Marx described religion as the opium of the people, he also indicated that it was "the heart of a heartless world" and "the spirit of a spiritless situation" (Marx & Engels, 1964, p. 42). Although Freud (1963) regarded religion as an illusion and mass

AUTHOR'S NOTE: Preparation of this chapter was supported by NIH Grant No. AG07904 from the National Institute on Aging. The author wishes to thank Max Herman for research assistance and Ann Fitzpatrick for preparing the manuscript.

neurosis, he also stated that "religion succeeds in sparing many people an individual neurosis" (pp. 21-22).

Despite the current resurgence of interest in religion, the epidemiology of religion is still in its infancy, and one recent study noted that this area is "better characterized as faith than as science" (Idler & Kasl, 1992, p. 1054). Religion is difficult to define and consensus has not yet emerged around particular empirical measures. At the same time, the ubiquity of religious organizations, the theorized effects that religious involvement can have on health, and the involvement of most of the population in some aspect of religion suggest that it is a topic that can no longer be ignored. However, advancement of our understanding of the ways in which religion affects illness, disability, and health requires more attention to the conceptualization and measurement of the religious variable.

This chapter focuses primarily on the measurement of religion in studies of religious commitment and health, but it also discusses other methodological issues relevant to the analysis of data from large survey samples. It will review and evaluate existing measures of religion as used in broad-based epidemiologic studies. It will describe limitations of current measurement approaches as well as propose the development of new measures as necessary. Epidemiologic studies of religion have typically not been informed by the long tradition of interest in the measurement of the religious variable among sociologists and psychologists of religion. This chapter highlights the importance of placing the assessment of religion in health research into this larger theoretically informed context of efforts to measure religion in all its complexity. What is needed for the field to move forward is well-designed empirical research that evaluates theoretical ideas about the relation between religion and health. This is necessary to provide confidence in both the theory and the measures employed.

Unidimensional Measures of Religion

Religious Affiliation

Religious affiliation is the most commonly used measure of religion in research on religion and health (Craigie, Liu, Larson, & Lyons, 1988; Larson, Pattison, Blazer, Omran, & Kaplan, 1986; Levin & Schiller, 1987). This is most frequently operationalized as Catholic versus Protestant versus Jewish. This classification scheme is woefully inadequate and does not capture the great variation that exists among religious groups. Students of religion have long noted that the Catholic-Protestant distinction is not very meaningful, because there is more variation within the Protestant category than between Protestants and Catholics (Glock & Stark, 1965; Schuman, 1971).

This issue has been addressed in the literature (Levin & Schiller, 1987; Levin & Vanderpool, 1987), but the use of the simple Catholic-Protestant-Jewish distinction is still evident in recent research. One reason for this is that most epidemiologic studies of religion use secondary data in which religion was not of central interest during the original data collection. Today's researcher is thus locked into the available measures. For example, a recent study by Idler and Kasl (1992) found that the relationship between religion and health status indicators was strong for Catholics and Jews but weak or nonexistent for Protestants. These researchers indicated that their data lacked detail on the various Protestant denominations and branches of Judaism. It is likely that a different pattern of results would have emerged if they had been able to account for the heterogeneity of these religious faiths.

The question of how to group together different denominations that share common characteristics has received extensive attention from sociologists of religion. One of the most influential typologies in the field is the distinction between church and sect (Troeltsch, 1950; Weber, 1958). Numerous ways of classifying Protestant denominations into churches or sects have been suggested by a variety of researchers (Knudsen, Erle, & Shrivier, 1978). Johnson (1963) sees rejection of its social environment as the key defining sectarian characteristic. Stark and Bainbridge (1985) agree that subcultural deviance is a key identifier of a sect. Sects not only tend to develop their own subculture but have a tendency to become total institutions (Iannaccone, 1988).

Data from a study of San Francisco Bay Area church members reveal that across a broad range of social and behavioral variables, Protestant denominations fall along a unidimensional continuum that corresponds to the church-sect distinction (Glock & Stark, 1966; Iannaccone, 1988). Using large national surveys and a similar denominational ordering, Roof and McKinney (1987) obtained very similar results. Compared with members of churches, members of sects are poorer, less educated, contribute more money to their religious organizations, attend more services, hold stronger and more distinctive religious beliefs, belong to smaller congregations, and have more of their friends as members of their denomination.

Kelley (1972) used a typology similar to the church-sect classification scheme to explain different patterns of growth within Protestant denominations. Kelley distinguished exclusivist (sectlike) denominations from ecumenical (churchlike) ones, and found that the small exclusivist denominations were growing rapidly whereas the large ecumenical ones were losing membership. Kelley (1972) suggested that the key underlying characteristic that explained the patterns of growth was the strict attitudinal and behavioral demands that conservative denominations made on their members.

Similarly, Iannaccone (1988) indicates that what is common to most definitions of a sect is the denomination's emphasis on a distinctive lifestyle and morality. Consistent with this perspective, Hoge (1979) reported that a single item assessing the extent to which a Protestant denomination emphasized a distinctive lifestyle and morality accounted for all of the observed variations in growth rates of 16 major denominations between 1965 and 1975. The simple bivariate correlation between this measure and growth rates was 0.97. Controls for socioeconomic status and region of the country did not markedly reduce the strength of this association. Research on the church-sect distinction is an important direction for future work on religion and health. Researchers should not only classify religious denominations using the church-sect typology but should also measure the extent to which an individual's religious denomination emphasizes a distinctive lifestyle.

Religious Attendance

The frequency of religious attendance is the second most commonly used measure of religious involvement in health research (Larson et al., 1986; Levin & Schiller, 1987). The association between this indicator of religious participation and health status appears to be fairly robust. Levin and Vanderpool (1987) documented that religious attendance is positively associated with health status across a broad range of health outcomes. Similarly, a recent review of the religious variable in mental health research concluded that measures of actual religious behavior like religious attendance were more strongly linked to mental health than were more subjective measures of religiosity (Gartner, Larson, & Allen, 1991). Similarly, Adlaf and Smart (1985) found that religious attendance is more strongly linked to drug abuse than the intensity of religious feelings.

Despite its popularity, there are several problems associated with the use of religious attendance as a primary measure of religious involvement. First, it is not clear that religious attendance per se is indicative of anything intrinsically religious (Williams, Larson, Buckler, Heckmann, & Pyle, 1991). Religious attendance is frequently a badge of social status, secular in character, and of no greater religious significance than participation in other community organizations (Goode, 1966; Wilson, 1978). Religious attendance may also be a proxy for physical health status (Levin & Vanderpool, 1987). Especially in studies of older populations, public participation in religious activities requires a certain degree of physical health. Levin and Markides (1986) found that a positive association between religion and health was reduced to nonsignificance once controlled for activity limitation.

Second, a simple measure of the frequency of religious attendance is not an adequate measure of public religious participation. Measuring public religious involvement requires the assessment of religious attendance at meetings other than the main weekly worship service, financial support of religious organizations, and holding leadership and volunteer positions in religious groups (Ainlay & Smith, 1984).

Third, the conventional coding of the religious attendance variable provides data that may be badly skewed (Levin & Vanderpool, 1987). Typically, the highest category of religious attendance is once a week or more. Levin and Vanderpool (1987) indicate that at least half of persons who go to religious services attend them at least once per week. Given the high level of religious attendance in the United States, the most extreme category of attending services (once a week or more) is likely to be the mean, median, and mode for the frequency distribution of religious attendance. They indicate that this restricted variation at the high end of religious attendance probably leads to underestimation of positive associations between religion and health. These researchers suggest that the number of times per week that an individual attends religious services and other religious meetings should also be assessed.

Fourth, religious attendance captures only a small part of religious commitment and activity. Many researchers view religious attendance as a proxy for the larger universe of religious involvement, but the empirical evidence indicates that religious attendance is relatively insensitive to other forms of religious involvement (Jones, 1969; Kenney, Cromwell, & Vaughan, 1977; Stark & Glock, 1968). That is, measures of religious attendance do not capture attitudes, beliefs, religiously motivated behavior outside of religious settings, or the extent of religious commitment. Many persons who do not attend religious services report high levels of religious involvement according to other indicators of religion. In the United Kingdom, for example, only a small minority of the population regularly attends religious services, but the presence of religious belief is pervasive (Davie, 1990).

Multidimensional Measures of Religion

Both religious affiliation and attendance are unidimensional indicators of religion. They do not capture the quality of friendship and fellowship within congregations, the impact of religious ritual or symbolism on health, the therapeutic aspects of religious worship services, or the particular belief systems that may enhance or impair health. As a result, at the present time, researchers do not know with any precision what types, amounts, and aspects of religious involvement are most consequential for health. What is needed is a comprehensive but parsimonious set of conceptually based measures of religious involvement to study the effects of religion on health.

Epidemiologists can take heart, because religion scholars have long concluded that religious involvement is a multidimensional construct and have been wrestling with the appropriate ways to measure it (Fukuyama, 1961; Glock & Stark, 1965; King & Hunt, 1972, 1975). Although no consensus has emerged on the specific content and number of dimensions, the multidimensional measurement of religion is normative among sociologists and psychologists of religion, with research efforts continuing to validate, replicate, and extend various multidimensional models.

Glock's (1962) typology is one of the most influential in the field. It views religion as consisting of five distinctive dimensions. These are ideological (religious beliefs), ritualistic (religious practice), experiential (religious feelings), consequential (generalized effects of religion in an individual's life), and intellectual (religious knowledge). Hilty, Morgan, and Burns (1984) indicate that this five-dimensional model is the theoretical typology most frequently studied by sociologists of religion and that several studies have found empirical support for its dimensions. For example, both Fukuyama (1961) and Glock and Stark (1965) found empirical support for all but the consequential dimension.

Although not the most widely used, the most comprehensive typology of religious involvement is that proposed by King and Hunt (Hilty et al., 1984). Originally proposed as a 9-dimensional construct, the King and Hunt typology eventually evolved into an 11-dimensional model (King, 1967; King & Hunt, 1972, 1975). An important contribution of the King and Hunt approach is that it attempted to incorporate all of the typologies that existed at that time. No consensus has emerged about the specific dimensions identified by King and Hunt, but the seven-factor model (Hilty et al., 1984) appears to be a useful place to begin. These seven factors are personal faith, intolerance of ambiguity, orthodoxy, social conscience, knowledge of religious history, life purpose, and church involvement. Like many of the extant scales that measure religion, the specific items would need to be reworded to be applicable to non-Christian groups. The ensuing discussion of the consequences of religion in terms of social support, ritual and symbolism, and subjective religiosity overlaps with and extends the conceptualization of religious involvement that is in this typology.

Social Support

The church attendance measure explicitly incorporates the notion that religion may affect health by serving as a source of social integration and social support. The consequences of social relationships for health have been under intense scientific investigation in recent years. The empirical evidence indicates that supportive social relationships have pervasive effects on health status that rival those of the more traditional biomedical risk factors (House, Landis, & Umberson, 1988). For example, social relationships are as strongly linked to mortality as is cigarette smoking. Moreover, the literature on social support explicitly includes measures of religious attendance as indicators of social support (Berkman & Syme, 1979; House, Robbins, & Metzner, 1982).

Churches are critical sources of social integration, and congregation-based friendship networks may serve as a type of extended family and be a major basis of supportive social relationships as persons go through the life cycle (Taylor & Chatters, 1988). Congregations vary in the extent to which they provide emotional and instrumental support, and this variation needs to be assessed. A recent study found evidence of an interaction between parishioners' needs and the level of congregational support (Maton, 1989). Congregational support was measured based on members' self-report of the quantity and quality of contact with all members of their church. Persons who had high levels of economic stress had greater well-being in high-support churches than in low-support congregations. However, for members low in economic stress, levels of well-being were unrelated to the support level of the congregation. The size of a congregation may be an important determinant of the quality of fellowship and group cohesiveness found among its members. Some limited evidence suggests that members of small churches may enjoy higher levels of social support than those in large churches (Wicker & Mehler, 1971).

It is instructive that the social network structure of church members also helps to distinguish churches from sects. Unlike churches, sects provide their members with most of their closest friendships, and the low rate of participation of sect members in nonreligious organizations suggests that their church friendships substitute for secular ones (Iannaccone, 1988). Stark and Bainbridge (1985) view this communal attribute (the religious group functioning as the primary group for the formation of interpersonal bonds) as a critical factor that distinguishes sects from churches. This has been measured by asking respondents how many of their five closest friends are members of their congregation or parish. Two or more such friendships is indicative of a communal group (Stark & Glock, 1968). Sects are high on communal involvement, whereas churches score low on this attribute.

Consideration of the supportive role of religion has almost exclusively focused on the primary prevention functions of religion—that is, the extent to which religion can counteract stress and/or pathogenic conditions and promote health by enhancing conditions in the environment. Researchers also need to explore the role of religion in secondary and tertiary prevention. Secondary prevention refers to shortening the duration of illness through early diagnosis and effective treatment, while tertiary prevention encompasses strategies that can reduce the debilitating consequences of illness and disability.

The clergy may play an important role in secondary prevention. They are gatekeepers to the mental health system and play a crucial role in the delivery of mental health services (Veroff, Douvan, & Kulka, 1981). For nearly 40% of the U.S. population, the clergy is a primary help-seeking source with less than 10% of these persons being referred to mental health professionals (Meylink & Gorsuch, 1988; Veroff et al., 1981). Analyses of data from the largest study of mental health ever conducted in the United States indicate that the clergy do not differ from mental health practitioners in terms of the type or severity of psychiatric problems that they see (Larson et al., 1988). However, researchers are largely unaware of what services the clergy provide to persons with psychiatric problems, the conditions under which they refer patients to clinicians, or the factors that increase the likelihood of such referral. An important research issue is the identification of the role that religion plays as an alternative system of treatment, especially for mental health problems. Some religious traditions view the seeking of help for mental health problems as a sign of moral failure. Religious values and beliefs may prevent some parishioners from seeking help from the formal mental health system as well as make some clergy reluctant to refer individuals for help.

Churches also play a critical but neglected role in tertiary prevention by helping to maintain marginal persons in society (Haugk, 1976). At the time of discharge from a health facility an individual has an important need for stability in the community. A local church can offer fellowship and acceptance as well as activities and groups in which the individual can become involved. Idler and Kasl (1992) note that religious group membership also may provide an incentive for rehabilitation and recovery, especially among the elderly. It can provide an otherwise disengaged older person a public role to which he or she can return.

The literature on social support indicates that social relationships not only can provide emotional concern and caring but can also serve as critical agents of social control (Umberson, 1987). It is likely that these social control elements of religion may be stronger in sects than in churches. Stark (1984) emphasizes that religion shapes individual behavior not only through internalized religious beliefs but also as an aspect of groups. Thus an adequate understanding of religious effects requires the assessment of religion at both the individual and the group level. The literature recognizes the role of social control primarily through moral codes that require patterns of behavior that may be health enhancing (Jarvis & Northcott, 1987; Levin & Vanderpool, 1987), but less attention has been given to the ways in which social ties reinforce and sustain individual commitment to religious norms.

Levin and Vanderpool (1987) recommend that researchers should ask respondents, "Compared to most people in your denomination, are you more religiously involved and committed, just about the same as everyone else, less religiously involved and committed, or not very involved or committed?" In addition, Stark and Glock's (1968) communal involvement question as well as the question, "How many of your closest friends have religious values and beliefs similar to yours?" should be asked. The social support literature has begun to give attention to the negative aspects of relationships. Social ties can provide both stress and support. Social relationships can be unpleasant and conflictive, and some evidence suggests that these negative aspects of relationships are more strongly linked to health status than the supportive ones (Fiore, Becker, & Coppel, 1983; Rook, 1984). Thus, in addition to assessing the extent to which fellow members make an individual feel loved and cared for, researchers must also ascertain the degree to which they are critical and make too many demands on the individual.

Rituals and Symbols

A simple measure of the frequency of religious attendance provides no data on what transpires during the service. The health consequences of religious attendance may be linked to the dynamics of the service. Research is needed that would pay greater attention to both the content and the context of religious services. This requires more explicit attention to the role of ritual and symbolism in religion. Researchers also need to be reminded that religious attendance is an important, but by no means the only common religious ritual.

There is a substantial literature on the health effects of religious rituals. However, these studies focus primarily on non-Christian groups (Kiev, 1964; Simpson, 1980). There does not yet appear to have been a systematic effort to assess religious rituals, develop reliable survey measures of them, and examine their relationship to health functioning in broad-based populations. Efforts that assess and quantify the religious rituals of congregations and that examine the extent to which they may promote or impair health and well-being may enhance the understanding of religion and health status and fill a critical gap in the literature by moving epidemiologic studies beyond the mere assessment of religious attendance.

Griffith, English, and Mayfield (1980) and Griffith, Young, and Smith (1984) indicate that participation in prayer and testimony at religious services can provide benefits to participants that are equivalent to those that individuals receive in formal psychotherapy. The expression of emotion and active congregational participation that is characteristic of some African-American church services can promote "collective catharsis" in ways that facilitate the reduction of tension and the release of emotional distress (Gilkes, 1980). Some religious services may be distinctive in the provision of opportunities to articulate and manage both personal and collective suffering. Through testimony, song, prayer, and sermon, participants may be allowed to express inner feelings without much inhibition. The personal faith dimension of the revised Hunt and King scale (Hilty et al., 1984) has several good measures of religious rituals that are practiced privately. However, religion measures capable of tapping the religious rituals of public religious worship are needed.

McGuire (1987) emphasizes that ritual language and nonverbal symbolism can provide not only a sense of order and control but also a sense of personal empowerment that may be health enhancing. Although ritual language is ubiquitous in religious organizations, little research attention has been given to this issue. Sabbath observance is another religious ritual worthy of examination. The observance of a weekly 24-hour period of rest and religious activity is normative within some branches of Judaism and for some Christian groups, such as Seventh-Day Adventists. This weekly "minivacation" typically involves a withdrawal from the normal hustle and bustle of life. Some theological scholars have suggested that this combination of physical rest with the intensification of religious activity may have important stress-reducing effects (Bacchiocchi, 1980; Heschel, 1951).

Recently, Idler and Kasl (1992) documented that the ritual observance of religious holidays was related to mortality in a large sample of elderly persons. In this study, fewer deaths occurred immediately before and during religious holidays than in the month afterward. This effect was stronger for more observant religious members than for less observant ones. This positive effect of religion existed for both Christians and Jews. Idler and Kasl (1992) observe that this protective effect of religion in the period before and during ceremonial occasions suggests that participation in religious rituals may be an important health-enhancing aspect of religious involvement.

Organizational Climate

There also is a need for more systematic assessment of the ways in which the organizational culture and structure of religious institutions affect the health of members. Pargament, Tyler, and Steele (1979) and Pargament, Silverman, Johnson, Echemendia, and Snyder (1983) indicate that churches vary in their psychosocial climates. These differences are measurable and decisive for the worldviews and well-being of participants. Building on research that documents that the organizational climate of health care and educational institutions is a determinant of the attitudes and behavior of individuals, Pargament et al. (1979) studied the extent to which the organizational structures of churches and synagogues differ in their social control and belief-transmitting functions. Congregations were defined as hierarchical or horizontal. Compared with horizontal congregations, hierarchical congregations were more likely to have status distinctions with differential power and privilege, to regulate individual behavior, and to have authoritarian religious beliefs. The study found that members of hierarchical congregations were less trustful of others, more likely to indicate that their lives were under the control of powerful persons and of God, and were less self-critical than members of horizontal congregations.

In a second study of 13 churches, Pargament et al. (1983) developed a congregational climate scale to explore the extent to which specific dimensions of congregations might be psychologically consequential for members. The 10 dimensions assessed were autonomy, sense of community activity, level of social concern, openness to change, stability, expressiveness, order, clarity, intrinsic religious orientation, and extrinsic religious orientation. The study found that congregational autonomy was positively related to the self-esteem and life satisfaction of church members.

Longitudinal studies are needed to assess the direction of causality and identify the process through which these relationships develop. Several different processes or combinations thereof could have produced these results (Pargament et al., 1983). Members with high self-esteem and life satisfaction may seek out and remain in autonomous congregations. Similarly, members with high self-esteem and life satisfaction may be more likely than those who view their lives less positively to perceive autonomy within their congregations. Alternatively, congregations that encourage participation may produce more positive outlooks in their members, or be more easily shaped by members who view themselves or their lives positively.

This study also found that most members of a congregation had similar perceptions of their church, and that congregations had distinctive psychosocial climates. For example, the small black Protestant congregations in the study were characterized by high levels of stability, expressiveness, social concern, and sense of community. Members of the small white Protestant congregations reported lower levels of stability and social concern than their black peers, but had comparable levels of community and expressiveness. Large white Catholic churches, on the other hand, were high on stability and social concern but low on expressiveness and sense of community.

Architecture

Another important but understudied aspect of religious symbolism is religious architecture. The physical structure of religious buildings can create particular images and convey complex and meaningful systems of ideas, beliefs, values, and feelings. Beyond the superficial appearance of the physical structure, there is often a deeper level of a symbolic system of religious ideas. Architecture can express ideology. Religious houses of worship very self-consciously attempt to retain their distinctiveness and reinforce particular values through architecture. Thus church architecture can be a determinant of the climate of the worship service and affect how people behave, feel, and think. By reinforcing particular feelings and actions, architecture can shape the hearts and minds of worshipers.

The physical layout of a church can reinforce notions of distance, differentiation, and gradation. Churches vary in the elevation of the pulpit and in the relative proximity of the preacher to the congregation, but the psychological consequences, if any, of these variations are not known. However, groups and individuals are sensitive to their particular setting, including the physical characteristics of that setting. Architecture can play an important role in social control and in the transmission of belief systems. Some have argued, for example, that the experience of worship in a Gothic cathedral has great impact on the participant:

> The immense height, the vertically directed arches, the massive rectangular base rising to a vast arched dome, the darkness below and the gentle light above, the mystical atmosphere . . . all these orient him toward God in heaven, but also toward feeling himself to be within a protecting, powerful, trustworthy, transcendent being. . . . Similarly, the acoustics of the church and the invisibility of the musicians enable music to envelop the worshiper. Such an atmosphere intensifies the feeling of being small and humble in relation to the awesome God. (Group for the Advancement of Psychiatry [GAP], 1968, p. 704)

Processes of both social support and social control are reflected in religious symbols and rituals. For the religiously involved, these effects of religion may be, paradoxically, both the most consequential and the least visible. Researchers' current self-report measures cannot adequately assess these effects. Small qualitative studies may be initially necessary to identify and understand and finally to catalog and quantify these specific aspects of religion. Adequate epidemiologic assessment of the role of religion in health will ultimately require the development of a parsimonious set of survey measures.

Measures of Subjective Religiosity

Epidemiologic studies of religion have rarely included indicators of the subjective dimensions of religiosity. These typically include attempts to assess an individual's rating of the importance or centrality of religion, or belief in particular religious teachings. Most of these measures have not been theoretically driven and the empirical payoff has been small. In a recent review of the religion and mental health literature, Gartner et al. (1991) concluded that behavioral predictors of religious involvement, such as church attendance, are more strongly linked to health status than more subjective, attitudinal indicators of religious involvement. Similarly, using data from a national sample of black Americans, Ellison and Gay (1990) report that although public religious involvement was positively linked to life satisfaction, private religiosity was unrelated to well-being. These findings may reflect the failure of the literature to assess the most relevant aspects of subjective religious involvement.

Intrinsic-Extrinsic Religion

A dominant approach to the measurement of the centrality of religion is one that emphasizes the motivations for religiousness. This work is best exemplified in the Religious Orientation Scale (ROS) of Allport (1950; also see Allport & Ross, 1967). Weber (1964) emphasized that it is the meaning provided by religious ideas that makes religion consequential for human behavior. He distinguished conceptions of the supernatural based on taboo from those based on religious ethics. A religious orientation based on taboo focused on the prescription and proscription of behavior. In contrast, one based on religious ethics involved a more general orientation to all aspects of life and social relationships. Allport's distinction between intrinsic and extrinsic religious orientation is somewhat similar to the Weberian approach.

According to Allport, intrinsic religion is an internalized, all-pervasive, organizing principle, whereas extrinsic religion is external and instrumental, a tool that is used to provide needs such as status and security. Allport's ROS and its subsequent adaptations represent the most widely used questionnaire measure in the empirical study of religion (Kirkpatrick, 1989). It has proven to be empirically robust and theoretically enlightening in studies of prejudice and other social phenomena (see Donahue, 1985). Allport (1963) hypothesized that intrinsic but not extrinsic religion would promote mental health, and declared 30 years ago that assessing the relationship between intrinsic religion and mental health was one of the most important research problems. To date, the association between the ROS and health status has not been examined in any population-based study, although it has been considered in small studies of religious individuals (Payne, Bergin, Bielema, & Jenkins, 1991).

The ROS has also received severe criticism. Stark and Glock (1968) indicate that Allport's typology mixes the conceptualization of religious commitment with its consequences, making it impossible to explain anything about commitment. Kirkpatrick and Hood (1990) indicate that Allport's intrinsic-extrinsic (I-E) framework has several weaknesses. First, the intrinsic dimension is poorly defined, because it measures religious commitment without considering the content of the beliefs to which the individual is committed. The extrinsic dimension, on the other hand, is well defined, but it is unclear as to which specific motives or goals underlie this orientation. Second, the extrinsic scale is unrelated to other measures of religiousness but correlated with variables such as prejudice, dogmatism, and trait anxiety. Third, the intrinsic-extrinsic dimensions should not be viewed as types but rather as poles on a continuum. Finally, the ROS is relevant only to religious populations. Kirkpatrick and Hood (1990) recommend an alternative conceptualization of the ROS in which each dimension is defined as a continuum from "not at all" to "very," with the former category representing the nonreligious.

Ongoing work on the I-E scale is addressing at least some of the criticisms of Kirkpatrick and Hood (1990). It is now apparent, for example, that the extrinsic items can be divided into subscales of personally oriented items and socially oriented items (Gorsuch & McPherson, 1989; Kirkpatrick, 1989). An I-E scale with revised wording that makes it applicable to a broader spectrum of the population also is now available (Gorsuch & Venable, 1983). A shorter version (14 items) also has been developed (Gorsuch & McPherson, 1989).

Tolerance of Ambiguity

Fundamentalism is a term usually used to describe theologically conservative Protestants who hold doctrines such as the inerrancy of the scriptures as well as the virgin birth, deity, and resurrection of Jesus Christ. However, some view fundamentalism as a mind-set, distinct from specific religious teachings, that emphasizes a dogmatic, simplistic approach to life that is intolerant of ambiguity and uncertainty (Hartz & Everett, 1989). According to this perspective, the fundamentalist mind-set is inherently pathological. The health consequences of fundamentalism are yet to be explored empirically; this issue rather explicitly exemplifies the need to assess both the positive and negative consequences of religion. However, most denominations that would be regarded as fundamentalist (sects instead of churches) also are likely to exhibit high levels of social integration and support. Research is needed to identify the extent to which these effects may cancel each other out and how they combine to affect health status. An instrument measuring tolerance of ambiguity is available in both the original King and Hunt (1975) scale and its recommended revision (Hilty et al., 1984).

Spiritual Well-Being

Psychologists generally recognize that one task of identity formation in late adolescence and early adulthood is finding a sense of purpose and direction in life and feeling satisfied about it (Richards, 1991). Religious socialization, including identification with religious characters or groups, can play a critical role in the establishment and development of religious identity in particular, and identity formation in general (GAP, 1968). Measures of spiritual well-being have attempted to capture the integrative nature of healthy human personality and may prove useful in understanding the relationship between religion and mental health (Moberg, 1984).

The life purpose dimension of the revised King and Hunt scale (Hilty et al., 1984) is one example of a spiritual well-being measure. The most widely used instrument of this kind is the Spiritual Well-Being Scale (SWBS) (Ellison & Smith, 1991). The SWBS consists of two subscales. The existential well-being scale measures the extent to which the individual has a sense of purpose, direction, and satisfaction in life. The religious well-being subscale assesses the degree of belief that one is loved by God and enjoys a fulfilling and meaningful relationship.

Studies reveal that the SWBS is correlated with a broad range of health status indicators as well as indicators of general well-being, church attendance, and other measures of religious involvement (Ellison & Smith, 1991). The scale also has been shown to have reasonable reliability and validity (Ellison & Smith, 1991; Richards, 1991). However, most of the research on this scale has not come from broad-based probability samples of the population. It is not clear how well this scale will apply to populations other than conservative Christians, and to non-Christian religious persons.

An alternative and promising approach to measuring spiritual well-being is the Maturity of Faith scales that have been used in a large national sample of Protestant adults and adolescents (Benson & Elkin, 1990). The main scale consists of a vertical subscale (relationship with God) and a horizontal subscale (relationships with others). Impressive levels of reliability and validity have been reported for the scale (Benson & Elkin, 1990). An important contribution of this approach is the use of the related Growth in Faith maturity scale, which covers the same dimensions as the Maturity of Faith scale but focuses on change on each item within the last 2 or 3 years. This approach emphasizes that religious involvement is not static and that researchers should study change in religious commitment.

Other Methodological Issues

Much of the research literature on religion and mental health is based on cross-sectional studies. This raises the difficult issue of establishing causal priorities in the nature of observed associations. The issue of selection bias may not be trivial in research on religion and health. In a study of members of a small religious group, the Divine Light Mission, Galanter and Buckley (1978) found that a large proportion of individuals in this group had a high incidence of psychiatric treatment before joining the group. In addition, the type of psychiatric treatment, and presumably the degree of psychiatric impairment, varied by religious group.

Similarly, a study of converts to the Hare Krishna, Bahai, Jewish, and Catholic faiths reported that although these converts were similar in the overall frequency of psychiatric treatment, they differed in the type of psychiatric difficulties represented (Ullman, 1988). Catholic and Jewish converts had a history of seeking outpatient psychiatric help for emotional problems, whereas the other converts were more likely to have a history of psychiatric hospitalization. In addition, this study indicated that a marked increase in turmoil precipitated by a specific stressor in the previous 2 years was a more frequent precursor to conversion among Jewish and Catholic subjects, whereas ongoing long-term difficulties were more characteristic for converts in the other groups.

These findings suggest that religious groups differentially recruit individuals with a history of psychological disturbance. Alternatively, certain characteristics of a religious group may meet particular psychological needs and thus specially appeal to particular kinds of psychiatric patients. This is consistent with the long-observed reality that individuals turn to religion in times of crisis. Thus, in cross-sectional studies, a positive relationship between religion and poor health status may in fact reflect the severity of the underlying crisis. The more serious the difficulty, the greater the likelihood of reliance on religion. For example, Lindenthal, Myers, Pepper, and Stern (1970) found that prayer increased in response to stress.

Researchers also need to give more systematic attention to specifying the nature of expected religious effects. Several examples in the literature suggest that the failure to specify correctly religion effects can lead to erroneous conclusions about the underlying relationship between religion and health status. For example, Idler and Kasl (1992) found no association between public or private religiosity and mortality once health status and other sociodemographic variables were included in the model. If they had stopped at this point, the study would have concluded that religion was unrelated to mortality. Instead, their theoretically derived prediction that religion might exert its effects on mortality through the ritual observance of holidays led them to perform additional analyses that documented an important role for religion in the timing of mortality.

Similarly, in a prospective study of the relationship between religion and psychological distress, Williams et al. (1991) found that religious attendance was not related to psychological well-being once initial health status was controlled. However, because they had hypothesized that religion may exert its effects by shielding an individual from adverse consequences of stress, they proceeded to test for interactions between religion and stress, and found evidence of a classic stress-buffering effect: In the face of stress, religious attendance reduced the negative consequences of stress on psychological well-being. Brown,

Ndubuisi, and Gary (1990) also found that religious involvement buffered the stress of a personal injury on depressive symptoms among black males. Most researchers assume that the relationship between religion and mental health is linear. However, some evidence suggests that it might be important to test for nonlinearity in the association between religion and health status. Some studies have found a curvilinear relationship between religion and psychological symptoms (Ross, 1990; Shaver, Lenauer, & Sadd, 1980). That is, the very religious and the nonreligious enjoyed the best health. A similar curvilinear relationship also has been reported between religion and death anxiety (Nelson & Cantrell, 1980) and between religion and prejudice (Gorsuch & Aleshire, 1974).

Researchers should also pay more attention to the nature of the relationship between individual characteristics and religion. GAP (1968) noted that "the particular aspects of religion that are utilized by one individual . . . depend on what he brings to religion from previous development and present conflict, and from the ensemble of his liabilities, assets, and needs" (p. 702). Thus it is important to assess individual characteristics and test for interactions between the characteristics of the individual and religious involvement. Analyses of this kind may also provide insights into the underlying dynamics that influence the relationship between religion and health. Krause and Tran (1989) document, for example, that religious involvement counteracts the adverse effects of stress on feelings of self-esteem and mastery. One of the advantages of doing secondary analyses in large data sets is the typical availability of data on other predictors of health status. Researchers must capitalize on these opportunities to explore the mechanisms and processes through which religion exerts its effects and establish the importance of religion relative to other social and psychological resources (e.g., Idler, 1987).

The association between religion and health may also be affected by the larger social context. The literature suggests that the effects of religion may vary systematically by factors such as region, socioeconomic status, and race. Although levels of religious participation are high in the South, religion may be more consequential in the North than in the South. Stump (1987) indicates that southern religious behavior may reflect conformity to cultural norms, whereas religion in the non-South may be more strongly related to personal religious motivation. Consistent with this perspective, Ellison and Gay (1990), using a national sample of African-Americans, documented that religious participation was positively associated with subjective well-being only among nonsouthern blacks.

The effects of particular indicators of religion may also vary by socioeconomic status (SES). The rich and poor manifest their religion in different ways. Sociologists have long noted that although religious attendance is positively associated with SES, lower SES persons are more likely than their upper-class peers to pray in private, to believe in the doctrines of their faith, and to report personal religious experiences (Goode, 1966; Stark & Bainbridge, 1985). These findings are consistent with Weber's (1978) notion that an individual's location in social structure will determine both beliefs regarding personal salvation and the impact of these beliefs on attitudes and behavior.

Another neglected issue in the literature is the extent to which there may be racial and ethnic variations in the association between religion and health status. Historically, the black church has been the central institution in the African-American community, serving a broad range of religious and nonreligious functions. Some evidence suggests that religion may be more central in the lives of blacks than of whites. National data reveal, for example, that compared with 53% of whites, 74% of blacks indicate that religion is very important in their lives (Gallup Report, 1987). Similarly, a 1981 survey of the United States, Japan, South Africa, and 12 European countries found that black Americans, more than any other group, rate religion as extremely important in their lives (Gallup Report, 1985). Some limited evidence also suggests that religion and social class appear to be related differently for blacks and whites (Jacobson, Heaton, & Dennis, 1990), and that the factor structure of religion items for whites differs from that of blacks and Hispanics (Jacobson et al., 1990; Kenney et al., 1977).

The collection of data in the available epidemiologic studies of religion predated the current surge of interest in the relationship between religious involvement and health status. Accordingly, current studies are limited and deficient in the measurement of religion. A broader range of indicators of religion is probably linked to health status than those currently used. The next generation of epidemiologic studies will require the development of conceptually based, empirically validated, and cost-effective survey measures of the dimensions of religion that are consequential for health. This is not an easy task, as this chapter argues that at least some of the decisive effects of religion are not readily amenable to respondent self-report. However, health researchers can profit from the social-scientific literature on religion. Failure to listen and learn from this larger literature will lead to impoverished research and the publication of flawed conclusions.

References

Adlaf, E. M., & Smart, R. G. (1985). Drug use and religious affiliation, feelings, and behaviour. *British Journal of Addiction, 80,* 163-171.

Ainlay, S. C., & Smith, D. R. (1984). Aging and religious participation. *Journal of Gerontology, 39,* 357-363.

Allport, G. (1950). *The individual and his religion.* New York: Macmillan.

Allport, G. (1963). Behavioral science, religion and mental health. *Journal of Religion and Health, 2,* 187-192.

Allport, G. W., & Ross, J. M. (1967). Personal religious orientation and prejudice. *Journal of Personality and Social Psychology, 5,* 423-443.

Bacchiocchi, S. (1980). *Divine rest for human restlessness.* Rome: Pontifical Gregorian University Press.

Benson, P. L., & Elkin, C. H. (1990). *Effective Christian education: A national study of Protestant congregations.* Minneapolis, MN: Search Institute.

Berkman, L. F., & Syme, S. L. (1979). Social networks, host resistance, and mortality: A nine-year follow-up study of Alameda County residents. *American Journal of Epidemiology, 109,* 186-204.

Brown, D. R., Ndubuisi, S. C., & Gary, L. E. (1990). Religiosity and psychological distress among blacks. *Journal of Religion and Health, 29,* 55-68.

Craigie, F. C., Jr., Liu, I. Y., Larson, D. B., & Lyons, J. S. (1988). A systematic analysis of religious variables in the *Journal of Family Practice,* 1976-1986. *Journal of Family Practice, 27,* 509-513.

Davie, G. (1990). Believing without belonging: Is this the future of religion in Britain? *Social Compass, 37,* 455-469.

Donahue, M. J. (1985). Intrinsic and extrinsic religiousness: Review and meta-analysis. *Journal of Personality and Social Psychology, 48,* 400-419.

Durkheim, E. (1951). *Suicide.* New York: Free Press. (Original work published 1897)

Ellison, C. G., & Gay, D. A. (1990). Religion, religious commitment, and the life satisfaction among black Americans. *Sociological Quarterly, 31,* 123-147.

Ellison, C. W., & Smith, J. (1991). Toward an integrative measure of health and well-being. *Journal of Psychology and Theology, 19,* 35-48.

Fiore, J., Becker, J., & Coppel, B. (1983). Social network interactions: A buffer or a stress. *American Journal of Community Psychology, 11,* 423-440.

Freud, S. (1963). *Civilisation and its discontents.* London: Hogarth.

Fukuyama, Y. (1961). The major dimensions of church membership. *Review of Religious Research, 2,* 154-61.

Galanter, M., & Buckley, P. (1978). Evangelical religion and meditation: Psychotherapeutic effects. *Journal of Nervous and Mental Disease, 166,* 685-691.

Gallup Report. (1985). *Religion in America–50 years: 1935-1985.* Princeton, NJ: Princeton Religious Research Center.

Gallup Report. (1987). *Religion in America.* Princeton, NJ: Princeton Religious Research Center.

Gartner, J., Larson, D. B., & Allen, G. D. (1991). Religious commitment and mental health: A review of the empirical literature. *Journal of Psychology and Theology, 19,* 6-25.

Gilkes, C. (1980). The black church as a therapeutic community: Suggested areas for research into the black religious experience. *Journal of the Interdenominational Theological Center, 8,* 29-44.

Glock, C. (1962, July-August). On the study of religious commitment: Review of recent research bearing on religious and character formation. *Religious Education*, pp. S98-S110.

Glock, C. Y., & Stark, R. (1965). *Religion and society in tension*. New York: Rand McNally.

Glock, C. Y., & Stark, R. (1966). *Christian beliefs and anti-Semitism*. New York: Harper & Row.

Goode, E. (1966). Social class and church participation. *American Journal of Sociology, 72*, 102-111.

Gorsuch, R. L., & Aleshire, D. (1974). Christian faith and ethnic prejudice. *Journal for the Scientific Study of Religion, 13*, 281-307.

Gorsuch, R. L., & McPherson, S. E. (1989). Intrinsic/extrinsic measurement: I/E-revised and single-item scales. *Journal for the Scientific Study of Religion, 28*, 348-354.

Gorsuch, R. L., & Venable, G. D. (1983). Development of an "age universal" I-E scale. *Journal for the Scientific Study of Religion, 22*, 181-187.

Griffith, E. E. H., English, T., & Mayfield, V. (1980). Possession, prayer and testimony: Therapeutic aspects of the Wednesday night meeting in a black church. *Psychiatry, 43*, 120-128.

Griffith, E. E. H., Young, J. L., & Smith, D. L. (1984). Therapeutic elements in a black church service. *Hospital and Community Psychiatry, 35*, 464-469.

Group for the Advancement of Psychiatry. (1968). The psychic function of religion in mental illness and health. *Report of Group for the Advancement of Psychiatry, 6*, 647-730.

Hartz, G. W., & Everett, H. C. (1989). Fundamentalist religion and its effect on mental health. *Journal of Religion and Health, 28*, 207-217.

Haugk, K. C. (1976). Unique contributions of churches and clergy to community mental health. *Community Mental Health Journal, 12*, 20-28.

Heschel, A. J. (1951). *The sabbath: Its meaning for modern man*. New York: Noonday.

Hilty, D. M., Morgan, R. L., & Burns, J. E. (1984). King and Hunt revisited: Dimensions of religious involvement. *Journal for the Scientific Study of Religion, 23*, 252-266.

Hoge, D. R. (1979). A test of denominational growth and decline. In D. R. Hoge & D. A. Roozen (Eds.), *Understanding church growth and decline: 1950 to 1978* (pp. 179-197). New York: Pilgrim.

House, J. S., Robbins, C., & Metzner, H. L. (1982). The association of social relationships and activities with mortality: Prospective evidence from the Tecumseh Community Health Study. *American Journal of Epidemiology, 116*, 123-140.

House, J. S., Landis, K. R., & Umberson, D. (1988). Social relationships and health. *Science, 241*, 540-545.

Iannaccone, L. R. (1988). A formal model of church and sect. *American Journal of Sociology, 94*, 241-268.

Idler, E. L. (1987). Religious involvement and the health of the elderly: Some hypotheses and an initial test. *Social Forces, 66*, 226-238.

Idler, E. L., & Kasl, S. V. (1992). Religion, disability, depression, and the timing of death. *American Journal of Sociology, 97*, 1052-1079.

Jacobson, C. K., Heaton, T. B., & Dennis, R. M. (1990). Black-white differences in religiosity: Item analyses and a formal structure test. *Sociological Analysis, 51*, 257-270.

James, W. (1902). *The varieties of religious experience*. New York: Longmans.

Jarvis, G. K., & Northcott, H. C. (1987). Religion and differences in morbidity and mortality. *Social Science and Medicine, 25*, 813-824.

Johnson, B. (1963). On church and sect. *American Sociological Review, 28*, 539-549.

Jones, K. S. (1969). An enquiry into some aspects of religion in relation to psychiatry. *Sociological Review, 17*, 27-46.

Kelley, D. M. (1972). *Why conservative churches are growing*. New York: Harper & Row.

Kenney, B. P., Cromwell, R. E., & Vaughan, C. E. (1977). Identifying the socio-contextual forms of religiosity among urban ethnic minority group members. *Journal for the Scientific Study of Religion, 16,* 237-244.

Kiev, A. (Ed.). (1964). *Magic, faith and healing.* New York: Free Press.

King, M. B. (1967). Measuring the religious variable: Nine proposed dimensions. *Journal for the Scientific Study of Religion, 6,* 173-85.

King, M. B., & Hunt, R. A. (1972). Measuring the religious variable: Replication. *Journal for the Scientific Study of Religion, 11,* 240-251.

King, M. B., & Hunt, R. A. (1975). Measuring the religious variable: A national replication. *Journal for the Scientific Study of Religion, 14,* 13-22.

Kirkpatrick, L. A. (1989). A psychometric analysis of the Allport-Ross and Feagin measures of intrinsic-extrinsic religious orientation. *Research in the Social Scientific Study of Religion, 1,* 1-31.

Kirkpatrick, L. A., & Hood, R. W., Jr. (1990). Intrinsic-extrinsic religious orientation: The boon or bane of contemporary psychology of religion. *Journal for the Scientific Study of Religion, 29,* 442-462.

Knudsen, D. D., Erle, J. R., & Shrivier, D. W. (1978). The conception of sectarian religion: An effort at clarification. *Review of Religious Research, 20,* 44-60.

Krause, N., & Tran, T. V. (1989). Stress and religious involvement among older blacks. *Journal of Gerontology, 44,* S4-S13.

Larson, D. B., Pattison, E. M., Blazer, D. G., Omran, A. R., & Kaplan, B. H. (1986). Research on religious variables in four major psychiatric journals, 1978-1982. *American Journal of Psychiatry, 143,* 329-334.

Larson, D. B., Hohmann, A., Kessler, L., Meador, K., Boyd, J., & McSherry, E. (1988). The couch and the cloth: The need for linkage. *Hospital and Community Psychiatry, 39,* 1064-1069.

Levin, J. S., & Markides, K. S. (1986). Religious attendance and subjective health. *Journal for the Scientific Study of Religion, 25,* 31-40.

Levin, J. S., & Schiller, P. L. (1987). Is there a religious factor in health? *Journal of Religion and Health, 26,* 9-36.

Levin, J. S., & Vanderpool, H. Y. (1987). Is frequent religious attendance *really* conducive to better health?: Toward an epidemiology of religion. *Social Science and Medicine, 24,* 589-600.

Lindenthal, J. J., Myers, J. K., Pepper, M., & Stern, M. S. (1970). Mental status and religious behavior. *Journal for the Scientific Study of Religion, 9,* 143-149.

McGuire, M. B. (1987). Ritual, symbolism and healing. *Social Compass, 34,* 365-379.

Marx, K., & Engels, F. (1964). *On religion.* New York: Schocken Books. (Original work published 1844)

Maton, K. I. (1989). Community settings as buffers of life stress: Highly supportive churches, mutual help groups, and senior centers. *American Journal of Community Psychology, 17,* 203-233.

Meylink, W. D., & Gorsuch, R. L. (1988). Relationship between clergy and psychologists: The empirical data. *Journal of Psychology and Christianity, 7,* 56-72.

Moberg, D. O. (1984). Subjective measures of spiritual well-being. *Review of Relgious Research, 25,* 351-355.

Nelson, L. D., & Cantrell, C. H. (1980). Religiosity and death anxiety: A multi-dimensional analysis. *Review of Religious Research, 21,* 148-157.

Pargament, K., Silverman, W., Johnson, S., Echemendia, R., & Snyder, S. (1983). The psychosocial climate of religious congregations. *American Journal of Community Psychology, 11,* 351-381.

Pargament, K. I., Tyler, F. B., & Steele, R. E. (1979). The church/synagogue and the psychosocial competence of the member: An initial inquiry into a neglected dimension. *American Journal of Community Psychology, 7,* 649-664.

Payne, I. R., Bergin, A. E., Bielema, K. A., & Jenkins, P. H. (1991). Review of religion and mental health: Prevention and the enhancement of psychosocial functioning. *Prevention in Human Services, 9,* 11-40.

Richards, P. S. (1991). Religious devoutness in college-students: Relations with emotional adjustment and psychological separation from parents. *Journal of Counseling Psychology, 38,* 189-196.

Roof, W. C., & McKinney, W. (1987). *American mainline religion.* New York: Holt.

Rook, K. S. (1984). The negative side of social interaction: Impact on psychological well-being. *Journal of Personality and Social Psychology, 46,* 1097-1108.

Ross, C. E. (1990). Religion and psychological distress. *Journal for the Scientific Study of Religion, 29,* 236-245.

Schuman, H. (1971). The religious factor in Detroit: Review, replication, and reanalysis. *American Sociological Review, 36,* 30-48.

Shaver, P., Lenauer, M., & Sadd, S. (1980). Religiousness, conversion, and subjective well-being. *American Journal of Psychiatry, 137,* 1563-1568.

Simpson, G. (1980). *Religious rituals of the Caribbean.* Rio Piedras, Puerto Rico: Institute of Caribbean Studies.

Stark, R. (1984). Religion and conformity: Reaffirming a sociology of religion. *Sociological Analysis, 45,* 273-282.

Stark, R., & Bainbridge, W. S. (1985). *The future of religion.* Berkeley: University of California Press.

Stark, R., & Glock, C. Y. (1968). *American piety.* Berkeley: University of California Press.

Stump, R. W. (1987). Regional contrasts within black Protestantism: A research note. *Social Forces, 66,* 143-151.

Taylor, R. J., & Chatters, L. M. (1988). Church-based informal support among elderly blacks. *The Gerontologist, 26,* 637-642.

Troeltsch, E. (1950). *The social teaching of the Christian churches* (O. Wyon, Trans.). London: Allen & Unwin.

Ullman, C. (1988). Psychological well-being among converts in traditional and nontraditional religious groups. *Psychiatry, 51,* 312-322.

Umberson, D. (1987). Family status and health behaviors: Social control as a dimension of social integration. *Journal of Health and Social Behavior, 28,* 306-319.

Veroff, J., Douvan, E., & Kulka, R. A. (1981). *The inner American.* New York: Basic Books.

Weber, M. (1958). *The Protestant ethic and the spirit of capitalism* (T. Parsons, Trans.). New York: Free Press.

Weber, M. (1964). *The sociology of religion.* Boston: Beacon Press.

Weber, M. (1978). The soteriology of the underprivileged. In W. G. Runciman (Ed.), *Weber* (pp. 174-191). New York: Cambridge University Press.

Wicker, A. W., & Mehler, A. (1971). Assimilation of new members in a large and small church. *Journal of Applied Psychology, 55,* 151-156.

Williams, D. R., Larson, D. B., Buckler, R. E., Heckmann, R. C., & Pyle, C. M. (1991). Religion and psychological distress in a community sample. *Social Science and Medicine, 32,* 1257-62.

Wilson, J. (1978). *Religion and American society.* Englewood Cliffs, NJ: Prentice-Hall.

6

The Anti-Tenure Factor in Religious Research in Clinical Epidemiology and Aging

KIMBERLY A. SHERRILL
DAVID B. LARSON

Introduction

For decades, scholars have asserted that religion plays a potentially important role in the promotion of health and well-being (Levin & Vanderpool, 1991), yet research in this important area has not been forthcoming. Systematic reviews by Larson and coworkers have demonstrated the latter point quite convincingly. For example, Craigie, Larson, and Liu (1990) assessed all references to religion in the *Journal of Family Practice* (*JFP*) from 1976 through 1986, and Larson et al. (1992) assessed references to religion in the two leading psychiatry journals (*American Journal of Psychiatry* and *Archives of General Psychiatry*) over a 12-year period (1978-1989), and found few studies were published. Only 4.8% of 1086 quantitative articles published in *JFP*, and 132 (2.0%) of 6659 quantitative articles published in the two leading psychiatry journals contained a quantified religious variable. In most of those cases, the only measure used was an initial study demographic—denomination.

AUTHORS' NOTE: The first author's work on this chapter was supported by the National Institute of Mental Health under Geriatric Mental Health Academic Award No. MH00915.

149

Poloma and Pendleton (1991) commented on the neglect of the study of religiosity generally in research on well-being and pointed out that it was noted a decade earlier by Moberg and Brusek (1978) and more recently by Witter, Stock, Okun, and Haring (1985). Levin and Vanderpool (1991) also comment:

> Paradoxically, while many researchers continue to produce empirical evidence for salutary religious effects, the emergence of this field of inquiry has suffered from a sort of collective amnesia on the part of social scientists, epidemiologists, and biomedical professionals whose tacit professional knowledge tends to downplay the role of religious belief and involvement as salient influences upon health. (p. 42)

One possible exception has been research on religion, health, and mental health in the field of aging. Investigators such as Moberg (1953a, 1953b), Kaplan (1976), Blazer and Palmore (1976), Levin (1989), Levin and Vanderpool (1987), and Koenig, Smiley, and Gonzales (1988) have contributed substantially in recent years. Compared with other clinical fields such as psychology, psychiatry, and family medicine, these researchers have been accepted more willingly by some of the leading aging journals (see Chapter 7 in this volume).

What might account for this relative indifference to the study of religion in fields and leading journals? We speculate that this unenthusiastic welcome by leading clinical journals could be secondary to a process operating in academic clinical research circles that has not been described previously or recognized in a way that brings out the mechanism by which relatively minor, disparate forces can act in concert to create barriers to the advancement of research. We have designated this process the anti-tenure factor (ATF) because the net effect is to discourage new investigators from entering a potentially important field, such as the study of religion and health, for fear of negative repercussions on the potential for career advancement.

The Anti-Tenure Factor

The ATF process can be described in terms of several interrelated phases in the early stages of development of a field of research that interact in negative ways to inhibit further growth in the field. Starting with characteristics common to any new field, certain other forces may gain strength or initiate a cascade of other elements whose net result is the suppression of research. We posit the following stages.

Simplicity of Early Work

In the early stages of research in a field, when the importance of an area or a particular factor (e.g., religion) is not yet strongly established as relevant to clinical care, studies are almost by definition simplistic. Descriptive, hypothesis-generating studies are the rule, and investigators most often use simple study designs such as case series, cross-sectional, or retrospective designs.

Although small numbers of publications and conceptual simplicity are not necessarily stumbling blocks to the continued development of a field of research, this initial phase sets up the next crucial one in the ATF process.

Research Viewed as Flawed

A second step serves to discourage further research efforts: confusion of the distinction between studies that are fledgling—that is, simplistic, exploratory studies that represent the early conceptual stage of research in a given field—and studies that are flawed—that is, those with conceptual and methodological weaknesses. The critical element that distinguishes these two attitudes is the expectation or standard associated with each one.

Unrealistic Standards Applied

The ATF dictates the next step: When research in a field is viewed as flawed when in fact it is not, unrealistically high expectations are established regarding the acceptable (i.e., publishable) standards of research for that field. Unrealistic expectations are a two-edged sword: On the one hand, peer-reviewed journals may not publish such unacceptable studies; on the other hand, investigators need the conceptual and theoretical background material provided by more basic studies if they are to achieve higher standards. The ATF thus sets up a double bind, telling the investigator to do better but preventing the means necessary to do so.

To clarify this argument, consider the stage of development in the field of social support and health. Over the last several decades, dozens of measures have been developed and used in widely ranging clinical settings. Conceptual approaches have been refined so that social support is seen as a multidimensional construct involving different types of support (e.g., instrumental, emotional, and so forth) and that it operates within a coping framework (e.g., the stress-buffering role of social support).

In contrast, the concept of the multidimensionality of religion, which has been accepted in sociology and psychology for decades, has yet to penetrate clinical epidemiologic research. Furthermore, there are less than a handful of measures that have been developed and standardized for use in clinical populations. Thus research standards that are appropriate for the study of social support and health would be inappropriate if applied to the study of religion and health.

Is there evidence that inappropriate standards have been applied to the study of religion and health? The authors note from personal experience in presenting their research that expectations run high, lending subjective support to the claim. Additional support is provided by comments from peer reviewers regarding publications submitted to well-known journals. One investigator known to both authors submitted a study that used a retrospective study design and was rejected by a journal editor because it was "not prospective."

Few Researchers

An unfortunate outcome of the ATF is that few researchers overcome the obstacles we have described. Facing unrealistic standards of research, and observing the lack of interest in leading journals, new investigators may question whether the particular area is worth pursuing. Because mentors in the area are virtually nonexistent, that perception remains unchallenged, and the new investigator concludes that the field (e.g., religion and health) is a fringe area with little potential for assuring him or her of job security.

Perpetuation of Low-Quality Research

Although some researchers may retain a personal interest in the doomed area, and attempt to address it peripherally as an adjunct to another primary area of interest, they almost inevitably use the variable in conceptually and methodologically unsophisticated ways. For example, as noted in Chapter 7 of this volume, the vast majority of studies using quantified religious variables published in leading psychiatric, family practice, and geriatric journals use denomination as the only measure of religiosity.

If studies fail to demonstrate results, or provide mixed findings, suspicions regarding the perceived irrelevance of the variable are confirmed. By perpetuating low-quality research, the ATF ultimately ensures Type II errors, the phenomenon of finding the null hypothesis to be true when in fact it is not (Fletcher, Fletcher, & Wagner, 1988). Negative findings also are difficult to publish, making the field that much less appealing to new researchers. In reality, such findings may be attributable largely to poor methodology or inadequate conceptualization of the factor. Nevertheless, decision makers, clinicians, and researchers may accept these findings uncritically as providing further evidence that religion is, indeed, an unimportant or fringe topic of concern to health.

Craigie et al. (1990) provided evidence consistent with this stage of the ATF in a review of religious variables in the *Journal of Family Practice*. Out of 64 uses of religious variables (in 52 articles), 16 of them were references to religious denominations. In all 16 cases, the religious denomination variable was associated with neutral outcomes. In other words, when the measure of religion used was denomination, a measure considered to be a poor conceptual representation of religion, religion was assessed to have no effect. In contrast, out of 27 references to religion across three dimensions other than denomination (ceremony, relationship with God, and social support), 24 (89%) demonstrated a positive or beneficial effect of religion. One can see that when religion was operationalized poorly (i.e., as denomination), the outcomes regarding the effect of the religious variable were neutral or mixed.

These observations are reminiscent of the controversy surrounding the efficacy of the BCG vaccine for prevention of tuberculosis, described by Clemens, Chuong, and Feinstein (1983). They note that those clinical trials that used weaker methodology (i.e., failed to provide protection against the introduction of certain biases and did not demonstrate adequate statistical precision) reported low efficacy of the vaccine, but results had wide confidence intervals, so that benefit could not be ruled out. Those few studies that used higher-quality methodology reported that the vaccine was efficacious (i.e., provided definite benefit) and results had narrow confidence intervals, which ruled out low efficacy. Thus, if study methodology is as important for the reliability of reported results in clinical trials of medications as it is for assessment of the role of psychosocial factors in health, the domain of religion may not be receiving the kind of research attention it deserves.

The Anti-Tenure Effect

The final nail in the coffin of a potential research career in religion and health comes from an unwritten rule that seems to exist regarding the publication of articles in areas considered to be fringe: An academician may dabble in a few such dubious areas, but should not exceed one or two publications, lest the investigator be considered fringe him- or herself. Those few academicians who overstep the unspoken publication limit do so at risk of their peers disapproval, further increasing the likelihood that they will be denied promotions.

Ideally, if research on the role of religion and health is to achieve respectability as a nonfringe area of study, it should have at least the following characteristics: (1) clinical relevance, (2) conceptual foundations, and (3) methodological soundness. Ironically, the accumulation of evidence so far actually meets those criteria (Larson & Larson, 1992; Larson et al., 1992). However, much of the research to date in individual disciplines, particularly outside of clinical gerontology, is lacking in one or more of these elements. Although a comprehensive review of the singular approaches of every discipline is outside the scope of this chapter, three in particular other than aging have demonstrated long-standing, albeit somewhat inconsistent, traditions of empirical research on the effects of religion: epidemiology, psychology, and sociology. It is worth noting that the leading gerontological publication, the *Journals of Gerontology,* is broken into separate journals that address each of these three areas, emphasizing again the strength of the multidisciplinary focus and its relevance for the field of aging.

An exploration of these independent fields of study might illuminate further the processes that have allowed the ATF to exist. As we explore them, we will demonstrate that each one has (1) strengths that allow for important and unique contributions and (2) weaknesses that place them at a relative disadvantage in trying to conduct conceptually founded, clinically relevant religious research. We will further discuss how the advantages and disadvantages could balance each other if the three disciplines collaborated. Let's examine these disciplines more closely, and then discuss recommendations concerning research directions that could improve the development of the study of religion in these three fields as well as in aging.

ATF Vulnerabilities in Other Key Disciplines

Epidemiology's Clinical Roots

Epidemiology is historically rooted in phenomenology, not theory. As such, its contributions are usually targeted to be practical and clinically relevant. When Snow (1936), one of the historical founders of epidemiology, mapped the cholera epidemics in London in the mid-1800s, the cholera bacillus had not been discovered, nor was its mechanism of action on the gastrointestinal tract understood. When Snow traced one localized epidemic to the famous Broad Street pump and convinced city leaders to remove the pump handle to halt the epidemic, the only theoretical knowledge at work was Snow's conviction of the disease's association with the water system. In fact, we know now, of course, that the culprit was bacterial contamination of sewage, but effective treatment, at least at the level of physical spread, required no deeper theoretical understanding. Certainly, incorporation of subsequent knowledge of disease mechanisms allowed for more effective treatment strategies, but epidemiologists were not the discoverers of those mechanisms. They only applied them.

The bulk of epidemiologic research in religion and health reflects this tradition. Religion is viewed atheoretically, as if it were best considered a demographic factor like age or sex, a fact pointed out in Chapter 7 of this volume. Although theologians, sociologists, or psychologists (among others) would argue that the term *Protestant* or *Catholic* or *Jew* contains little real information representative of individual religiosity or of any clinically significant differences among individuals, outside of ethnic or genetic meanings, epidemiologists, with their relative lack of experience in conceptual issues, would typically be disinterested in such an argument. Reviews of epidemiologic research in religion and health bear this statement out (Levin & Vanderpool, 1987).

Schiller and Levin (1988) criticize the overrepresentation of denomination in the health services literature:

> In short, if health services researchers are indeed interested in uncovering meaningful, independent religious effects, then the conventional, uninformed way of treating this issue must change; there is little reason to believe that the effects of religion—however defined or measured—have been satisfactorily investigated in this field. This characterization may seem unduly harsh, but it is not clear that dozens of additional studies providing zero-order comparisons

of, say, the frequency of private dental visits between Jews and Gentiles will represent much of a substantive contribution either to the study of religion and health or, more importantly, to health services research. (p. 1376)

If understanding theories and concepts is a lower priority for epidemiologists than for some other disciplines, by the same token the language of epidemiologists—terms like *risk ratios, odd ratios, confidence intervals, morbidity, mortality,* and *clinical trials*—holds little meaning for others such as theological, psychological, or sociological disciplines. Thus, although one of the primary strengths of epidemiology is the focus on clinical outcomes, a weakness, insofar as it inhibits the development of religious research, is the lack of a theoretical and conceptual focus.

Psychology's Conceptual Complexity

Researchers could turn to psychology for conceptual expertise in terms of clinical relevance, but if they did so they might encounter several problems. One is that much of the prominent literature in religion and psychology comes from a psychoanalytic perspective. Although certainly of great interest and influence in mental health, the psychoanalytic perspective inherently conflicts with the epidemiologic, and at times with the religious (Ellis, 1980; Kung, 1984, 1986; Vitz, 1988). At risk of oversimplifying such rich traditions, one could say that psychoanalysis delves into the workings of one individual at a time, hoping to apply that understanding to many, whereas epidemiology studies many individuals, hoping to apply the understanding to one (Fletcher et al., 1988).

An analogy may shed light on the argument. Meteorologists may be able to predict the likelihood (or odds or risk) of lightning striking in a given location but cannot, as might the clinician or the physiologist, determine the physiologic effects lightning has on the person it strikes; neither does the physiologic damage of the lightning help the meteorologist predict weather patterns any more accurately. However, if the clinician and the meteorologist worked together and informed individuals of the risk of being in a certain location during a thunderstorm as well as the likely physiologic damage, an individual at risk may be motivated more strongly to change his or her behavior. Similarly, psychoanalysis can complement clinical epidemiology in the study of religion and health from a motivational, attitudinal, or health-behavior perspective.

Another problem may be encountered in the psychoanalytic perspective toward religion, which is that, for the most part, psychoanalysis casts religion in a conceptually negative or psychopathological light. Examples include the well-known critical attitude of Freud, and of other contemporary psychiatrists such as Ellis (1980), although there are some recent exceptions (Rizzutto, 1979) that interpret religion's potential for clinical benefit as well as harm.

It should be added that a negative conceptual assessment of the contribution of religion to health and mental health is not in itself problematic for the epidemiologic researcher, in that negatively framed hypotheses can be tested as well as can positively framed ones. A contribution of the epidemiologic perspective, then, is that it introduces the possibility of a two-tailed test: Religion may be harmful regarding certain clinical indices, but it also may be beneficial in regard to other clinical indices, and both are testable hypotheses. Psychology and psychoanalysis are not typically found to assess hypotheses of both harm and benefit in reference to religion.

A potentially fruitful source of information to support the study of religion and health in the psychological tradition is social psychology, which shares with epidemiology a community or population-based perspective. However, another problem may be encountered here: A field that is so conceptually rich can become bewildering. For example, Sherrill recently obtained a current reading list for an introductory graduate course in psychosocial theory as applied to health behavior and found an article with the following abstract:

> The present article examines the nature and function of human agency within the conceptual model of triadic reciprocal causation. In analyzing the operation of human agency in this interactional causal structure, social cognitive theory accords a central role to cognitive, vicarious, self-reflective, and self-regulatory processes. The issues addressed concern the psychological mechanisms through which personal agency is exercised, the hierarchical structure of self-regulatory systems, eschewal of the dichotomous construal of self as agent and self as object, and the properties of a nondualistic but nonreductional conception of human agency. The relation of agent causality to the fundamental issues of freedom and determinism is also analyzed. (Bandura, 1989, p. 1175)

Given that this abstract underwent peer review and was authored by one of the field's leaders, it is clear that there exists a gap in experience and familiarity that may be difficult for the clinical researcher to overcome and who, as a result, may fall prey to the ATF. For a notable exception in the field of social psychology, Martin and Carlson (1988) provide an excellent review of a large body of clinically oriented research on health-related religious behaviors and attitudes, including intervention studies that have used spiritual approaches in dealing with a number of difficult to treat health problems. Although many of the studies they review are anecdotal or represent preliminary data, the clinical researcher can obtain a sense of the work that can—or is beginning to—develop in health psychology.

Two specific exceptions to the excessive complexity in the field of social psychology that we wish to highlight are provided by the work of Maton (1989) on the stress-buffering role of spiritual support and the work of McIntosh and Spilka (1990) on faith and control beliefs, both of which will be discussed below.

Sociology's Methodological Specialization

Similar to epidemiology, sociological approaches to the study of religion have been oriented traditionally toward groups, determining religion's relationship to group cultural phenomena, such as racial prejudice, or to large-scale community or national trends in measurable social phenomena, such as suicide. Unlike epidemiology, however, they have been weighted toward the conceptual, frequently at the expense of clinical validity or applicability. Durkheim (1961), for example, developed his theories regarding the role of religion in promoting social cohesion, and discussed European trends in suicide, which he believed were connected with religious factors. Sociological findings like these are not assessed or presented with clinical usefulness in mind. For example, Durkheim's data do not provide any guidance for the physician who is treating a suicidal patient or who wishes to prevent one from becoming suicidal.

Another problem in sociological study of religion contributing to the ATF, a perspective argued most forcefully by Beckford (1985), is the insulation of the sociology of religion as a subdiscipline within sociology. He notes that the position of religion in sociological research is weakly institutionalized yet strongly integrated, meaning that the strength of internal bonds is much greater than is the integration into mainstream society (Beckford, 1985, p. 352). Larson, Lyons, Gartner, Sherrill, and Larson (1989) summarize Beckford's argument by noting that the sociology of religion has become like a too-close-knit family, and the failure of integration of religious research into the mainstream of sociology means, in family terms, that the adolescent does not wish to leave home. Furthermore, because conditions outside the sociology of religion have been unfavorable to the domain of religious interpretation, the authors conclude, "No wonder these adolescents don't want to leave home— their peers don't seem too interested in them" (Larson et al., 1989, p. 632).

In spite of the problems standing in the way of a full appreciation of the work in sociology, an important strength should be highlighted and incorporated in the developing area of religious research: methodological expertise regarding measurement. Silverman (1982) compiled some 462 references to measures and questionnaires that have been used in the social scientific study of religion. Although published by the American Psychological Association, most of the measures derive from the sociological study of religion. This wealth of experience would be of great help to the field if it could be adapted for use in clinically relevant epidemiologic research.

Battling the ATF: Clinical Gerontology's Relative Success

Fortunately, the field of clinical gerontology provides an exception, at least at a preliminary level, to many of the problems described above. From our perspective, the field of aging has one key characteristic to which much of the success in the growth of research on religion and health can be attributed: its multidisciplinary aspect. Few other health-related fields have so many disciplines represented within their boundaries.

The long-standing tradition of multidisciplinary collaboration in the field of clinical gerontology is one factor that may have given that field a relative advantage in the study of religion and health, thus operating as an antidote to the ATF. One outcome of the multidisciplinary focus may have been an early appreciation for clinical epidemiologic research on factors affecting longevity, a subject naturally of great interest to clinical gerontologists. For example, Zuckerman, Kasl, and Ostfeld (1984) studying 400 community-dwelling elderly in New Haven and using a case-control design, reported that, at 2-year follow-up, the less religious had mortality rates almost twice as high as the more religious, even controlling for age, marital status, education, income, race, gender, health, and previous hospitalizations. House, Robbins, and Metzner (1982) studied 2700 adults over an 8- to 10-year period and noted that increased church attendance was protective against mortality for women but not for men. Comstock and Partridge (1972) reported that the risk of dying from arteriosclerotic heart disease was much less for men who attended church services at least weekly, even controlling for the effects of smoking, socioeconomic status, and water hardness. The same was true for women, but the effect was even stronger. Furthermore, death rates from pulmonary emphysema and suicide were also more than twice as high for infrequent attenders, while death from cirrhosis of the liver was almost four times as high, possibly accounted for by differences in alcoholism rates between high and low attenders.

Another advantage of the multidisciplinary focus in clinical gerontology is a greater sensitivity to the critical conceptual importance of the role of psychosocial factors in general, and thus religion specifically, in health and mental health among older age groups. Blazer and Jordan (1986) comment that older persons may be more affected by social stressors. We will note some evidence along that line in a later section.

The multidisciplinary advantage in the aging field has not been realized by many other disciplines. In fact, one could argue that the single largest obstacle to improvements in conceptual and theoretical approaches to the study of religion and health is the multiplicity of disciplines that are separately involved in studying various aspects of religion.

Thankfully, the conceptual has not overridden the clinical in the study of aging and religion. Religion and aging research has dipped into combinations of the above-mentioned fields, with encouraging results. An excellent example of a careful balance, even synthesis of theoretical considerations with an epidemiologic perspective in the social gerontology literature is provided by Levin (1989). He reviews six theoretical models that may govern the relationship between religion and health as people grow older. To summarize his work briefly, these models are the following:

1. *Eschatological.* The inevitable life crises accompanying older age stimulate individuals to take inventory of their lives in preparation for death. This model predicts greater religious involvement, both organizational and nonorganizational, with increasing age.

2. *Deterioration.* As people age, they deteriorate physically and mentally and turn to religion as a source of comfort or healing. This model predicts that increased nonorganizational involvement (e.g., prayer, listening to religious music, and Bible reading) and decreased nonorganizational involvement are both salient to enhanced health in old age.

3. *Activity exchange.* Aging adults trade old activities for new ones, including increasing levels of religious participation. This model predicts increased participation up to very old age, when physical limitations cause a decline, but includes no prediction regarding the salience of such participation for health status.

4. *Disengagement theory.* People voluntarily pull back from activities, including religious activities, as they age, predicting a declining association between age and religious participation. The model provides no guidance for changes in the affective or attitudinal dimension of religious involvement that occurs with aging, but two variations of this model, noted in models 5 and 6 below, do.

5. *Social isolation.* This modifies disengagement theory by suggesting that the disengagement is involuntary and unwanted and that the resulting disengagement from religious participation is associated with lowered personal well-being and thus is itself potentially detrimental to health status.

6. *Multidimensional disengagement.* Aging is associated with decreased organizational religious involvement and an increase in health-salient nonorganizational involvement, similar to the deterioration perspective, but states that the decline in religious involvement, given an increase in satisfying nonorganizational activity, has relatively little salience for health.

Levin (1989) presents research findings that address these perspectives:

1. Religious attendance is fairly stable over the life cycle, and then may decline slightly among the very old or disabled.

2. Nonorganizational religious involvement and subjective religiosity remain stable as people age, but may increase slightly to offset those eventual declines in organizational religious involvement.

3. Nonorganizational religious involvement may be inversely related to health and well-being in older people, although results are mixed.

4. Among older people, religious attendance is positively related to general measures of personal adjustment and this association does not appear to decline with age.

5. Among older people, religious attendance is positively related to both subjective health and life satisfaction, the latter measure assessed by either single items or scales. (p. 142)

Finally, Levin notes that while the available data do not fit any model exactly, the findings to date are probably most in keeping with the multidimensional disengagement perspective, the sixth model described above.

Turning from the theory to how theory and clinical epidemiology can best be synthesized, the work of Koenig and colleagues provides an excellent example. These researchers illustrate the kind of integration of clinical and theoretical work that can be done and is needed. In one study Koenig, George, and Siegler (1988) demonstrated the frequent use of religion as a coping strategy by a group of geriatric subjects. Almost half of the study sample of 100 subjects mentioned the critical importance of religious coping, making it the most frequently mentioned coping strategy, followed by the strategies of focusing on other activities, accepting the situation, and—surprisingly in fourth place—seeking support and encouragement from family or friends. Of further interest is that respondents only infrequently turned to health professionals.

Another reason for the growth in religious research in gerontology is the stimulus of a number of excellent reviews bringing together a previously unrecognized body of research providing fairly compelling support for the salutary health effects of religion (Levin, 1989; Levin & Vanderpool, 1987). In addition, several prominent epidemiologic researchers have actively encouraged research in this area (Blazer & Palmore, 1976; Larson, Pattison, Blazer, Omran, & Kaplan, 1986). As a result, at least two federal granting agencies (the National Institute of Mental Health and the National Institute on Aging) have recently awarded support to researchers whose primary focus is the study of religion and health in aging populations. This success in the aging field derives in part from the fact that, among the disciplines that have indicated a willingness to consider the health effects of religion, the field of aging is perhaps the most open.

Integrative Work in Other Fields

We alluded earlier to the contribution by social psychology to the study of religion, health, and mental health. One particular theoretical perspective promises to become central in the study of religion: the concept of religious coping and the degree to which it facilitates an individual's sense of personal control in the face of stressful (i.e., uncontrollable) life events. Another way to describe the issue is to consider how religion affects an individual's ability to maintain a sense of well-being even when faced with difficult or traumatic circumstances.

McIntosh and Spilka (1990) in a very thoughtful paper state specifically their conviction that the association between religion and health may be a function of the relationship between religion and control. They suggest that the concepts of primary and secondary control have bearing on the coping utility of religion. In primary control, the individual strives to effect changes in the world, whereas in secondary control, the individual's perceptions are changed through a process of attitude modification. Activities such as prayer and religious participation may be seen as efforts at primary control if they are associated with the belief that prayer changes things or that material or emotional benefits—such as support from association with religious groups—are an advantage of religious participation. They may be seen as secondary control if they are viewed as affecting one's own attitude toward the unpleasant or stressful events—such as maintaining hope or a sense of well-being in spite of stressful circumstances. Thus religious coping may have both a social support aspect and a personal or attitudinal aspect, which hinge, respectively, on the concept of active control over stressful events or control over the anxiety associated with such events.

In a review of the literature on religion and mental health, Gartner, Larson, and Allen (1991) comment that low levels of religiosity are most often associated with disorders related to undercontrol of impulses, such as substance abuse, while problems of overcontrol, such as authoritarianism, are most often associated with high levels of religiosity.

The issue of control may be one that is particularly relevant for aging populations. Rodin's (1986) review concluded that studies show there are detrimental effects on the health of older people when their control of their activities is restricted; in contrast, interventions that enhance options for control by nursing home patients promote health.

Apart from aging populations or religious considerations, the concept of locus of control (LOC) has been prominent in the social psychological literature over the last two decades. Originally LOC pertained to an individual's explanations regarding the cause of important or stressful life events. Early conceptualizations suggested that people attributed the cause of important events to one of three loci: self, fate or chance, and powerful others. Of interest is that the role of God or divine control was not considered as a separate category, so that religious beliefs would be lumped under the category powerful others.

Thus religion has for the most part remained a forgotten factor (Larson & Larson, 1992) in LOC research. An exception is the work by DeVellis et al. (1985), who developed and tested the psychometric properties of a Child Improvement Locus of Control (CILC) scale. The scale measures parents' beliefs about five factors that could exert influence on their child's recovery from illness: the child, the parents themselves, professionals, chance, and divine influence. Parents are asked how effective they believed each of the five sources was in influencing their child's recovery.

Using the scale, DeVellis, DeVellis, and Spilsbury (1988) assessed specifically the effect of each of the five sources of influence on the actions parents said they would take regarding a sick child. In a regression that analyzed the endorsement of active help-seeking behaviors (seeking help from physicians, friends, and relatives) versus inactive behavioral responses in response to a hypothetical illness (asthma) in their child, divine influence was the only significant predictor variable for active help seeking ($F = 7.86$; $p < .01$), controlling for the effects of education, religiosity, and number of children. In other words, the stronger the belief in divine influence, the more likely the parents were to endorse seeking help from physicians, friends, and relatives. No other subscale of the CILC besides divine influence was predictive of help seeking. Of further interest is that parents who scored higher on the parental influence subscale of the CILC (i.e., those who saw themselves as strongly influencing their child's health) were also more likely to endorse seeking spiritual guidance in response to hypothetical illness in their child. These findings contradict the notion of religious faith as a hindrance or a deleterious substitute for taking action.

Findings from a study by Bearon and Koenig (1990) in a geriatric age group also suggest that belief in divine influence is associated with taking action about a perceived health problem. They asked 40 community dwelling adults aged 65 to 74 what physical symptoms they had prayed about and which symptoms had been treated with medication or discussed with a physician. They found that symptoms that were more serious (i.e., had been treated with medication or reported to a physician) were more likely to have been prayed about. Analysis of verbal responses indicated to the authors that people prioritize symptoms and do not waste prayer on what they perceive as inconsequential symptoms.

Sherrill and Larson (1988) assessed another facet of the issue of control, mastery, in a study of religious coping among 43 burn patients. They found that patients with greater religious commitment reported a diminished sense of personal mastery compared with those with lower religious commitment. Patients who used more psychotropic medication and had lower mastery were more religious. However, these same religious subjects were no more likely to be anxious or depressed than the nonreligious subjects, despite their lower mastery scores. These findings add support to the research by DeVellis et al. (1988) and Bearon and Koenig (1990), noted above, suggesting that patients with more serious physical outcomes may turn to religion for support and that the support may serve as a buffer for anxiety.

These studies indicate that, as one interpretation, religion may help an individual cope with stressful or health-threatening events or at least the anxiety associated with these events. Support for such an interpretation is provided by several lines of research (Lazarus, 1983). Janis (1974) suggested that denial or low fear in the face of eminent surgery was associated with high distress and behavioral difficulties during the later recovery period. The converse, that low denial and high fear are related to positive outcomes is a concept Janis and Mann (1977) have called the "work of worrying." Thus vigilance is viewed as a desirable trait. It follows then that the association of high levels of religiosity with low levels of mastery, in the setting of an acute medical illness or imminent health threat, may actually be beneficial for the patient in the long run because it diminishes the use of unhealthy denial as a major coping mechanism.

In another study addressing the potential coping utility of religion, Maton (1989) reported that spiritual support, distinguished from group social support, had a buffering effect for parents who had experienced the recent death of a child. Those parents with high spiritual support reported more favorable well-being than bereaved parents without such support. Among lower-stress parents (more than 2 years since death of the child occurred), spiritual support did not influence well-being, suggesting that spiritual support was of most benefit in the acutely bereaved, high-stress situation; that is, religion served as a stress buffer for high stress but was not active and did not play a role in well-being (was not needed) in the lower-stress situation.

A second study by Maton (1989) among college freshmen replicated the findings of the first study prospectively. Spiritual support reported by subjects at high school graduation predicted better personal and emotional adjustment to college 5 months later among students classified as high-stress, but not among the low-stress students. Williams, Larson, Buckler, Heckman, and Pyle (1991) analyzed data from a longitudinal community study of 720 adults and reported that religious attendance, but not affiliation, reduced the adverse psychological consequences associated with stressful events and physical health problems. Religious attendance was not found to have a direct effect on psychological distress but had an effect only during times of stress, indicating its role as a stress-buffering factor.

Taken as a whole, these studies strongly suggest a potentially fruitful theoretical direction for understanding the relationship between religion and health: the coping utility of religion and its relationship with maintenance or resilience of a sense of personal control, mastery, or hope in the face of stressful life circumstances. Future researchers would benefit from considering this or related concepts in the development of theoretical approaches to the study of religion and health.

ATF Treatment Recommendations

While the developments in gerontology and in other disciplines are heartening, the question remains as to what other factors might contribute to greater vitality and growth in the study of religion and health. Perhaps interventions at several points in the anti-tenure process could make a difference in the malaise afflicting this field of inquiry.

Dealing With Conceptual Simplicity

One point of intervention would be to strengthen conceptual and theoretical foundations in research on religion and health (Jenkins, 1976). As we have noted, however, it is one thing to tell clinical epidemiologic researchers to use theory and quite another to provide information and support on how to do it. Perhaps one step on the way to advancing the theoretical and conceptual foundations of the study of religion and health is to begin by accepting simple clinically oriented studies.

For example, one researcher who conducted early research focusing on the mental health effects of religion as a primary area of interest (as opposed to a focus on other areas, with religion as a side interest) was Wilson at Duke University Medical Center. His studies on the relationship between religion and mental health (Bishop, Larson, & Wilson, 1987; Cancellaro, Larson, & Wilson, 1982; Wilson, Larson, & Meier, 1983) would be considered methodologically weak by some standards, but they represented some of the first clinical research with a primary focus on religion and its relationship to diagnosable psychiatric disorders. Somewhat earlier than Wilson's work, Blazer, a geriatrician also at Duke, was publishing on religion and aging (Blazer & Palmore, 1976); and Kaplan, a social epidemiologist at Chapel Hill, was addressing the epidemiology of religion, social support, and coronary artery disease (Kaplan, 1976; Sherrill & Kaplan, 1989). These prominent senior researchers began a mentoring network that now involves a cohort of active investigators in this area, including Larson, Levin, Koenig, and Sherrill. It is no coincidence that all of them are also trained in geriatrics or gerontology. Thus the early acceptance of simplistic research and the subsequent availability of mentors representing key disciplines (psychiatry, sociology, geriatrics, and clinical epidemiology) have been keys to growth in the study of religion and health, especially in aging.

Promoting Higher-Quality Research

As we have noted, a strength of the purely epidemiologic approach is an emphasis on clinical outcomes and research methodology. A problem, however, in applying this strength to the study of religion and health is the lack of appropriate measures. This deficit is acknowledged by Baker and Gorsuch (1982) and Gartner et al. (1991), who note the mixed findings in the literature assessing the relationship between religion and mental health. Both sets of reviewers suggest that a measurement issue may underlie the confusion. They note that general measures of religiosity that do not account for more specific religious orientations may blur distinctions that have important mental health consequences.

Several schemata exist regarding the best conceptualization of religion for purposes of measurement in a research study population. One of the most popular is Allport's Internal-External (I-E) Religious Orientation scale (Allport & Ross, 1967). The conceptualization of religious motivations as two-dimensional—with an external, more social or utilitarian orientation toward religion and an internal, more emotional or experiential type—is relevant to our earlier discussion regarding control. The I-E religious dimensions may capture some of the same distinctions as internal LOC versus external LOC. If so, one would expect a similar pattern of findings, with the internal dimension associated with positive mental health outcomes compared with the external dimension.

A number of studies bear out such a prediction. Baker and Gorsuch (1982), using Allport's Religious Orientation Scale, demonstrated in a sample of 52 subjects that intrinsics were less anxious than nonintrinsics, while extrinsics were more anxious than nonextrinsics. Thus, if studies for which anxiety is an outcome failed to take into account different distributions of this characteristic, the results would vary, depending on the distribution of intrinsicness and extrinsicness in the study group.

Another example supporting the notion that internality is associated with mental health is provided by Watson, Morris, and Hood (1988), also using the Allport and Ross scales. They reported that an intrinsic religious orientation was associated with healthy psychological characteristics, while an extrinsic orientation was associated with greater levels of anxiety and depression. Similarly, Bergin, Masters, and Richards (1987) reported that in an inherently highly religious population (students at Brigham Young University), intrinsic religious orientation was positively correlated with a number of measures of psychological health, including self-control, sociability, sense of well-being, responsibility, and tolerance. Extrinsic orientation, as predicted, was negatively correlated with most of the same variables.

Laaser (1981) took the notion of intrinsic and extrinsic religious orientation into the personality realm and hypothesized an association between extrinsicness and Type A personality, and intrinsicness and Type B personality. However, he failed to demonstrate such associations and concluded that the Allport scale may not be able to distinguish cognitive assent to one religious orientation from emotional participation in that type. Thus, for example, while a number of the Type A subjects scored high on the intrinsic scale, their ability to affirm its content emotionally may have been lacking. This study raises questions about the strict applicability of the I-E orientation scale outside of rather straightforward studies of mental health symptoms.

Kirkpatrick and Hood (1990) summarized decades of work using the Allport and Ross I-E scales and concluded that all told the I-E framework is theoretically impoverished; they argued for more sophisticated approaches. A second view of the way to conceptualize religion for measurement purposes is the multidimensional perspective. Kauffman (1979) summarizes the earliest work in that regard by Lenski (1961) and Stark and Glock (1968), which has been the most widely used and consists of five dimensions:

1. *Belief.* Adherents to the church's doctrines.
2. *Religious practices.* Acts of worship and devotion, subdivided into ritual (e.g., church attendance and mealtime prayer) and devotional (e.g., private prayer and Bible study).

3. *Religious experiences.* Feelings or sensations of being in relationship with God or supernatural beings.
4. *Religious knowledge.* Information about the Bible, church history, and church rites and traditions.
5. *Consequences.* The effects of religious belief, practice, experience, and knowledge in persons' day-to-day lives.

In light of our discussion regarding the strengths and weaknesses of the different key disciplines involved in studying religion, it is interesting to note the confusion in Stark and Glock's dimensional scheme between predictors and outcomes, a distinction that epidemiologists would make very readily. One can see that the fifth dimension in their schema is actually a description of outcomes. Stark and Glock (1968), Kauffman notes, had some appreciation for this fact as evidenced by their comment that it "is not entirely clear the extent to which religious consequences are a part of religious commitment or simply follow from it" (p. 16). They did later omit this dimension from their analyses. Additional excellent discussions on the dimensionality of religion are provided by Gorsuch (1984), King and Hunt (1975), and, in the gerontological literature, by Koenig, Smiley, and Gonzales (1988).

As we have mentioned, the concept of the multidimensionality of religion has not been integrated in the medical and psychiatric literature. However, by convention, if not by design, religion has been viewed from many dimensional perspectives, usually one per study. The study by Craigie et al. (1990) (described previously) and a similar study by Larson et al. (1992) note that certain dimensions such as social support, ceremony, prayer, and one's relationship with God appear to be associated with benefit, whereas one other dimension (meaning) appears to be associated with mixed clinical effects.

Clinical gerontology also has room for improvement in the multidimensional assessment and measurement of religion. Sherrill, Larson, and Greenwold (1993) assessed religious variables in three leading clinical gerontologic journals. From 1985 to 1991, a total of 78 (3.6%) of 2127 quantitative studies included a religious variable, but only 14 (0.6%) used what could be considered minimally acceptable methodology, asking at least two questions over at least two religious dimensions. Most articles (71%) asked a single question (usually denomination). We believe that the incorporation of multidimensional measures in future research would lead to a substantial improvement in the conceptual and methodological quality of publications, a step in the right direction toward alleviating the effects of the ATF.

Epistemological Issues

Another treatment recommendation implied but not explicitly stated in our discussion of the factors affecting the persistence of the ATF is the need to grapple with epistemological differences that exist among disciplines and among individuals. Several researchers have argued that at a fundamental level epistemological diversity—that is, differences in what one considers knowable and by extension, researchable—may underlie the fragmented quality of research on religion and health (Larson et al., 1986; Levin & Vanderpool, 1987).

One could argue that from the standpoint of epidemiologic research acknowledgment of the potential clinical use of a perspective does not mean having to embrace that perspective oneself. Thus opposing views on the philosophical or theological meaning of religion would not stand in the way of research on the clinical utility of religion, even if it were only a marker for certain pathological syndromes or symptom clusters. Yet the acceptance of a view of religion as potentially of clinical interest has not been consistent. One colleague, upon submitting a paper on religion and health to a respected peer-reviewed journal, received a letter from the journal editor remarking that the topic itself was "execrable." Anti-religious bias in simulated psychology graduate school applications was demonstrated by Gartner (1986). And the indifference to religion in leading clinical specialty journals, such as psychiatry (Larson et al., 1992), family practice (Craigie et al., 1990), and gerontology (Sherrill et al., 1993), suggests the possibility of similar biases.

The clinical epidemiologic perspective addresses these concerns quite well. In a brief but elegant article regarding the role of clinical epidemiology, Fletcher (1990) suggests that although personal experience and knowledge of physiologic mechanisms are two time-honored and often useful approaches in making decisions in clinical medicine they often fail because of the complexities of humans and their often unpredictable responses to logically applied medical interventions. A solution, he states, is to include a third way of knowing, the clinical epidemiologic perspective, in which the aim is "to discover how frequently a clinical phenomenon occurs, under relatively real life conditions, more than whether it could occur at all (the usual perspective of case reports) or how it occurred (the orientation of basic science)" (Fletcher, 1990,

p. 310). He also suggests that the clinical epidemiologic perspective helps to balance the other two.

Similarly, the study of religion has been dominated by conflicting epistemological positions regarding its validity as a factor affecting health. On the one hand are those who view it almost structurally, as if it were part of our community physiology. Religion from this perspective is most likely assessed as a demographic variable and may behave in certain culturally predictable ways, but those same predictions fall short when applied to individual, more complex, clinical situations. On the other hand are those whose positions for or against the salience of a role of religion in health are experientially based. The lack of attention to religion in leading psychiatric and medical journals suggests as one interpretation that those making decisions have little experience to convince them that religious factors have anything to do with health or mental health. The clinical epidemiologic perspective can balance these other two perspectives by promoting the study of religious factors in health and mental health phenomenologically and by encouraging openness to different perspectives that can be tested empirically.

The issue of being open to different perspectives has applications at several levels. At one level is the notion of two or more academic disciplines sharing expertise while working toward a common goal. At another level is that of being open to another's perspective within a professional relationship, such as the patient-physician relationship. Larson et al. (1986) has argued that one obstacle to progress in research on religion and mental health comes from psychiatry's lack of knowledge and experience concerning religion, due in part perhaps to the discrepancy between the high degree of faith in the general public (Gallup, 1985) compared with professionals in the mental health disciplines. Bergin and Payne (1991) draw attention to this same issue in the context of psychotherapy. They argue that it may be appropriate to become acquainted with major teachings and dilemmas typical of clients of diverse religious orientations.

Coles (1990), a psychoanalyst and child psychiatrist, describes grappling with similar concerns while treating a child whose committed religious orientation was initially viewed as an obstacle in therapy. He describes a pivotal session with his psychoanalytic supervisor:

> Dr. Fineman [the supervisor] went on: Here is a bright child who is intensely involved in Catholicism. She is also having enough psychological trouble— truculence at school and in the neighborhood—to warrant psychiatric treatment

(no small step for a working-class, culturally conservative, Irish Catholic family in the late 1950s, I now realize). Now, you are trying to get her to speak our language, to use the psychological words and images we find useful, congenial. She resists you, brings you lots of religious stories, themes and metaphors. You resist her, but she hasn't budged, and here we are trying to calculate how to work with her, how to make inroads on a neurosis, how to win her over, really, to a commitment toward therapy. Why not shift tactics, why not let her educate us about her Church, and also about her? No doubt she would offer us some trite remarks, some memorized cliches—but who doesn't? Psychology can generate them as well as religion. . . . There's a spirituality at work in her, and we might explore her spiritual psychology. (Coles, 1990, p. 15)

Coles records his response:

I had no idea what he [Dr. Fineman] meant by the use of that phrase [spiritual psychology], and I told him so with a polite question—only to hear he was as perplexed and uncertain as I was, though obviously more sure of himself than I, and hence ready for a gamble.

At wits end, I also gambled—changed direction in my work with this young patient. For the first time in my short-lived, inevitably anxious and striving career as a hospital resident, I told a patient that I wanted some advice. (p. 16)

Coles's willingness to gamble, supported by the confidence and guidance of his supervisor, is an all too rare event in academic circles. While his experience focuses on one aspect of the interface of religion and health, psychotherapy, the process he advocates is relevant to the broader concerns of the interface between psychology and epidemiology. That process includes a willingness to acknowledge the potential value of another discipline's approach to religion, whether it fits within one's own epistemological framework or not. One may have to be willing, as Coles was, to face and deal with a certain discomfort about the topic.

Edlund (1986) notes one of the tensions inherent to this kind of openness:

Multi-causal models produce results that are inherently harder to accept. The results of the Framingham study, where a host of different factors explain only a minority of the variance of coronary disease, with many of these variables themselves probably proxies for more directly causative variables, leaves many people unsatisfied. The shift from these contingency models, where individuals are assigned aggregate statistical risk scores, is that much more removed from daily practice, and does not provide physicians with the emotional certainty they feel about the causes of infectious disease. (p. 713)

Thus tension and, to some degree, dissatisfaction are probably intrinsic to research on multicausal research models. Unfortunately, when such tension is augmented because of association with research on religion, the barriers to the advancement of research may become insurmountable.

Conclusion

A pivotal problem in overcoming the inertia that inhibits progress in the study of religion and health is the ATF: Researchers fear that it is a dead-end area on which to build an academic career. Ironically, as we have noted, the mass of research on religion and health strongly suggests that it is an important area, with beneficial effects reported on a range of clinical outcomes (Larson & Larson, 1992). However, for religion to join the research mainstream of psychosocial factors in health requires not only a recognition of this previous body of work but also an active effort by policymakers to support more research. So far, with the exception of clinical gerontology, that support has been lacking to a large extent.

Despite the lack of support, a collection of theoretical perspectives that view religion in a coping role has emerged in the gerontology literature, supported by findings in several nonaging areas. These perspectives suggest that religious coping is an effort to maintain emotional control in the face of threatening events. Issues of control may be particularly relevant as a psychosocial factor in health among the elderly.

Research on religion and health is inherently a multidisciplinary effort, but the disciplines it involves are not accustomed to working together simultaneously toward both clinically and theoretically relevant goals. Viewing religion from markedly contrasting perspectives—and tending to operate in isolation—key disciplines, such as psychology, sociology, and epidemiology, have developed unique strengths that, when combined, could contribute toward an effective research strategy.

A model for combining the strengths of different disciplines is found in clinical gerontology. The field's relative success may be attributed to its emphasis on multidisciplinary collaboration, its reliance on clinical epidemiologic approaches to research, and the incorporation of a multidimensional view of the conceptualization and measurement of religious variables.

References

Allport, G. W., & Ross, J. M. (1967). Personal religious orientation and prejudice. *Journal of Personality and Social Psychology, 5,* 432-443.

Baker, M., & Gorsuch, R. (1982). Trait anxiety and intrinsic-extrinsic religiousness. *Journal for the Scientific Study of Religion, 21,* 119-122.

Bandura, A. (1989). Human agency in social cognitive theory. *American Psychologist, 44,* 1175-1184.

Bearon, L. B., & Koenig, H. G. (1990). Religious cognitions and use of prayer in health and illness. *The Gerontologist, 30,* 249-253.

Beckford, J. A. (1985). The insulation and isolation of the sociology of religion. *Sociological Analysis, 46,* 347-354.

Bergin, A. E., Masters, K. S., & Richards, K. S. (1987). Religiousness and mental health reconsidered: A study of an intrinsically religious sample. *Journal of Counseling Psychology, 34,* 197-204.

Bergin, A. E., & Payne, I. R. (1991). Proposed agenda for a spiritual strategy in personality and psychotherapy. *Journal of Psychology and Christianity, 10,* 197-210.

Bishop, L. C., Larson, D. B., & Wilson, W. P. (1987). Religious life of individuals with affective disorders. *Southern Medical Journal, 80,* 1083-1086.

Blazer, D. G., & Jordan K. (1986). Epidemiology of psychiatric disorders and cognitive problems in the elderly. In G. L. Klerman, M. M. Weissman, P. S. Appelbaum, & L. H. Roth (Eds.), *Social, epidemiologic, and legal psychiatry* (Psychiatry Series, Vol. 5) (pp. 261-272). New York: Basic Books.

Blazer, D., & Palmore, E. (1976). Religion and aging in a longitudinal panel. *The Gerontologist, 16,* 82-85.

Cancellaro, L. A., Larson, D. B., & Wilson, W. P. (1982). Religious life of narcotic addicts. *Southern Medical Journal, 75,* 1166-1168.

Clemens, J. D., Chuong, J. H., & Feinstein, A. R. (1983). The BCG controversy: A methodological and statistical reappraisal. *Journal of the American Medical Association, 249,* 2362-2369.

Coles, R. (1990). *The spiritual life of children.* Boston: Houghton Mifflin.

Comstock, G. W., & Partridge, K. B. (1972). Church attendance and health. *Journal of Chronic Diseases, 25,* 665-672.

Craigie, F. C., Larson, D. B., & Liu, I. Y. (1990). References to religion in the *Journal of Family Practice:* Dimensions and valence of spirituality. *Journal of Family Practice, 30,* 477-479.

DeVellis, R. F., DeVellis, B. M., Revicki, D. A., Lurie, S. J., Runyan, D. K., & Bristol, M. (1985). Development and validation of the Child Improvement Locus of Control (CILC) scales. *Journal of Social and Clinical Psychology, 3,* 308-325.

DeVellis, B. M., DeVellis, R. F., & Spilsbury, J. C. (1988). Parental actions when children are sick: The role of belief in divine influence. *Basic Applied Social Psychology, 9,* 185-196.

Durkheim, E. (1961). *The elementary forms of religious life.* New York: Collier Books.

Edlund, M. J. (1986). Causal models in psychiatric research. *British Journal of Psychiatry, 148,* 713-717.

Ellis, A. (1980). Psychotherapy and atheistic values: A response to A. E. Bergin's "Psychotherapy and Religious Values." *Journal of Consulting and Clinical Psychology, 48,* 635.

Fletcher, R. H. (1990). Three ways of knowing in clinical medicine. *Southern Medical Journal, 83,* 308-312.

Fletcher, R. H., Fletcher S. W., & Wagner E. H. (1988). *Clinical epidemiology: The essentials* (2nd ed.). Baltimore: Williams & Wilkins.

Gallup, G. (1985). *Religion in America—50 years: 1935-1985.* Princeton, NJ: Princeton Religious Research Center.

Gartner, J. D. (1986). Anti-religious prejudice in admissions to doctoral programs in clinical psychology. *Professional Psychology Research and Practice, 17,* 473-475.

Gartner, J., Larson, D. B., & Allen, G. D. (1991). Religious commitment and mental health: A review of the empirical literature. *Journal of Psychology and Theology, 19,* 6-25.

Gorsuch, R. L. (1984). Measurement: The boon and bane of investigating religion. *American Psychologist, 39,* 228-236.

House, J. S., Robbins, C., & Metzner, H. L. (1982). The association of social relationships and activities with mortality: Prospective evidence from the Tecumseh Community Health Study. *American Journal of Epidemiology, 116,* 123-140.

Janis, I. L. (1974). Vigilance and decision-making in personal crises. In G. V. Coelho, D. A. Hamburg, & J. E. Adams (Eds.), *Coping and adaptation* (pp. 139-175). New York: Basic Books.

Janis, I. L., & Mann, L. (1977). *Decision making: A psychological analysis of conflict, choice, and commitment.* New York: Free Press.

Jenkins, C. D. (1976). Recent evidence supporting psychological and social risk factors for coronary disease. *New England Journal of Medicine, 294,* 987-994.

Kaplan, B. H. (1976). A note on religious beliefs and coronary heart disease. *Journal of the South Carolina Medical Association, 15*(5, Suppl.), 60-64.

Kauffman, J. H. (1979). Social correlates of spiritual maturity among North American Mennonites. In D. O. Moberg (Ed.), *Spiritual well-being: Sociological perspectives* (pp. 237-254). Washington, DC: University Press of America.

King, M. B., & Hunt, R. A. (1975). Measuring the religious variable: National replication. *Journal for the Scientific Study of Religion, 14,* 13-22.

Kirkpatrick, L. A., & Hood, R. W. (1990). Intrinsic-extrinsic religious orientation: The boon or bane of contemporary psychology of religion? *Journal for the Scientific Study of Religion, 29,* 442-462.

Koenig, H. G., George, L. K., & Siegler, I. C. (1988). The use of religion and other emotion regulating coping strategies among older adults. *The Gerontologist, 28,* 303-310.

Koenig, H. G., Smiley, M., & Gonzales, J. A. P. (1988). *Religion, health, and aging: Review and theoretical integration.* Westport, CT: Greenwood.

Kung, H. (1984). *Freud and the problem of God.* New Haven, CT: Yale University Press.

Kung, H. (1986, May 10-16). *Religion: The last taboo.* Paper presented at the 139th annual meeting of the American Psychiatric Association, Washington, DC.

Laaser, M. R. (1981). *Religion and heart disease: An investigation of their association as expressed in the religious dimensions of the coronary prone behavior pattern—Type A.* Ph.D. dissertation, Department of Religion, University of Iowa, Iowa City.

Larson, D. B., & Larson, S. S. (1992). *The forgotten factor in physical and mental health: What does the research show?* (Independent Study Seminar). Arlington, VA: National Institute for Healthcare Research.

Larson, D. B., Lyons, J. S., Gartner, J., Sherrill, K. A., & Larson, S. S. (1989). Demonstrating the neglect of religion in the social sciences and researching the effectiveness of religious volunteer interventions: Some steps in responding to a crisis of research identity. In R. Wuthnow (Ed.), *Philanthropy and the religious tradition* (pp. 631-650). Washington, DC: The Independent Sector and the United Way Institute.

Larson, D. B., Pattison, E. M., Blazer, D. G., Omran, A. R., & Kaplan, B. H. (1986). Systematic analysis of research on religious variables in four major psychiatric journals, 1978-1982. *American Journal of Psychiatry, 143,* 329-334.

Larson, D. B., Sherrill, K. A., Lyons, J. S., Craigie, F. C., Thielman, S. B., Greenwold, M. A., & Larson, S. S. (1992). Associations between dimensions of religious commitment and mental health reported in the *American Journal of Psychiatry* and *Archives of General Psychiatry*: 1978-1989. *American Journal of Psychiatry, 149,* 557-559.

Lazarus, R. S. (1983). The costs and benefits of denial. In S. Breznitz (Ed.), *Denial and stress* (pp. 1-30). New York: International Universities Press.

Lenski, G. E. (1961). *The religious factor.* Garden City, NY: Doubleday.

Levin, J. S. (1989). Religious factors in aging, adjustment, and health: A theoretical overview. In W. M. Clements (Ed.), *Religion, aging and health: A global perspective* (pp. 133-146). New York: Haworth.

Levin, J. S., & Vanderpool, H. Y. (1987). Is frequent religious attendance *really* conducive to better health?: Toward an epidemiology of religion. *Social Science and Medicine, 24,* 589-600.

Levin, J. S., & Vanderpool, H. Y. (1991). Religious factors in physical health and the prevention of illness. *Prevention in Human Services, 9,* 41-64.

Martin, J. E., & Carlson, C. R. (1988). Spiritual dimensions of health psychology. In W. R. Miller & J. E. Martin (Eds.), *Behavior therapy and religion: Integrating spiritual and behavioral approaches to change* (pp. 57-110). Newbury Park, CA: Sage.

Maton, K. I. (1989). The stress buffering role of spiritual support: Cross-sectional and prospective investigations. *Journal for the Scientific Study of Religion, 28,* 310-323.

McIntosh, D., & Spilka, B. (1990). Religion and physical health: The role of personal faith and control beliefs. *Research in the Social Scientific Study of Religion, 2,* 167-194.

Moberg, D. O. (1953a). The Christian religion and personal adjustment in old age. *American Sociological Review, 18,* 87-90.

Moberg, D. O. (1953b). Church membership and personal adjustment in old age. *Journal of Gerontology, 8,* 207-211.

Moberg, D. O., & Brusek, P. M. (1978). Spiritual well-being: A neglected subject in quality of life research. *Social Indicators Research, 5,* 303-323.

Poloma, M. M., & Pendleton, B. F. (1991). The effects of prayer and prayer experiences on measures of general well-being. *Journal of Psychology and Theology, 19,* 71-83.

Rizzutto, A. (1979). *The birth of the living God: A psychoanalytic study.* Chicago: University of Chicago Press.

Rodin, J. (1986). Aging and health: Effects of the sense of control. *Science, 233,* 1271-1276.

Schiller, P. L., & Levin, J. S. (1988). Is there a religious factor in health care utilization?: A review. *Social Science and Medicine, 27,* 1369-1379.

Sherrill, K. A., & Kaplan, B. H. (1989, May 31-June 2). *Adult burn patients, religious coping and recovery: Classic issues in primary care for psychiatric epidemiology.* Paper presented at the World Psychiatric Association, Toronto, Canada.

Sherrill, K. A., & Larson, D. B. (1988). Adult burn patients: The role of religion in recovery. *Southern Medical Journal, 81,* 821-825.

Sherrill, K. A., Larson, D. B., & Greenwold, M. A. (1993). Is religion taboo in geriatrics? Systematic review of research on religion in three major gerontologic journals, 1985-1991. *American Journal of Geriatric Psychiatry, 1,* 109-117.

Silverman, W. (1982). *Bibliography of measurement techniques used in the social scientific study of religion* (Psychological Documents, Ms. 2539). Hicksville, NY: American Psychological Association.

Snow, J. (1936). *On the mode of communication of cholera.* New York: Hafner Press.

Stark, R., & Glock, C. Y. (1968). *American piety.* Berkeley: University of California Press.

Vitz, P. C. (1988). *Sigmund Freud's Christian unconscious.* New York: Guilford Press.

Watson, P. J., Morris, R. J., & Hood, R. W. (1988). Sin and self-functioning, Part 2: Grace, guilt, and psychological adjustment. *Journal of Psychology and Theology, 16,* 270-281.

Williams, D. R., Larson, D. B., Buckler, R. E., Heckman, R. C., & Pyle, C. M. (1991). Religion and psychological distress in a community sample. *Social Science and Medicine, 32,* 1257-1262.

Wilson, W. P., Larson, D. B., & Meier, P. D. (1983). Religious life of schizophrenics. *Southern Medical Journal, 76,* 1096-1100.

Witter, R. A., Stock, W. A., Okun, M. A., & Haring, M. J. (1985). Religion and subjective well-being in adulthood: A quantitative synthesis. *Review of Religious Research, 26,* 332-342.

Zuckerman, D. M., Kasl, S. V., & Ostfeld, A. M. (1984). Psychosocial predictors of mortality among the elderly poor. *American Journal of Epidemiology, 119,* 410-423.

7

Neglect and Misuse of the R *Word*

Systematic Reviews of Religious Measures in Health, Mental Health, and Aging

DAVID B. LARSON
KIMBERLY A. SHERRILL
JOHN S. LYONS

Adherents to all religions attest to the influence of faith in their lives. From the development of values to comfort during times of need to feelings of community, religious commitment is often discussed as an important and valuable part of many people's lives. In the health care setting, religious faith is frequently cited as important to individuals dealing with the stress of illness or pain. It is quite possible that academic research assessing the association between religious commitment and medical, psychological, psychiatric, and social status would demonstrate important findings for each of these fields.

The goal of this chapter is to review and critique the state of the art of the study of religion among several academic disciplines, including psychiatry, family practice, gerontology and geriatrics, psychology, other social sciences, pastoral care, and philanthropy research. Recognizing the profound impact that literature reviews may have in shaping

AUTHORS' NOTE: The second author's work on this chapter was supported by the National Institute of Mental Health under Geriatric Mental Health Academic Award No. MH00915.

a field of research, we begin with a discussion of how the literature in controversial areas, such as religion and health or mental health, should best be reviewed. To that end, we focus on the *methodology of review* rather than methodology of research, per se. We then assess the above-noted academic disciplines in that light, interpret our findings, and provide suggestions regarding the development of academic research concerning religion and health.

Reviewing Research Literature

An unrecognized aspect of development of a field of research is the influence of research reviews. Particularly in underdeveloped fields, growth can be stimulated based on the findings and recommendations of research reviews—especially when they are published in peer-reviewed journals.

Literature Reviews as Art

Although there are several approaches to reviewing research literature, traditional reviews rely on the reviewer's expertise to gather key sources in a given field, assess their strengths and weaknesses, integrate the research findings, and then make specific recommendations about what research is needed and what is not (Light & Pillemer, 1984; Mulrow, 1987). The reviewers could be described as exercising more art in the review process than science, in that the review process is for the most part determined by the expertise of the particular reviewer. Traditionally, the reviewer exercises his or her individual judgment to make decisions about which articles will be included, which portions of those articles are of most significance, and how the findings will be interpreted.

This strategy offers flexibility, and allows for the individual expression of expert opinion within a given field. While these are important advantages, a disadvantage to this approach is the potential for introducing personal biases. Furthermore, because the review process is relatively unstructured, even if biases are suspected it may be difficult if not impossible to replicate the review, and thus assess it objectively for possible biases. Alternatively, even if the review is an accurate reflection of a field of research, it is vulnerable to criticism by others who may themselves hold biased perspectives.

The disadvantages are particularly relevant when the topic under review is a controversial one. The study of religion and health is such an area, and thus reviews are vulnerable to insertion of bias as well as to criticisms of subjectivity in both the selection and the interpretation of the data. It should come as no surprise that scientists have, therefore, historically lacked the temerity to undertake reviews concerning religious variables, and publishers likewise may have avoided publishing such reviews.

Literature Reviews as Science

An alternative review strategy to the more traditional and less systematic art form of review is the meta-analysis (Glass, 1976; Light & Smith, 1971; Sacks, Berrier, Reitman, Ancona-Berk, & Chalmers, 1987). In this type of review, statistical findings are combined across studies to give literaturewide estimates of particular effects. This review strategy has a clear methodology and thus is useful for minimizing bias in handling controversial topics.

However, accomplishing a meta-analysis requires that studies have acceptable design considerations including randomization and a control group. In addition, meta-analyses are intended for series of studies with (1) homogeneous study populations, (2) similar interventions, and (3) process or (more usually) outcome variables measured on the same dimension. Thus the more objective meta-analysis is not useful when reviewing a wide-ranging topic with diverse study populations, diverse study methodologies, or diverse measure assessments.

With one review approach too lax in its method, another highly objective but too restrictive in its inclusion criterion, we are left with a "Goldilocks-porridge" dilemma. That is, with one too hot and one too cold, we must hope for one just right, or at least more acceptable.

Systematic Reviews of Research

A more acceptable review strategy has been somewhat recently developed. This review strategy has been called a *systematic review* (SR) and uses a method that permits a quantitative or replicable review of a specific research literature. In this way, the SR minimizes the opportunity for bias found in the more traditional review approach but is much more inclusive than meta-analysis in terms of the kinds of studies that may be assessed. The SR could be considered a cousin of meta-analysis in that both owe their conceptualization to work by Light and Pillemer. Light and Pillemer's (1984) book *Summing Up* laid the groundwork for the development of the SR, whereas meta-analysis derives from their work about a decade earlier.

Larson and Lyons developed further some of Light and Pillemer's general concepts by narrowing the focus and making the technique simple enough to undertake without extensive statistical or methodological expertise. In a nutshell, SRs take an epidemiologic look at the scientific core (methods and results sections) of a specific "population" of studies to reach a consensus on a given topic.

In the SR, all aspects of the review design are quantified, including inclusion and exclusion criteria regarding the "subjects" to be sampled (usually quantified studies from the one or two best peer-reviewed journals in a field), the method for analyzing the quality of study for each study sample, determining and specifying interrater reliability, and summing the results across all reviewed studies. Results can be simply presented and understood as numeric items. Thus the review and its results, like any good research protocol, are replicable. In areas of controversy, replication of a literature review should be an available option.

The SR surveys a specified sample of representative research, using the field's leading journals (Bareta, Larson, Zorc, & Lyons, 1990; Beardsley et al., 1989; Larson, Lyons, Hohmann, et al., 1989; Lyons et al., 1990) to define the field's state of the art. Thus, unlike the metaanalytic review, an SR can sample diverse studies with diverse samples and diverse research methodologies.

SRs have most frequently been used to assess the frequency, or quantity, along with the quality of use, of a variable within a research field. As a result, SRs can be used to demonstrate how frequently and effectively one research field (e.g., religion, or the use of religious variables) has penetrated into another.

Like meta-analyses, systematic reviews are quite objective, with reported interrater reliabilities generally above 0.90. A clear advantage of SRs is that, like meta-analyses, the findings can be replicated. Therefore, the systematic review represents an optimal choice for reviewing within a broad scientific literature how a specific potentially controversial topic (frequently operationalized using a specific variable) is scientifically handled. A brief outline of the SR technique is provided below.

**Framing Hypotheses and
Selecting Variables**

Because SR is an application of epidemiologic techniques, the first step involves framing a hypothesis and determining the variables of interest. However, the population of interest is a specified group of publications rather than a population of individuals. For example, some of Larson's first SRs were based on the hypothesis that the quantity and quality of research on religious variables in several fields would be low (Larson, Pattison, Blazer, Omran, & Kaplan, 1986).

Setting the Sampling Frame

The next step is to specify the sampling frame. Usually this involves selecting the journals of interest and the years that will be searched. For example, for each of the SRs that will be reviewed later (psychiatry, family practice, gerontology and geriatrics, and pastoral care) key journals were selected because they were expected to contain papers most relevant to the hypotheses and variables of interest (e.g., religion) and because they were the most prominent publication outlets in their respective fields.

Obtaining the Sample

The reviewer then searches by hand through every article within the specified sampling frame for articles that pertain to the subject of the review. Usually, editorials or other opinion pieces are omitted because they do not contain quantified data. Running totals are kept of the number of articles scanned and the number of articles on the topic of interest that are found.

A computerized search is not an adequate substitute for hand searching. The variables of interest are often buried in tables or text, and many times represent such a minor part of the article that they are not denoted as keywords for purposes of computer searching. Bareta et al. (1990) demonstrated that the SR appears to be more sensitive than computerized literature searches. They compared SR with librarian-assisted computerized database literature searches and found that the computer searches detected only 65% of relevant articles in a specific set of journals. Although this step is the most time-consuming and tedious, it is the most critical for identifying the articles to be reviewed.

Assessing the Variable(s) of Interest

Once the sample of articles is obtained, the final step is abstracting data regarding specific methodological variables of interest. The variables must be quantifiable, such as numeric variables (e.g., size of the article's study sample) or variables that can be counted (e.g., number of references articles pertaining to religion).

Systematic Reviews of Religion

As we have noted, the SR technique is well suited to assess both the quantity and quality of studies in a potentially sensitive or controversial area. One such area is the study of religion and health.

It is most interesting that in the last decade a number of research reviews concerning religion have been published in peer-reviewed journals assessing the quantity and quality of studies, and pointing out methodological deficits. The deficits have included both the small number of variables used to assess religious commitment, and the quality of those same variables. In light of this, the authors will discuss the results of a number of systematic reviews that have been published by us and several other research colleagues in psychiatry.

Psychiatry

Since the time of Freud, the relationship between psychiatry and religion has been tenuous, if not conflicted. Freud's writings speak of religion as a "universal obsessional neurosis" (Freud, 1907/1959). Ellis (1980), a contemporary psychologist best known for his work on rational emotive therapy, asserts the same view more forcefully, stating that the more emotionally healthy a person is, the less religious he or she will be.

Attitudes such as these have no doubt served to discourage empirical research in this area. However, given at the very least anecdotal evidence, as well as empirical evidence reviewed elsewhere in this volume, it is certainly reasonable to propose that a person's religious beliefs and practices might have a relationship to his or her mental health status.

To study the state of this research, Larson et al. (1986) conducted a systematic review of all research studies found in the four leading psychiatric journals (*American Journal of Psychiatry, British Journal of Psychiatry, Canadian Journal of Psychiatry,* and *Archives of General*

Psychiatry) published during a 5-year period from 1978 to 1982. This systematic review evaluated the penetration of the scientific study of religion into psychiatry. Research penetration was assessed by evaluating the frequency of psychiatric studies that included a measure of religious status and the research quality of measuring religious status. Of the 2348 psychiatry research articles reviewed, only 59 (2.5%) included an empirical (quantified) measure of religion. In the vast majority of these studies, the only measure of religion taken was denomination. Subtracting the studies that assessed the more static measure of religious denomination, fewer than 1% of all psychiatric research studies assessed the more appropriate measures of religious commitment, including religious beliefs, practices, and attitudes. In addition, only 1 of the 59 studies that assessed religious status used a multidimensional measure. Furthermore, most of the studies assessed religion descriptively without any statistical analyses.

Finally, only 3 studies addressed traditional religion as the central study theme. More than 90% of the U.S. population are affiliated with one of three traditional religious faiths: Protestantism, Judaism, and Catholicism. In comparison, 17 studies addressed a religious cult or sect as the central study theme. Less than 0.5% of the U.S. population are affiliated with one of the many existing cults or sects.

This research generally failed to analyze more dynamic measures of religious belief, commitment, or practice; thus it could say little concerning either the importance (or lack of importance) of religion in those who provide, receive, or need psychiatric care. Because most of the studies that assessed religion did so using more static, denominational measures, we evaluated the authors' handling of denomination.

Another interesting finding was the discrepancy between the distribution of religious groups in the U.S. population compared with the distribution of those groups in the research studies. Although Protestant groups predominate with 62% of the U.S. population, they were represented by only 32% of the study samples. Although Jews are 2.5% of the U.S. population, the proportion in the research samples was 15%. Catholics represent 27% of the U.S. population but 35% of the combined study samples (Larson, Donahue, et al., 1989). Finally, in U.S. samples, 9.5% claim "none or other" religious affiliation but 23% of the study groups make this claim. None of the psychiatric authors noted any of these discrepancies between their psychiatric populations and the overall U.S. population.

Finally, in a recent review, Larson et al. (1992) demonstrated the benefit of religious commitment according to findings from the *Archives of General Psychiatry* and the *American Journal of Psychiatry*. The authors systematically reviewed and then summed religious commitment-mental health associations over a 12-year period (1978-1989). Religious commitment variables were first classified along six dimensions: (1) religious ceremony, (2) prayer, (3) church attendance, (4) religion as a social support, (5) relationship with God, and (6) meaning. Next, the association between the religious commitment variable and mental health variable was classified according to three choices: (1) a negative valence (i.e., religious commitment was associated with psychopathology), (2) a positive valence (i.e., religious commitment was associated with either well-being or no psychopathology), or (3) a neutral valence (no association was found).

The findings were quite surprising. The valence for four of the six religious commitment dimensions (religious ceremony, prayer, church attendance, and religion as a social support) was found to be positive in 92% of the cases. The remaining 8% were negative or neutral. In addition, the psychiatric science of assessing religious commitment was flawed. Only 22% of the studies had a respective a priori hypothesis. Conversely, only 40% of those studies that did state an a priori hypothesis presented the final result.

Family Practice

Family practice is the specialty of medicine most likely to interface broadly with patients' lives and lifestyles. As such, this specialty should be most likely to view patients with a wider lens; that is, it should be expected to take a psychosocial perspective. Craigie, Larson, and Liu (1990) and Craigie, Liu, Larson, and Lyons (1988) studied the treatment of religion in the most prominent journal of this medical specialty, the *Journal of Family Practice*.

In the first review of 1086 articles, 52 (4.8%) contained at least one measure of religious status. A total of 64 religious variables were studied. Similar to the psychiatry review, the family practice review found frequent measures of denomination and frequent descriptive and infrequent inferential, or statistical, handling of the data. As with the psychiatric literature, only one study included a multidimensional measure of religion (Craigie et al., 1988).

Craigie et al. (1990) also undertook a valence review. As with the psychiatry valence review, after classifying the type of religious measure, the authors then assessed whether the type of religious variable was found to have a positive, negative, or neutral valence associated with clinical health (or disease) status. Generally, 89% of the religious measures concerning (1) ceremony, (2) relationship with God, and (3) social support were found to be positive, or beneficial, in their effects on clinical status. The other 11% had no effect, and no studies reported a negative or harmful valence. However, of the 15 studies that included a measure of meaning, only 1 presented potentially beneficial effects, 5 reported negative effects, and the other 9 studies reported no effect.

Not surprisingly, the 16 assessments concerning the more static variable denomination all had neutral or no effects on health status. Thus 100% of the denominational measures had a neutral valence. In contrast, for the other 5 dimensions of religious status assessed, only 14 of 48 (29%) religion-mental health associations had a neutral valence.

Gerontology and Geriatrics

In a seminal review of religion and health in the aging literature, Moberg (1965) addressed issues considered then to be the state of the art in the assessment of religion, such as the multidimensionality of religion. He presented evidence suggesting that although religious practices tend to decline with age, presumably because of limitation by functional disability, religious attitudes and feelings apparently increase. He furthermore noted that religious beliefs and practices seem positively related to good personal and social adjustment in old age. Blazer and Palmore (1976), in a longitudinal assessment of religious attitudes and behaviors, documented that although there is a stability of positive religious attitudes throughout life the importance of religion appears to increase over time and is significantly and strongly associated with happiness, feelings of usefulness, and adjustment. Like Moberg, they also noted a decline in religious participation with age.

Whereas others, such as Koenig, George, and Siegler (1988), Koenig, Kvale, and Ferrel (1988), Markides (1987), and Levin (1989) have documented the importance of religious activities and religious coping for the elderly, research has been slow in arriving (Sherrill, Larson, & Greenwold, 1993). Larson et al. (1992) conducted a systematic review of articles published in the three major aging journals (*Journal of the American Geriatrics Society, Journals of Gerontology,* and *The Geron-*

tologist) from 1985 to 1991. Over the time frame reviewed, only 3.6% of 2127 quantitative studies included a religious variable. In most cases (71%), measures consisted of a single question, usually denomination. Furthermore, only 18% of the studies with a religious variable cited at least one article in reference to previous religious research.

Compared with the psychiatry literature, the proportion of studies with a religious variable in the aging literature reviewed was greater (χ^2 = 5.01; df = 1; p < .05). Publications in the aging field were also significantly more likely than psychiatry to use a multidimensional measure: 18% compared with psychiatry's 8%.

Psychology

In 1983, Strommen delivered the American Psychological Association's William James Lecture. The address was titled "Psychology's Blind Spot: A Religious Faith." He noted the irony of religion being so important to many Americans but of such little importance to social scientists. For example, Strommen (1983) pointed out that between 1942 and 1968, less than 2% of all social science dissertations dealt with religion. Psychology outdid sociology for the "low-ball" award, because fewer than 0.5% of all psychology dissertations dealt with religion and religiousness.

Strommen echoed concerns expressed 8 years earlier in Campbell's 1975 American Psychological Association presidential address. Campbell (1975) noted that "behavioral scientists relapse into an epistemic arrogance and literalism when dealing with religious claims for truth. They hold up for a direct realism, a literal veridicality, even though they may recognize that this [standard] is impossible for science itself" (p. 1120). We doubt that the context has changed significantly since Campbell delivered his address.

In a thorough analytic review of the study of religion in the field of psychology, Bergin (1983) examined a rather extensive literature and found religiousness to be a complex, multidimensional phenomenon. For a better understanding of the role of religious status, Bergin recommended that better specification of concepts and improved measurement of religiousness is necessary. Failure to study religious beliefs and practices in their full complexity appeared to have a tendency to wash out findings and could thus lead to an underestimation of the importance of religion associated with mental health status.

Despite previous claims to the contrary (Ellis, 1980), there appeared to be no evidence of a positive relationship between religious commitment and psychopathology. Ellis, as noted previously, stated that religiosity was a marker for psychopathology. In contrast, Bergin reviewed the literature and found that religion-mental health associations were more frequently beneficial, with 47% of the studies having positive associations, 30% neutral associations, and 23% negative associations. These findings were quite similar to the religion-health status results of Craigie et al. (1990), summarized above, in which, excluding the 16 denominational measures, 52% of associations were positive, 19% neutral, and 29% negative.

Other Social Sciences

It should be noted that the findings concerning religious variables in psychiatry and family practice are similar to the results found in other social science fields. Reviews by Poloma and Pendleton (1989) concerning quality of life measures, Kaplan and Blazer (in press) concerning stress and adaptation research, and Schiller and Levin (1988) concerning health services research have all found a similar infrequent assessment of religion status. These findings are perplexing given both the theoretical models to assess religious domains (Levin, 1989; Martin & Carlson, 1988; Schiller & Levin, 1988) and the beneficial impact of religious commitment found concerning both preventing and coping with social problems, physical illness, and psychiatric disorders (Gartner, Larson, & Allen, 1991; Levin & Schiller, 1987; Levin & Vanderpool, 1989, 1991; Payne, Allen, Bielema, & Jenkins, 1991).

Pastoral Care

One area in which religious status would be a fertile field of inquiry is the scientific literature studying pastoral care and counseling. Four peer-reviewed journals—*Journal of Pastoral Care, Journal of Pastoral Counseling, Journal of Religion and Health,* and *Pastoral Psychology*—publish pastoral care research.

To determine the research quality of this literature, Gartner, Larson, and Vachar-Mayberry (1990) studied the pastoral care research from 1975 to 1984. Only 5% of the 1045 studies systematically reviewed included even a single analysis.

Comparing the quality and quantity of research in pastoral care journals to that found in similar journals in psychiatry, nursing, and geriatrics, this review found that pastoral care research suffered from major methodological flaws. These studies were less likely to (1) state hypotheses, (2) use control groups, (3) state a sampling method, (4) report a response rate, (5) include a prospective or longitudinal design, and (6) discuss the limitations of their results. These findings are of concern given previous calls for improved research methodology in the field (Arnold & Schick, 1979) more than a decade before the publication of the systematic review.

The authors concluded that these shortcomings are evidence that pastoral care research has failed to develop adequately as a behavioral science. As such, training in research design and statistics for individuals interested in this area should be encouraged. In addition, funding opportunities should be enhanced with an effort to encourage established investigators to devote at least some of their efforts to research in this field.

Philanthropy Research

Another field that should be producing frequent, quality religious research is the volunteer sector, or philanthropy. Rudney (1987) has noted that churches and denominationally tied organizations provide nearly 66% of all U.S. charitable contributions. In addition, this same group provides at least 33% of all volunteer labor and 20% of the volunteer sector wage earners (Hall, 1989).

Rudney's findings do not take into account the 20% to 25% of the U.S. population who are very committed to their religious beliefs and practices and who provide volunteer services at a level far more frequently than do their less religious counterparts (*Connecticut Mutual Life Report,* 1981). There is a need to determine the additional proportion of volunteer contributions or services being provided because of volunteer religiousness—that is, through nonreligious organizations but due to personal religious commitment.

Despite the critical importance of organized religion and religiousness making possible the very existence of philanthropy and volunteerism, little volunteer sector research has been undertaken. In the early 1980s, Smith (1983) noted the benign neglect of religious research by the volunteer sector research field. Six years later, Hall (1989) and others (Larson, Lyons, Gartner, et al., 1989) noted what by now could better be described as malign neglect. Hall (1989) found that in three key compendiums of volunteer sector research, on the average, less than 3% of the publications addressed religiousness or religious organizations.

Other Systematic Reviews

Both the Department of Health and Human Services (DHHS) and the Department of Justice funded systematic reviews in 1990 and 1991. The DHHS reviews assess research concerning the quantity and quality of family, marital, and community research variables (including measures of religiosity) across 20 fields of academia. The Department of Justice funded a similar set of reviews, focusing on adult and juvenile crime.

In 1992, because of the difficulties in accurately reviewing policy research, the federal government also began to fund systematic reviews on pornography, minority families, family therapy, and abortion. Thus the systematic review technique is now receiving significant support as a literature-synthesis methodology.

Evidence of Bias in Research on Religion

From the above reviews, it is apparent that religion often receives scant attention, and when it does receive attention it is not well measured or studied. Given these methodological deficits, it is no surprise to find that when researchers deal with religious issues, they do so with some bias.

Gartner (1986) documented such bias within the field of clinical psychology. Using a mock admissions process, he demonstrated discrimination against graduate school applicants who reported more conservative, Protestant Christian beliefs, even though the applications were identical in other respects.

In a study of introductory psychology textbooks, Lehr and Spilka (1989) reported that although there appeared to be some improvement in attention paid to religious issues from the 1960s to the 1980s, little attention was paid to the research on religion. In addition, the influence of religion in psychology was often painted in a negative light in texts. This finding contrasts with the two-to-one positive-to-negative relationship between religiosity and mental health found by Bergin (1983).

In a study of denominational variables found in the four major psychiatry journals (Larson, Donahue, et al., 1989), Protestants, likely conservative Protestants, were underrepresented across all studies that reported data on denomination. None of the researchers had noted the studies' consistent underrepresentation of Protestants and Catholics or the studies' consistent overrepresentation of Jewish respondents and those reporting other or no affiliation (Tamney, Powell, & Johnson, 1989).

In a previous review, Larson et al. (1986) discussed several possible explanations for mental health researchers' inadequate handling of religious issues. Along with a lack of scientific interest and regular misinterpretation, additional factors included (1) low rates of theistic beliefs among mental health professionals (Ragan, Malony, & Beit-Hallahmi, 1980); (2) high rates of intergenerational *apostasy,* that is, being raised in a theistic family of origin, but currently reporting agnosticism or atheism (Henry, Simms, & Spray, 1971); (3) the impact of psychoanalytic specialization; and (4) the failure of mental health professionals to work together with the clergy for the benefit of clients with a significant religious commitment.

Implications for Research in Health and Aging

This review of the treatment that religion receives in several socio-medical literatures should inform the future academic study of the role of religion in health- and aging-related disciplines. Although this issue has been addressed empirically, little attention has been paid, and thus it is a field of inquiry that still requires some stimulation. Future research should be undertaken in several areas.

First, epidemiologic research is needed to establish the presence of religion's impact on human health. Such data would provide a context in which to understand the nature of this relationship and the impact of religious commitment in general. This step would also provide an important baseline for understanding changes in religiosity or religious effects over time. Such research is especially needed on substantive issues germane to several basic clinical specialties, including pediatrics, general internal medicine, surgery, and obstetrics-gynecology as well as certain other specialties and subspecialties for which religious commitment has been already shown to play an important mediating or healing role. These include adult and child oncology, preventive medicine, geriatric medicine and geropsychiatry, cardiology, diabetes care, drug and alcohol treatment, and rehabilitation medicine.

Second, clinical economic research on the costs and savings of religious commitment in both the prevention and treatment of specific diseases should be pursued. Assessments should be made of both direct and indirect costs for the individual and for the individual's family. To communicate optimally with the health care industry, empirical study of the cost benefit of religious interventions (Byrd, 1988) and of religious commitment in general (Pressman, Lyons, Larson, & Strain, 1990) is critical to impact effectively on decision makers in the health care market who—like scientists and academic clinicians—continue to overlook the vital role of religious commitment.

Third, the effects of religion on the development of clinical and academic values and beliefs should be studied. Although it may be the case that prevailing clinical and academic values are merely a reflection of culture, it also is quite possible that these values are a powerful causal agent in the development of culture-wide values and beliefs. Demonstration of such relationships might facilitate an understanding of the responsibilities incumbent on individuals and corporations in a free society when such power is given to so few.

Fourth, the presentation and incorporation of religious material into teaching programs and texts in medicine and other academic fields should prove a fertile ground for study.

In sum, the systematic study of the relationship of religion to health and aging and of religion's neglect and misinterpretation in academia are areas of potentially great importance. The results of systematic reviews of research on religion across a variety of fields point to two central findings. First, there appears to be a reluctance to assess potentially relevant religious constructs in research on health, mental health, and aging. Second, when religious variables are included, they appear to exhibit consistent, positive relationships with health and well-being. Religion is a large part of many people's lives. It is not a large part of scientific and clinical research. Unless this disparity is reconciled, researchers will limit unnecessarily their ability to understand complex phenomena in human health and aging.

References

Arnold, J. D., & Schick, C. (1979). Counseling by clergy: A review of empirical research. *Journal of Pastoral Counseling, 14,* 76-101.

Bareta, J. C., Larson, D. B., Zorc, J. J., & Lyons, J. S. (1990). A comparison of the MEDLARS and systematic review of the consultation-liaison psychiatry literature. *American Journal of Psychiatry, 147,* 1040-1042.

Beardsley, R. S., Larson, D. B., Lyons, J. S., Gottlieb, G., Rabins, P. V., & Rovner, B. (1989). Health services research in nursing homes: A systematic review. *Journal of Gerontology: Medical Sciences, 41,* 30-35.

Bergin, A. E. (1983). Religiosity and mental health: A critical re-evaluation and meta-analysis. *Professional Psychology: Research and Practice, 14,* 170-184.

Blazer D., & Palmore E. (1976). Religion and aging in a longitudinal panel. *The Gerontologist, 16,* 82-85.

Byrd, R. C. (1988). Positive therapeutic effects of intercessory prayer in a coronary care unit population. *Southern Medical Journal, 81,* 826-829.

Campbell, D. (1975). On the conflicts between biological and social evolution and between psychology and moral tradition. *American Psychologist, 30,* 1103-1126.

The Connecticut Mutual Life report on American values in the 1980s. (1981). Hartford, CT: Connecticut Mutual Life.

Craigie, F. C., Larson, D. B., & Liu, I. Y. (1990). References to religion in the *Journal of Family Practice. Journal of Family Practice, 30,* 477-480.

Craigie, F. C., Liu, I. Y., Larson, D. B., & Lyons, J. S. (1988). A systematic analysis of religious variables in the *Journal of Family Practice,* 1976-1986. *Journal of Family Practice, 27,* 509-513.

Ellis, A. (1980). Psychotherapy and atheistic values. *Journal of Consulting and Clinical Psychology, 48,* 635-639.

Freud, S. (1959). Obsessive actions and religious practices. In *Standard edition of the complete works of Sigmund Freud* (Vol. 9) (pp. 126-127). London: Hogarth. (Original work published 1907)

Gartner, J. D. (1986). Anti-religious prejudice in admissions to doctoral programs in clinical psychology. *Professional Psychology: Research and Practice, 17,* 473-475.

Gartner, J. D., Larson, D. B., & Allen, G.D., (1991). Religious commitment and mental health: A review of the empirical literature. *Journal of Psychology and Theology, 19,* 6-25.

Gartner, J., Larson, D. B., & Vachar-Mayberry, C. D. (1990). A systematic review of the quantity and quality of empirical research published in four pastoral counseling journals: 1975-1984. *Journal of Pastoral Care, 44,* 115-129.

Glass, G. V. (1976). Primary, secondary, and meta-analysis of research. *Education Research, 5,* 3-8.

Hall, P. D. (1989). A bridge founded upon justice and built of human hearts: Reflections on religion, science and the development of American philanthropy. In R. Wuthnow (Ed.), *Philanthropy and the religious tradition* (pp. 239-264). Washington, DC: The Independent Sector and the United Way Institute.

Henry, W. E., Simms, J. H., & Spray, S. L. (1971). *The fifth profession: Becoming a psychotherapist.* San Francisco: Jossey-Bass.

Kaplan, B. H., & Blazer, D. G. (in press). Religion in the stress and adaptation paradigm. In P. R. Barchas (Ed.), *Essays in sociophysiology.* New York: Oxford University Press.

Koenig, H. G., George, L. K., & Siegler, I. C. (1988). The use of religion and other emotion-regulating coping strategies among older adults. *The Gerontologist, 28,* 303-310.

Koenig, H. G., Kvale, J. N., & Ferrel, C. (1988). Religion and well-being in late life. *The Gerontologist, 28,* 18-28.

Larson, D. B., Donahue, M. J., Lyons, J. S., Benson, P. L., Pattison, E. M., Worthington, E. L., & Blazer, D. G. (1989). Religious affiliation in mental health research samples as compared to national samples. *Journal of Nervous and Mental Disease, 177,* 109-111.

Larson, D. B., Lyons, J. S., Gartner, J., Sherrill, K. A., & Larson, S. S. (1989). Demonstrating the neglect of religion in the social sciences and researching the effectiveness of religious volunteer interventions: Some steps in responding to a crisis of research identity. In R. Wuthnow (Ed.), *Philanthropy and the religious tradition* (pp. 631-650). Washington, DC: The Independent Sector and the United Way Institute.

Larson, D. B., Lyons, J. S., Hohmann, A. H., Beardsley, R. S., Huckeba, W. M., Rabins, P. V., & Lebowitz, B. D. (1989). A systematic review of nursing home research in three psychiatric journals. *International Journal of Geriatric Psychiatry, 4*, 129-134.

Larson, D. B., Pattison, E. M., Blazer, D. G., Omran, A. R., & Kaplan, B. H. (1986). Systematic analysis of research on religious variables in four major psychiatric journals, 1978-1982. *American Journal of Psychiatry, 143*, 329-334.

Larson, D. B., Sherrill, K. A., Lyons, J. S., Craigie, F. C., Thielman, S. B., Greenwold, M. A., & Larson, S. S. (1992). Associations between dimensions of religious commitment and mental health reported in the *American Journal of Psychiatry* and *Archives of General Psychiatry: 1978-1989. American Journal of Psychiatry, 149*, 557-559.

Lehr, B., & Spilka, B. (1989). Religion in the introductory psychology textbook: A comparison of three decades. *Journal for the Scientific Study of Religion, 28*, 366-371.

Levin, J. S. (1989). Religious factors in aging, adjustment, and health: A theoretical overview. In W. M. Clements (Ed.), *Religion, aging and health: A global perspective* (pp. 133-146). New York: Haworth.

Levin, J. S., & Schiller, P. L. (1987). Is there a religious factor in health? *Journal of Religion and Health, 26*, 9-36.

Levin, J. S., & Vanderpool, H. Y. (1989). Is religion therapeutically significant for hypertension? *Social Science and Medicine, 29*, 69-78.

Levin, J. S., & Vanderpool, H. Y. (1991). Religious factors in physical health and the prevention of illness. *Prevention in Human Services, 9*, 41-64.

Light, R. J., & Pillemer, D. B. (1984). *Summing up: The science of reviewing research.* Cambridge, MA: Harvard University Press.

Light, R. J. and Smith, P. V. (1971). Accumulating evidence: Procedures for resolving contradictions among different research studies. *Harvard Educational Review, 41*, 429-471.

Lyons, J. S., Larson, D. B., Bareta, J. C., Hohmann, A. H., Liu, I. Y., & Sparks, C. H. (1990). A systematic analysis of the quantity of AIDS publications and the quality of research methods in three general medical journals. *Evaluation and Program Planning, 13*, 73-77.

Markides, K. S. (1987). Religion. In G. L. Maddox (Ed.), *The encyclopedia of aging* (pp. 559-561). New York: Springer.

Martin, J. E., & Carlson, C. R. (1988). Spiritual dimensions of health psychology. In W. R. Miller & J. E. Martin (Eds.), *Behavioral therapy and religion: Integrating spiritual and behavioral approaches to change* (pp. 57-110). Newbury Park, CA: Sage.

Moberg, D. O. (1965). Religiosity in old age. *The Gerontologist, 5*, 78-87.

Mulrow, C. D. (1987). The medical review article: State of the science. *Annals of Internal Medicine, 106*, 485-491.

Payne, R., Allen, B. E., Bielema, K. A., & Jenkins, P. H. (1991). Review of religion and mental health: Prevention and the enhancement of psychosocial functioning. *Prevention in Human Services, 9*, 11-40.

Poloma, M. M., & Pendleton, B. F. (1989). Religious domains and general well-being. *Social Indicators Research, 22*, 1-22.

Pressman, P., Lyons, J. S., Larson, D. B., & Strain, J. J. (1990). Religious belief, depression, and ambulation status in elderly women with broken hips. *American Journal of Psychiatry, 147*, 758-760.

Ragan, C., Malony, H. N., & Beit-Hallahmi, B. (1980). Psychologists and religion: Professional factors and professional belief. *Review of Religious Research, 21,* 208-217.

Rudney, G. (1987). The scope and dimensions of nonprofit activity. In W. W. Powell (Ed.), *The nonprofit sector: A research handbook* (pp. 55ff.). New Haven, CT: Yale University Press.

Sacks, H. S., Berrier, J., Reitman, D., Ancona-Berk, V. A., & Chalmers, T. C. (1987). Meta-analyses of randomized controlled trials. *New England Journal of Medicine, 316,* 450-455.

Schiller, P. L., & Levin, J. S. (1988). Is there a religious factor in health care utilization?: A review. *Social Science and Medicine, 27,* 1369-1379.

Sherrill, K. A., Larson, D. B., & Greenwold, M. (1993). Is religion taboo in geriatrics?: Systematic review of research on religion in three major gerontologic journals, 1985-1991. *American Journal of Geriatric Psychiatry, 1,* 109-117.

Smith, D. H. (1983). Churches are generally ignored in contemporary voluntary action research: Causes and consequences. *Review of Religious Research, 24,* 293-321.

Strommen, M. P. (1983, August). *Psychology's blind spot: A religious faith.* William James Award acceptance address presented to Division 36, American Psychological Association.

Tamney, J. B., Powell, S., & Johnson, S. (1989). Innovation theory and religious nones. *Journal for the Scientific Study of Religion, 28,* 216-229.

Religious Involvement Among Older African-Americans

LINDA M. CHATTERS
ROBERT JOSEPH TAYLOR

Introduction

The nature, patterns, and functions of religious involvement among African-Americans have been the topic of enduring academic interest since the early 1900s (e.g., Du Bois, 1899). Extensive scholarly traditions in the areas of African-American studies, African-American history, religious studies, anthropology, and the sociology of religion attest to the persistence of these themes and their capacity to capture the imagination of students of the social sciences and religion alike. Part of this fascination for religious involvement among African-Americans stems from the apparent pervasiveness and persistence of the religious context for this group. The historical literature demonstrates that black religious traditions and their formalized institutions have possessed a permanence within African-American communities over time, geographic location, and social context and circumstance. Specialized treatments of the black church indicate that, as it has endured over time, several of its distinguishing characteristics and features have changed and adapted in response to external forces and conditions and diverse

AUTHORS' NOTE: The work of the authors was supported by the National Institute on Aging under NIH Grant No. AG10135.

social contexts. Throughout these transformations and modifications, the pervasiveness and centrality of the black church within its host communities have been documented over the years. Diverse perspectives on the black church describe its central importance to the economic, political, and civic functioning of African-American communities and its positive influences on the spiritual, psychological, and physical well-being of families and individuals.

Despite this rich legacy of scholarly work on African-American religious traditions and the black church, relatively few of the substantive topics in these areas have been the subject of focused and systematic quantitative investigation. This is despite the fact that the investigation of these topics has the potential for illuminating a variety of issues bearing on the nature, form, and functions of religious involvement for this group. More generally, African-American religious involvement provides a specific context and domain for the study of the intersection of individuals, families, community, and society. This chapter attempts to remedy the situation by surveying the current empirical literature on these topics and suggesting further domains and topics for investigation. For the most part, the chapter will mirror the predominant religious preferences of African-Americans in describing theory and research pertaining to specifically Christian traditions. Information concerning other faiths is discussed typically with respect to profiles of denominational preference. Furthermore, unless otherwise noted, the literature and research reviewed here focuses on African-Americans holding U.S. citizenship (native born or naturalized); ethnicity and immigrant status are not explored as major stratifying variables in the present discussion. Although these are significant and important factors for understanding religious involvement in their own right, the status of current knowledge prevents a comprehensive assessment of their influence on the form and function of religious expression.

The chapter begins with a review and summary of what is currently known about religious involvement among African-Americans and, specifically, older persons. Research describing the role of religion and religious institutions in the black experience will be highlighted. Following this, we briefly review extant models of religious expression among African-Americans and a number of assumptions concerning religiosity that result from these models. The recent work of Lincoln and Mamiya (1990) serves as an organizing framework for understanding black religious expression.

Next, the chapter describes research findings on the black church and on religiosity among African-Americans. The selective review concentrates on patterns and components of religiosity, sociodemographic predictors of religious involvement, and the social and health correlates and outcomes of religious involvement. Research based on national samples of respondents, and particularly programmatic research from the National Survey of Black Americans (NSBA) data set, will be emphasized. Data of this type provide a number of advantages related to (1) the size and quality of the samples available, (2) the distribution on major sociodemographic factors evident in those samples, and (3) the ability to use multivariate analyses that allow for the assessment of the independent effects of various factors on religious involvement.

Finally, this chapter describes a research agenda that is presently being pursued by us in collaboration with Jeff Levin. This agenda considers several of the current conceptual, methodological, and analytical limitations in this area. Of particular importance are issues bearing on the conceptualization of African-American religious experience as a multidimensional and dynamic phenomenon as well as the continued development and articulation of models of the antecedents and consequences of religious involvement. We explore a number of methodological considerations that would advance these objectives, including the use of data sets that are appropriate to the study of black religiosity with respect to item and construct content, sample representativeness on major sociodemographic factors, and prospective design. We also discuss the employment of analytical techniques that provide for assessment of independent effects of factors on religious involvement and the multidimensional measurement of religiosity and modeling of religious effects on subsequent outcomes. Concluding comments consider the future of theory and research on black religion, with an emphasis on the particular strengths and challenges of interdisciplinary collaboration in gerontology and health research.

Religion and the
African-American Experience

The importance of religion and religious institutions to individual African-Americans and broader black communities has been documented in numerous research and scholarly efforts. This work describes the impact of religion on the historical experiences of blacks within

American society as well as its role in the development of independent black institutions and communities (Lincoln & Mamiya, 1990; Nelsen & Nelsen, 1975). Across these differing perspectives, black religious institutions are depicted as cohesive and integrated spiritual and social communities that foster the religious and social well-being of individuals. The primary position of black churches is demonstrated by the various secular activities and functions they perform within their communities. Among others, these functions include facilitating linkages to community health resources (Levin, 1984, 1986), providing instrumental social and psychological support (Neighbors, Jackson, Bowman, & Gurin, 1983), and serving as a base for political mobilization and social movements (Morris, 1981).

Integral to any discussion of the form and functions of religious involvement among African-Americans is some understanding of the historical origins of these traditions and the social, economic, and political experiences that served to define religious expression. Lincoln and Mamiya (1990) and others (e.g., Frazier, 1974) argue that African-American theological orientations and religious practices emanated from the unique and dynamic social, political, and historical contexts that characterized their position within American society. Because black religious expression occurred within the context of a frequently hostile larger society, the aims and purposes of religious belief and expression were uniquely oriented and adapted toward the amelioration, buffering, and/or abolishment of conditions that were deleterious to the well-being of African-Americans. In common with all religious traditions, black religious expression addressed itself to questions of ultimate concern and existential meaning (e.g., illness, personal suffering, and death). However, within the context of American society, these questions of ultimate concern were framed within the context of the conditions and life circumstances of African-Americans. As a consequence, African-American religious traditions also necessarily reflected the salient issues of emancipation, enfranchisement, civil and human rights, and social and economic justice (Lincoln & Mamiya, 1990). The enduring emphasis on the improvement of the tangible life circumstances of African-Americans suggests that spirituality, per se, was but one of the purposes of black religious traditions. To varying degrees and across different traditions, the conditions of immediate physical existence as well as spiritual life have exerted powerful and complementary influences on the nature and functions of black religious expression.

Models of the Black Church and
Religious Involvement

Several extant models of the black church and religious involvement have been developed that attempt to characterize the form and function of black religious expression. These models, however, have been found wanting in a number of respects, principally in regard to their inadequate appreciation for the impact of social and historical context and the processes of change and an overemphasis on individual and discrete manifestations of black religious expression. As a result, traditional models of black religious involvement are, to a great degree, static and ahistorical in nature (Stump, 1987) and tend to investigate a limited set of characteristics in defining black religious expression. Lincoln and Mamiya's (1990) overview of traditional models of black religious expression suggests that the black church (and its roles and functions in black communities) is viewed as a product of lower-status black culture, and, consequently, is depicted in a largely negative manner. Among the prominent themes articulated in this literature are that black religious traditions have served to isolate black communities, impeded the assimilation of blacks within broader society, promoted "other-worldly" religious orientations, and functioned to compensate for deprivations experienced within American society (e.g., Marx, 1967).

Certainly, one of the more conventional and popular notions concerning black religious expression is that it, in some sense, functions to compensate for deprivations (e.g., social, economic, political, and personal) in other areas of life (Glock, Ringer, & Babbie, 1967). However, the contention that mere "deprivation" with respect to various social statuses motivates black religious involvement is not supported by the majority of the data bearing on this question (e.g., Taylor, 1988a, 1988b). In a similar vein, the family surrogate model (Glock et al., 1967), a variant of the deprivation-compensation perspective, suggests that unmarried persons and childless couples compensate for the absence of spouse and/or family through religious involvement. Again, the data do not support the claim that higher religiosity is evident among persons who are unmarried and childless couples. In contrast, recent work indicates that the relationship between social status factors and religious involvement among African-Americans is more complex than previously thought (Stump, 1987).

In contrast to the traditional models of black religious involvement, Lincoln and Mamiya (1990) propose what they term a dialectical model of the black church. The principal elements of this model include (1) an appreciation for the historical origins of the institutional structures in black religion, (2) a dynamic orientation emphasizing change and adaptation to both immediate circumstances and conditions and larger societal forces, and (3) a conceptualization of the black church that reflects its position along a number of dimensions that are organized as polar opposites (dialectical tensions). These dialectical tensions are identified as reflecting the polarities of (1) priestly versus prophetic function, (2) other-worldly versus this-worldly, (3) universalism versus particularism, (4) communal versus privatistic, (5) charismatic versus bureaucratic, and (6) resistance versus accommodation. These dimensions of the black church have been the subject of study in previous research, but because they were typically examined in isolation, they provided only a limited understanding of the nature of black religious expression. The resulting dialectical model provides a more comprehensive treatment of the black church, incorporating notions of dynamic interaction with historical forces, ongoing change and adaptation in response to contemporaneous factors, and an inherent multidimensional character.

Lincoln and Mamiya's (1990) work provides a useful conceptual framework for understanding several features of black churches and religious involvement, in particular the central and pivotal role of the church in many communities and the multiplicity of manifest functions and objectives. They argue that specific features of African-American culture, in dynamic relationship with the larger American context, has given rise to a religious tradition in which religious and secular concerns are only partially differentiated. In essence, because black religious traditions have sought to address the social and political conditions that impact on the lives of African-Americans as a group, religious pursuits have not become fully differentiated (i.e., privatized) from secular concerns. As evidence of this, among other things, black churches are viewed as being instrumental in the development of the black self-help tradition (i.e., mutual-aid societies) and in providing the institutional foundations for educational, civic, and commercial endeavors within black communities. Historical and ethnographic research on the nature of black religious involvement verify its multidimensional character (Cone, 1985). With respect to black churches, they are noted for their role in social welfare, political, and civic and community functions (Frazier, 1974; Taylor & Chatters, 1986a, 1988; Taylor, Thornton, & Chatters, 1987). The apparent diversity of function within black churches and black religious involvement, more generally, suggests a number of means by which the spiritual, emotional, social, and political strivings of African-Americans might be achieved. As will be discussed later, multidimensional characterizations of black religious involvement have been empirically validated in recent studies. Furthermore, models emphasizing the multifarious nature of religious involvement provide a useful framework for understanding the possible mechanisms whereby religious factors impact a number of outcomes of interest (Ellison, 1991; Levin & Vanderpool, 1989, 1991).

Religious Involvement Among African-Americans: Research Findings

This section discusses existing research findings addressing the nature, form, and function of religious involvement among African-Americans. This review is selective and assesses information derived primarily from national data sets of the population. Topics to be covered are religious affiliation, predictors and outcomes of religious involvement, and patterns and components of religiosity. Programmatic research based on the NSBA data set is highlighted in this review.

Religious Affiliation

Topics considered here include African-Americans' attitudes toward the black church, correlates of religious nonaffiliation and apostasy, and descriptive profiles of denominational preference among blacks. An assessment of African-Americans' attitudes regarding the role of black churches (Taylor et al., 1987) demonstrated both positive sentiments toward the church and a recognition of the diverse functions they have performed within black communities. The majority of respondents (82.2%) described the church's impact on the circumstances of blacks in America as being beneficial, 4.9% reported that the church has been detrimental to the status of blacks, and 12.1% reported that the church has made no difference. Multivariate analyses indicated that positive assessments of the church's sociohistorical role tended to be voiced by older persons, those who resided in the South (versus the Northeast), women, and persons with more years of formal education. Specific positive examples of the church's impact described its role in providing spiritual assistance, sustaining and strengthening both individuals and communities, giving individual social support and assistance, providing guidelines for moral behavior, functioning as a source of cultural unity, operating as a community resource and center, and advancing the goals of social and political progress for blacks.

Stark and Bainbridge's (1981) preliminary analysis of American sects provides information of a slightly different type with respect to the religious beliefs and orientations of blacks. A religious sect is defined as a group that separates from a dominant religious body while remaining within the religious tradition that is regarded as normal (nondeviant) within the society in which the sect originates. In contrast, groups within so-called deviant religious traditions are identified as cults. The authors found that the proportion of sects having a primarily black membership (10%) is very close to the proportion of blacks found in the general population. They argue that this finding suggests that despite greater relative deprivation, the black population has not produced more sects than has the white population.

A profile of religious affiliation among African-Americans (Taylor & Chatters, 1991b) found that a total of 40 different religious affiliations were reported, indicating considerable breadth and variety in religious preference. Respondents identified largely with the Baptist tradition, with 52.1% indicating that they were Baptist. A total of 11.7% reported being Methodist, 6.3% indicated a current affiliation with Roman Catholicism, 3.2% of the respondents indicated that they were Holiness, and 2.1% reported being Jehovah's Witnesses. Approximately 15% of the sample indicated a current affiliation with 1 of 35 other religious groups, 1 out of 10 respondents indicated that they had no religious preference, and 8 persons indicated that they were atheist or agnostic. A similar affiliation profile among persons 55 years and older indicated a total of 28 different religious groups (Taylor, 1992). The percentages of elderly persons reporting affiliations with Baptist, Methodist, or Roman Catholic traditions were largely comparable with those reported for the entire adult sample. However, compared with younger blacks, elderly adults were somewhat more likely to be Methodist, were less likely to report no religious affiliation and, overall, reported a narrower collection of religious denominations (28 as opposed to 40).

Taylor (1992) examined older black adults' current religious affiliation in conjunction with reports as to their own childhood (i.e., religion when growing up) and both parents' affiliations. The comparison of older respondents' own current religious affiliation with that of their parents (both mother and father) revealed substantial similarities. The overwhelming majority of elderly black adults identified their own current affiliation, as well as that of their parents, as either Baptist or Methodist. However, contrasts involving respondents' current religious affiliation compared with (1) their own childhood affiliation and (2) their parents' affiliation revealed important differences. With respect to current affiliation, respondents were slightly less likely (compared with childhood and parent affiliation) to indicate being Baptist or Methodist and were slightly more likely to indicate that they held another religious affiliation. Furthermore, although relationships between current religious affiliation and both childhood and parents' religious affiliation were generally robust, mothers' religious affiliations demonstrated a somewhat stronger association with respondents' current religious affiliations than did fathers' affiliations.

Although these and other data suggest that affiliation with a religious tradition, in some manner or form, is a relatively common circumstance among African-Americans (Nelsen, 1988; Welch, 1978), we know little about persons who apparently are disengaged from a religious context (i.e., apostates). Taylor's (1988a) investigation of persons who were religiously noninvolved (i.e., no current religious affiliation and absence of religious service attendance since adulthood) found that very few respondents (10%) indicated a complete absence of all overt religious involvement. Religious noninvolvement was associated with being male, younger, and residing outside the southern region. Furthermore, persons who were never married and those with low levels of income and education were more likely to forgo religious involvement than their counterparts. However, even among persons identified as religiously noninvolved (i.e., nonaffiliation, church absence), a substantial number indicated that they prayed on a frequent basis and characterized themselves as being fairly religious.

Ellison and Sherkat (1990) conducted an extensive analysis of patterns of religious affiliation among African-Americans. Their work focused on change in religious preference between 1972 and 1988 using data from the General Social Survey (1972-1988) and the NSBA. Overall, their findings indicated that religious affiliation or denominational preference was relatively stable. Over this period, there were small declines in the percentage of persons who were Baptist, Methodist, Catholic, or affiliated with predominantly white organizations. Among those who did change affiliations, Baptists were more likely to switch to small conservative Protestant groups and Methodists were more likely to become Baptist. Catholics, on the other hand, were more likely both to indicate no current religious preference and, similar to persons raised without formal religious ties, to affiliate with nontraditional religions. This line of research was extended in a recent analysis (Sherkat & Ellison, 1991) using NSBA data that examines the demographic and racial group identity correlates of both religious nonidentification and change in denominational identification among religious adherents. Compared with persons who remained in black mainline religious denominations (i.e., Baptists and Methodists), religious apostates (those raised in black mainline denominations, but now unaffiliated) were more likely to be male, younger, and reside outside of the South. Furthermore, apostates tended to hold negative attitudes about black churches, had lower levels of racial group identification, had less frequent contact with family members, and were less likely to be a member of a national or neighborhood organization. Religious switchers (persons raised in a black mainline denomination, but with a different current religious affiliation) were more likely than persons remaining in mainline denominations to be married, reside in urban areas, and to support political protest to gain equal rights. However, religious switchers demonstrated lower levels of racial group identity than their religious mainline counterparts.

Structural Determinants of Religious Involvement

Recognizing a general lack of basic information concerning the structural antecedents of religiosity among African-Americans, research studies reviewed here document the nature and extent of sociodemographic differences (i.e., age, gender, marital status, urbanicity, socioeconomic status, and region) in religious involvement. The religious outcomes of interest include organizational (or public) and nonorganizational (or private) religious behaviors as well as religious attitudes and sentiments.

Despite a general pattern of frequent religious attendance, high rates of church membership, and an overwhelming tendency to characterize oneself as religious, Taylor (1986) found significant differences in religious involvement among older black adults. With respect to age, the oldest members of this group of respondents were more likely than their younger counterparts to describe themselves as religious. Men and persons divorced from their spouses demonstrated lower levels of religious involvement on all three measures (i.e., attendance, membership, and subjective religiosity) than their counterparts (women and married persons, respectively). Individuals who were widowed attended church less frequently and had lower levels of subjective religiosity compared with married persons. Although living in rural areas was associated with higher rates of attendance and membership, there were no significant regional differences in religious involvement among this older group. An examination of nonorganizational religious participation among this same age group (Taylor & Chatters, 1991a) found that the majority of respondents engaged in daily prayer, read religious materials, watched or listened to religious programs on a weekly basis, and requested prayer on their own behalf several times a month. Taken together with previous work, an emerging profile of religiosity among older black adults emphasizes a high degree of organized religious participation such as religious attendance and church membership coupled with extensive involvement in private religious activities.

A comparable study of adults from 18 to 101 years of age (Taylor, 1988b) examined the determinants of religious service attendance, church membership, and private religious activities. Approximately 70% of respondents reported attending religious services at least a few times a month, and 66% were official members of a church or place of worship. With respect to frequency of devotional behaviors, 78% of respondents indicated that they prayed, 27% indicated reading religious books, 21% watched or listened to religious programs on television or radio, and 13% reported that they ask someone to pray for them on nearly a daily basis. Significant differences by sociodemographic factors document generally higher rates of participation for older persons, women, married individuals, those with higher levels of income and education, and rural and southern residents. These findings clearly underscore a considerable degree of heterogeneity with respect to religious participation among African-Americans.

Chatters and Taylor (1989a) examined the specific effects of age on seven indicators of organizational, nonorganizational, and attitudinal forms of religious involvement among adults across the entire age range. Among women, age was positively associated with each of the religiosity measures, while for men, "requests for prayer from others" was the only indicator for which age was not a significant predictor. Current models of age and religious involvement were evaluated, along with a discussion of possible age, period, and cohort differences. Together with other empirical data on religiosity among black Americans, these findings suggest that the religious experiences of African-Americans are characterized by both relatively high levels of overall religious involvement and, further, a general linear and positive age trend whereby religious involvement increases with advanced age. Finally, Stump (1987) analyzed regional differences (North versus South) in the determinants of religious attendance among African-American Protestants. His findings suggested that religious attendance in the South is predicted by social variables (e.g., age, education, and presence of young children) to a greater degree than in the North, where religious factors are more prominent (e.g., commitment and confidence in clergy). Furthermore, despite a narrowing of differences between northern and southern religious experiences, persistent disparities with respect to moral asceticism are thought to reflect historical regional differences in the centrality of religious institutions across these settings.

The body of findings for sociodemographic differences in the religious involvement of African-Americans suggests several tentative conclusions. First, within the black population there is considerable heterogeneity that is reflected in consistent differences in the extent of public and private religious involvement. Age and gender reflect the most pervasive of these influences, although marital status, socioeconomic status, region, and urbanicity also demonstrate important effects on religious involvement. Second, the direction and patterns of effects for sociodemographic factors are largely comparable to those observed for the general population. However, the data as a whole tentatively suggest that baseline rates of indicators of religious involvement may be particularly elevated for African-Americans generally as well as within discrete subgroups (i.e., older persons and women). Third, although not elaborated here, the particular interpretations of sociodemographic effects are largely compatible with more current models of religious involvement. That is, the findings observed among African-Americans are congruous with explanations of religious involvement differences that emphasize factors such as social roles, social location, social networks, and place of residence effects. This conclusion is tentative, as the systematic examination of the operation of sociodemographic factors has only begun and more complex models (e.g., including interaction terms) may be required.

Social and Health Correlates
and Outcomes

In this section, we describe a group of studies that suggest that involvement in religious pursuits is related to various social and health factors and outcomes. We specifically examine the nature and operation of religious- or church-based social networks, the use of religiously derived coping strategies and mechanisms, and the position of religious factors as correlates and antecedents of psychological health and well-being. Although several of these efforts provide only a descriptive profile of these processes and phenomena, attempts to delineate significant sociodemographic variability are noted.

Historical and contemporaneous research on the black church emphasize its status as an important and central institution within black communities and its role as a context for social support and group cohesion (e.g., Watson, 1990). Moore's analysis (1991) of the black church describes its historical place as a crucial intermediary between society and black communities and individuals. The role of the church with respect to individual and community empowerment, social change, and mutual assistance is highlighted. The principal emphasis of a number of investigations has been to examine the nature and determinants of church-based social networks, their role in providing social support (i.e., frequency, amount, and type of aid), and important determinants of these helping relationships. Among older black adults who were the recipients of assistance from their church networks, levels of church membership, religious attendance, and expressed importance of attending religious services were predictive of receiving aid (Taylor & Chatters, 1986a). Findings revealed an interactive effect of age with parental status (i.e., having an adult child) for the frequency and amount of assistance provided. Specifically, among persons who have children, advanced age was associated with increases in assistance from church networks; for childless elderly, however, older age reflected decreases in church support. Official status as a member of a church interacted with age as an important determinant of church-based assistance. For persons who were official members, there were no significant age differences in the amount of assistance received. However, among persons who were not church members, those who were relatively older received significantly more assistance than did their younger counterparts.

An investigation of church-based support (Taylor & Chatters, 1988) across the entire adult age range found that close to 66% of respondents indicated that church members provided some level of assistance. A roughly comparable set of church-related factors (i.e., religious attendance, church membership, and subjective religiosity) predicted receiving aid. Significant differences for denominational affiliation indicated that Catholics received less aid than the comparison group of Baptists.

However, as distinct from the elderly analysis (Taylor & Chatters, 1986a), across the entire age range, older persons and women were less likely to receive assistance (similar to previous work, divorced persons tended to receive less support as well). An investigation of patterns of informal assistance (Taylor & Chatters, 1986b) indicated that family, friends, and church members were differentially influential as support resources of older black adults. A total of 80% of older persons received support from either a best or close friend, approximately 60% reported aid from church members, and more than 50% received support from extended family members. Analysis of type of support indicated that while there is some overlap in forms of assistance offered by the three networks, older persons were more likely to receive advice, encouragement, and help during sickness from church members.

Turning to a consideration of the use of religion and religious resources as a coping strategy, Brown and Gary (1987) found that religious effects on health status were different for men versus women. Religiosity was not related to health among men, while among women greater religiosity was associated with poorer health status. Black women who experienced several life events (such as problems involving the health of family members) tended to report poorer health status and greater religious involvement. The authors speculate that religious participation was a mechanism used by black women to cope with the poor health of family members and acted to minimize the effects of stress on their own physical health. Bryant and Rakowski (1992) found that religious attendance reduced the risk of mortality among older African-Americans even when the effects of physical health problems were controlled. The increased risk of mortality was particularly strong among older men who did not attend church.

In a similar vein, Krause and Tran (1989) examined religious factors in a stress and coping framework among older black adults. They found that religiosity tended to counterbalance the negative effects of life events by bolstering feelings of self-worth and personal control. In an expanded treatment of these issues, Krause (1992) incorporated measures of social support to examine the relative impact of religious factors for psychological distress. The findings indicated that, independent of the effects of emotional support from significant others, religious factors counteract the impact of life events on depressive symptoms via their effects on evaluations of self-esteem. Chatters and Taylor (1989b) examined the distribution and types of self-reported personal life problems among older black adults. Respondents reported using prayer to deal with the distress associated with money and health problems. Various functions of prayer were noted, including attempts to gain direct (i.e., divine) intervention for a problem or to alter one's perspective on the situation (e.g., an acceptance of God's will) or one's emotional response to the difficulty. Neighbors (1991) investigated the use of formal helpers by persons experiencing a serious personal problem. About 30% of respondents reported seeking assistance from a member of the clergy (i.e., minister). Although age, gender, income, and education did not emerge as significant predictors, the type of problem experienced had a major impact on the use of ministers. Persons who indicated that their personal problem involved coping with the death of a loved one were much more likely to use ministers than were those who indicated that they had experienced an interpersonal, emotional, economic, or physical health problem.

Wilson and Netting (1988) offer several reasons why churches are uniquely suited to act as informal service providers. Their strategic location in general proximity to older persons within the community and the existence of a number of volunteer-based services make them particularly well equipped to serve as informal providers to older adults. Griffith and associates (Griffith, 1983; Griffith, English, & Mayfield, 1980; Griffith & Mahy, 1984; Griffith, Young, & Smith, 1984) have identified a number of positive therapeutic benefits of religious involvement among African-Americans. This work also suggests that church congregations function as informal helper networks that assist in the identification of individuals with problems and through referral to formal services. Caldwell, Chatters, Billingsley, and Taylor (in press) investigated supportive programs for older adults within black churches and found that organizational characteristics (e.g., age, size, location, and financial solvency), the mission and dynamics of congregations, clergy leadership attributes, and existing relationships with health and social agencies were each related to whether or not a church provided outreach programs to older persons in their communities.

A program of work undertaken by Hatch and associates (Eng & Hatch, 1991; Eng, Hatch, & Cunningham, 1985; Hatch & Eng, 1983, 1984; Hatch & Lovelace, 1980) has addressed the possible interfaces existing between churches and health and human service agencies. The development of the lay health adviser (LHA) model (Eng & Hatch, 1991) reflects systematic efforts to identify and use the natural support resources within African-American congregations as important linkages between individuals at risk and formal service agencies. The authors describe a typology of interventions based on the LHA model that specifies the roles and aims of network member involvement. The LHA model and its intervention approach represent the most sophisticated application and integration of information on social support networks, help-seeking behaviors, community development, and health behaviors as they relate to African-American churches.

Patterns and Dimensions of Religious Involvement

Previous theoretical work in this area supports a conceptualization of religious involvement embodying different component dimensions (Ainlay & Smith, 1984; Chatters & Taylor, 1989a; Hunsberger, 1985; Jacobson, Heaton, & Dennis, 1990; Levin, 1989; Mindel & Vaughan, 1978). Research investigations reviewed in this section are concerned with exploring diverse measures of religious involvement (i.e., behaviors versus attitudes; organizational versus nonorganizational versus subjective religiosity) and the development of multidimensional measurement models of religiosity among the African-American population. Common to these efforts (e.g., Chatters, Levin, & Taylor, 1992; Chatters & Taylor, 1989a; Taylor, 1988a, 1988b; Taylor & Chatters, 1991a) is the conceptualization and measurement of religious involvement as a metaconstruct that encompasses both formal and informal practices as well as religious beliefs, sentiments, and attitudes. Accordingly, analyses have used several measures of religious involvement in an attempt to explore (1) the role of social-status factors as correlates of religious involvement as it is broadly defined and (2) the influence of religious dimensions on various health and well-being outcomes.

Justification for a multidimensional conceptualization of religious involvement is derived from basic profiles of religious sentiments, commitments, and activities as well as research examining the differential predictive abilities of sociodemographic factors. Taylor's (1988a) study of apostates indicated that even among religious nonaffiliates (i.e., those reporting no organized religious involvement), reports of frequent prayer and self-characterizations as being fairly religious were evident. Taylor (1988b) also found that social-status factors were differentially predictive of various forms of religious involvement; education and income were significant predictors of organized religious participation, but not of private religious involvement. Taylor and Chatters (1991a) examined the relationship of demographic factors and health disability to different types of nonorganizational religious involvement among older blacks.

The findings indicated that gender, education, age, health disability, and denominational effects varied across the nonorganizational behaviors that were examined. Health disability was positively associated with frequency of watching or listening to religious programs, but was unrelated to personal prayer, reading religious materials, and requests for prayer from others. These particular findings, in conjunction with other work using the NSBA sample (Taylor, 1986), suggest that rather than substituting nonorganizational practices for organizational religious activities, persons in poor health engage in both types of behaviors simultaneously. Although they are comparable to their healthier counterparts with regard to religious attendance, their higher rates of viewer/listenership suggest that they use broadcast religious programming to supplement rather than substitute for formal activities.

Chatters et al. (1992) proposed and tested a measurement model of religiosity among older adults, incorporating three dimensions of religious involvement—namely organizational (or formal or public) religious behavior, nonorganizational (or informal or private) religious behavior, and subjective religious attitudes or feelings. The proposed model provided a good fit to the data, was preferable to other alternative models of these relationships, and was acceptable in regard to convergent validity. Exogenous factors (i.e., age, gender, marital status, income, education, urbanicity, and region) performed largely as expected as predictors of religious involvement and were differentially predictive of the three latent religiosity constructs. Greater variance was explained for subjective religiosity compared with the two behavioral constructs. Noted status-group differences in religiosity were discussed in relation to socialization experiences (e.g., gender roles), contemporaneous experiences (e.g., age differences), and social-environment factors (i.e., region effects) that might promote a religious worldview.

A related analysis (Levin, Chatters, Taylor, & Jackson, 1989) tested a structural-equation model linking the three dimensions of religiosity to health status and life satisfaction among black adults. These findings indicated that specific aspects of religious involvement, notably organizational religious participation, exerted significant effects on life satisfaction net of both health and several important exogenous variables. A number of different explanatory mechanisms (e.g., instrumental support, value and belief affirmation, therapeutic properties of religious ritual) were discussed (Levin & Vanderpool, 1989) whereby involvement in religious pursuits and communities could exert a positive impact on well-being. Investigations continuing this line of inquiry attempt to identify the operative dimensions in the religious experiences of African-Americans and to isolate their relative impacts on physical and mental health and psychological well-being.

Theoretical, Conceptual, Methodological, and Analytical Issues

The research investigations reviewed thus far have addressed several important theoretical, conceptual, methodological, and analytical considerations in relation to religious research generally and to work among African-Americans in particular. Levin's work (e.g., Levin, 1989; Levin & Vanderpool, 1987, 1989) has been influential in the identification and discussion of these issues (see these critiques for a comprehensive treatment). Despite the fact that several of the issues and theoretical problems that will be addressed have been critiqued elsewhere in the literature, it is nonetheless worthwhile to address them briefly here. Within the context of these broader issues, four interrelated problems will be discussed that have an important bearing on theory and research on religious involvement among African-Americans.

Theories and Models of Religious Involvement

The first question concerns a critique of the nature of theory as it relates to the religious experiences of African-Americans and the predominant role of status-group factors as defining events for religious involvement. Traditional models of black religiosity have prompted fairly rudimentary depictions of religious commitment in which the variety and forms of religiosity have been left largely undifferentiated. Although these perspectives have recognized the position of sociodemographic factors as antecedents of religious involvement, it has been primarily to emphasize the significance of these factors for characterizing the (lower) social status of African-Americans as a group, viz. the wider society. Lower status position, then, having been largely presumed, has been perceived as effectively and uniformly determining the (compensatory) nature and functions of religious expression. African-American religion has become identified variously with otherworldly orientations, isolation of the black community from the mainstream, and the operation of deprivation-compensation mechanisms (Lincoln & Mamiya, 1990). In effect, a number of essentially untested and/or inadequately verified assumptions with respect to African-American religious involvement and institutions have been promulgated. These assumptions, in turn, have fostered the view that blacks as a group are routinely religiously oriented, with little if any variation in the form, degree, or pattern of religious involvement.

Emerging theoretical work on black religious orientations (Lincoln & Mamiya, 1990) and recent empirical investigations of religiosity among this group (Ellison, 1991; Ellison & Gay, 1990; Sherkat & Ellison, 1991; Taylor et al., 1987) suggest that more complex models of black religiosity are necessary. In particular, reevaluations of the relationships of social status factors to various facets of religious involvement have suggested the need for further examination and clarification.

Conceptualization of Religiosity

Related to the problem of theory and models of black religiosity are issues of how religious phenomena are conceptualized. Given that predominant models have emphasized a fundamental similarity in the experience and functions of religion for African-Americans, explorations of diversity in overall patterns of religious involvement have been largely neglected. Similarly, conceptualizations of religious involvement that involve individual and distinct components and differentiations of public and private behaviors and religious sentiments and attitudes have not been pursued. Related to this, information as to the operative mechanisms (e.g., social support and group cohesion) for understanding religious effects is lacking (Koenig, Smiley, & Gonzales, 1988; Levin & Vanderpool, 1987, 1989). Finally, little attention has been devoted to the development of causal models of how external factors uniquely determine various aspects of religious involvement and, in turn, how religious components function in distinctive ways as predictors of other outcomes and factors. We recognize that these have been enduring issues in the conceptualization of religious phenomena more generally. However, they have been especially persistent and pervasive concerns with respect to conceptualizations of religiosity among African-Americans.

Methodological Issues

Literature on the black church and African-American religious traditions reveals a significant background and tradition of research employing both ethnographic and survey research methodologies. However, because the methodological approaches employed to examine these issues reflect the prevalent theoretical and conceptual orientations of religious involvement among African-Americans, there are a number of identified limitations of this research. Although the significant strengths of ethnographic research methods are reflected in the depth of inquiry that is possible and the appreciation of social context, several critical theoretical questions cannot be answered definitively given the character and scope of information (i.e., nonrandom samples) typically available from qualitative research. Quantitative investigations, too, frequently rely on convenience samples or the in-depth study of small communities. Findings from previous studies characterized by use of small, nonprobability samples of African-Americans and/or concentration on persons or communities of lower socioeconomic status possess limited generalizability. Overall, the appropriate operationalization and measurement of religious phenomena are pertinent issues for both qualitative and quantitative research efforts.

These identified weaknesses in method have conversely frustrated an adequate and thorough testing of existing theoretical propositions concerning religious involvement. Reflecting limitations in the conceptual definition of religious involvement, the significance and relative salience of different aspects (e.g., ritual, experience, belief) of religious expression generally, and for specific denominations and traditions, have not been appreciated. Religious phenomena are typically assessed using public-behavioral measures (e.g., religious attendance) or using a proxy measure such as religious or denominational affiliation. In some instances, denominational differences among African-Americans are not assessed, nor do researchers consider how other factors (e.g., region) might modify various aspects of religious involvement within denominations (e.g., southern versus northern Baptists). The measurement strategies employed to examine religious behaviors frequently ignore important distinctions (e.g., socioeconomic status) both across and within denominations with respect to normative expectations for particular behaviors such as religious attendance (i.e., weekly versus daily). Furthermore, the operation of religious or denominational affiliation as a proxy for other identifiable factors (e.g., lifestyle preferences and social support) is not readily appreciated. Overall, the operationalization and measurement of religious involvement all too often reflect a lack of sophistication and inadequate understanding as to the range, diversity, and contextual meaning of religious phenomena (Levin & Vanderpool, 1987, 1989).

Analytical Issues

The concern with analytical issues primarily focuses on the need for multivariate investigations of religious involvement (as both dependent and independent variable) in which the effects of potentially confounding factors such as health, socioeconomic statuses, region, and religious denomination are controlled. Methodological innovations such as the presence of adequate sample size and representativeness on major sociodemographic factors allow the opportunity to investigate the social-status antecedents of religious involvement. Coupled with these important sample features, the application of controls for the effects of health status would allow a clearer and more definitive assessment of the independent predictive abilities of important sociodemographic and health factors for religious involvement. For example, Chatters and Taylor (1989a) found that independent of controls for the effects of health and sociodemographic factors, age remained a significant and positive predictor of both formal and informal religious involvement. This finding suggests that, despite extensive levels of religious involvement, there remains significant variation in religiosity that is attributable to differences in social status characteristics.

An additional concern with respect to methods is the reconciliation of apparent discrepancies in the correlates of religious involvement that arise from sample differences on factors such as age of respondent. Investigations of religious involvement that employ samples with a truncated age range (e.g., older persons only) frequently yield findings that conflict with evidence based on more age-comprehensive samples. These discrepancies are most noticeable for the effects for age on religious involvement. For example, positive age effects for religious involvement across the entire adult age range may not be apparent when examining a sample of exclusively older individuals, due to possible differences in the underlying variability of the religious factor in question. Current research in this area reflects studies involving the entire adult age range (Chatters & Taylor, 1989a; Taylor, 1988a, 1988b; Taylor & Chatters, 1986a, 1988b; Taylor, Thornton, & Chatters, 1987) as well as investigations focusing solely on older persons. Taken together, these efforts provide a comprehensive understanding of the influence of age and other factors on religious involvement both within specified age groups and across the full adult age range.

In summary, the empirical study of African-American religiosity and the black church suffers from a number of serious but modifiable problems in theory, concepts, methods, and analytical strategies. Among traditional models of black religiosity and the black church, social status position has been particularly prominent and influential for defining the nature and functions of religious involvement among African-Americans. Despite the existence of a number of testable hypotheses concerning the impact of social status on religious involvement for directly examining these assumptions, several related factors have operated to obstruct a rigorous investigation of these hypotheses. Insufficient elaboration of the conceptual definition of religious involvement has precluded an appreciation of its various components and their individual antecedents and consequences. Identified methodological and analytical limitations reflected in the use of small convenience samples that are not representative of the underlying population of interest and the absence of important controls for potentially confounding factors are further impediments to gaining a comprehensive picture of religious involvement among African-Americans.

Analyses that are based on representative samples of respondents and that allow for an assessment of the relative impacts of race and a diverse set of social-status and health factors on various forms of religious involvement provide pivotal tests of previous propositions concerning religiosity among African-Americans. Ultimately, such an approach is crucial to an understanding of religious phenomena among African-Americans from diverse backgrounds and circumstances. It is to that task that we now turn our attention.

Future Research Directions

In this final section, we highlight several promising avenues for research on religious involvement that we have undertaken. This program of research places a special emphasis on the effects of aging and on older adults. The purpose of this research agenda is to propose a general investigative framework that will generate appropriate data that will provide a better appreciation of the nature, extent, and significance of religious involvement among adult African-Americans. The research agenda described here addresses four general issues: (1) racial differences in religiosity, (2) confirmation of measurement models of religiosity, (3) generational differences in religiosity, and (4) panel analysis of religiosity. These four classes of research problems are not discrete, but overlap in a number of ways (e.g., panel analyses of racial differences and generational differences in measurement models). Within the present context, these research problems are described and formulated in such a manner to examine these questions both within the African-American population (i.e., intragroup analyses) and comparatively with the general white population. Ultimately, a more complete understanding of religious phenomena requires that parallel approaches and analyses are employed among racially and ethnically diverse groups of respondents.

Racial Differences in Religiosity

One of the most persistent questions regarding religious involvement among African-Americans is whether real and significant race differences exist in these phenomena. The existence of race differences in religious involvement has been presumed on the basis of data documenting the importance and centrality of religion and its institutions for African-Americans. A collection of research findings indicates generally that, across various religious measures, African-Americans report higher levels of religious involvement than do whites. Blacks attend religious services (Nelsen, Yokley, & Nelsen, 1971; Sasaki, 1979) and engage in daily prayer at higher rates (Greeley, 1979) and feel more strongly about their religious beliefs (Alston, 1973). Gallup Poll data (Gallup, 1984) indicate that African-Americans are more religiously involved than are whites across a number of indicators, with higher rates of religious attendance and membership in a church or synagogue, and an overall increased likelihood of attaching greater significance to religion and to contend that religion's impact on American life is diminishing.

Beeghley, Van Velsor, and Bock (1981) found that black Methodists attended religious services more frequently than did white Methodists. These findings underscore racial differences within particular religious traditions that, ostensibly, are theologically homogeneous. Roof and McKinney's (1987) comparison of rates of religious participation for several religious traditions (i.e., black Protestants, liberal Protestants, moderate Protestants, conservative Protestants, Catholics, Jews, and persons reporting no religious preference) found that black Protestants and conservative Protestants reported the highest levels of religious attendance, church membership, and denominational commitment (Roof & McKinney, 1987). It is difficult to offer definitive interpretations of these findings given noted difficulties in the measurement of denominational affiliation. Furthermore, because blacks and whites differ with respect to overall denominational affiliations, comparisons between these groups will provide very different profiles of religious involvement (i.e., differences in the variance of religious phenomena). In essence, black Protestants, who are predominantly Baptists and Methodists, tend to be similar to conservative Protestants by virtue of shared religious orientations, ideology, and normative behaviors. Similarly, within-denomination comparisons fail fully to capture the different emphases of black and white Methodist traditions. Taken together, these studies demonstrate apparent and pervasive racial differences in diverse forms of religious involvement and, furthermore, suggest additional lines of inquiry requiring more in-depth examination.

While this work is generally supportive of a race-differences interpretation, several observed findings are based on comparisons of percentage differences or on simple bivariate relationships between race and religious involvement. Observed racial differences in these measures are potentially confounded by other factors; adequate testing for racial differences in religious participation requires the application of controls for the effects of important intervening or exogenous factors that are potentially related to both race and religious involvement (George, 1988). Black-white differences in socioeconomic status, regional distribution, and denominational affiliation indicate that, in the aggregate, blacks (1) possess substantially lower levels of income, financial assets and wealth, and educational attainment; (2) are more likely to reside in the South; and (3) are less heterogeneous with respect to religious preference (higher affiliation with Baptist and Methodist traditions). Furthermore, findings of higher reported levels of religious involvement among rural blacks (Lincoln & Mamiya, 1990; Taylor, 1986) suggest that urban-rural variation in religious involvement may be important for understanding race differences as well. In addition, studies typically employ relatively simple models of the effects of race (i.e., additive) and do not consider more complex models incorporating possible race-interactive effects (Beeghley et al., 1981). Socioeconomic status (George, 1988), region (Fichter & Maddox, 1965; George, 1988; Stump, 1987; Taylor, 1988b; Taylor et al., 1987; Wuthnow & Christiano, 1979), and religious affiliation (Greeley, 1979; Roof & McKinney, 1987) are three factors that are of particular salience for investigations of race differences, whether employed as controls or potential moderators of the relationship between race and various forms of religious involvement.

Finally, differences between black and white populations with respect to compositional factors (i.e., age, gender, socioeconomic, and marital statuses) suggest that bivariate racial differences involving social relationships and other social phenomena may in fact be due to the differential distribution of various demographic characteristics within these groups (George, 1988). We view these cautions as being particularly relevant for public religious behaviors such as religious affiliation, church membership, religious attendance, and tithing and religious giving. However, differences in population composition also may help to illuminate racial disparities in various social processes that occur within the church as a corporate body (e.g., church-based social support) as well as in private religious behaviors and beliefs (e.g., reading religious materials, watching religious television programs). Controlling for compositional variables, in addition to socioeconomic status, region, and religious affiliation, is crucial for establishing authentic racial differences in religious involvement.

With few exceptions, extensive and adequate tests of the impact of race on religious involvement (i.e., analyses with controls for the effects of health and other sociodemographic factors) have not been conducted. Taylor, Chatters, Jayakody, and Levin (1993) investigated racial differences in religious involvement across seven national data sets, multiple data collection points, and numerous measures of religious involvement. Their findings revealed that, across diverse measures of public and private religious behaviors and subjective religiosity, a significant and independent racial difference in religious involvement was empirically identified and isolated. Possible explanations for this racial disparity focused on the roles and functions of religious institutions within African-American communities and differences in level of differentiation (i.e., religious privatization) of secular and religious spheres. Similar findings of a distinct racial difference also were obtained in another multisample analysis of specifically older adults (Levin & Taylor, 1993).

In line with current work on the conceptualization of religious involvement, future research efforts examining race differences should employ diverse measures of religious attitudes (e.g., subjective religiosity, importance of spiritual concerns in daily life) as well as both organizational (e.g., religious attendance, membership, and affiliation) and nonorganizational (e.g., prayer and reading religious materials) religious behaviors. Data of this type from national probability samples of the black and white populations are the most pertinent for achieving this research objective, as they provide the advantages of wider generalizability of the findings and a fuller appreciation of the heterogeneity that exists in sociodemographic predictors of religious involvement. The presence of heterogeneous samples of black and white respondents will make it possible to determine whether observed racial differences in religiosity are, to some degree, accounted for by the effects of socioeconomic status or other factors (e.g., region, religious affiliation) that exert independent influences (i.e., main effects) on religious involvement or that moderate relationships between race and religiosity (i.e., interactive effects).

In sum, one of the goals of a developing program of research on religion among African-Americans should be to determine patterns and identify predictors of religious involvement among blacks and whites, with a concomitant emphasis on the impact of sociodemographic and religious factors such as age, socioeconomic status, region, and religious affiliation. We view this objective as enhancing our understanding of religious concerns among African-Americans and thereby informing the nature of racial comparisons of religious involvement. This research goal will provide important baseline information on the religious attitudes and behaviors of blacks and whites and create a more meaningful context for the investigation of racial-group comparisons. Ultimately, investigations of racial differences that demonstrate theoretical, conceptual, methodological, and analytical sophistication hold promise for strengthening and enriching the study of religious involvement more generally.

Confirmation of Measurement Models of Religiosity

A second major goal of our research program is to confirm multidimensional measurement models of religious involvement for use with African-Americans both across the life course and among older populations as well as within diverse subgroups of the population. This approach to instrument development is valuable and effective because it permits one to posit a theoretically supported and empirically verifiable latent-factor model for a particular construct (e.g., religiosity) which can then be used in theoretically specified structural-equation (or path) models in which similar models of both exogenous and endogenous constructs are simultaneously examined in relation to the construct in question and to each other.

These powerful techniques, known collectively as covariance-structure-modeling or CSM (Bollen, 1989), also allow the investigator to replicate the validity, across different groups, of a proposed measurement model of religious involvement. Specifically, a proposed measurement model of religiosity could be verified across age groupings (i.e., young, middle-aged, and old), regions (i.e., South and non-South), and religious affiliations (e.g., Baptists and Methodists) among African-Americans and within both age- and race-stratified subsamples of black and white adults. One such effort that verified a three-dimensional measurement model of organizational, nonorganizational, and subjective religious involvement was originally developed and tested in a sample of older black adults (Chatters et al., 1992). As a part of this overall research agenda, similar analyses could be conducted among African-Americans spanning the full adult age range as well as among comparable samples of white respondents. Previously significant religious effects on outcomes such as personal adjustment may be invalid in light of the potentially dubious and unreliable measurement of religious constructs and the absence of appropriate controls for the effects of factors known to be consequential to these relationships, notably health status (Levin & Vanderpool, 1989). The application of CSM procedures to clarify and specify the measurement of religious involvement is particularly critical for investigations in which religiosity is employed as an independent variable. For example, CSM techniques would allow us to address the question of whether the structure of religiosity is invariant across African-Americans of different denomination affiliations (e.g., Baptists versus Methodists). Furthermore, these techniques could provide an assessment of the independent and relative impact of organizational, nonorganizational, and subjective religious dimensions, as well as sociodemographic and health-related factors, on outcomes such as personal adjustment both within and across identified subgroups of respondents.

Generational Differences in Religiosity

The third objective of our research program explores generational influences on religious involvement. As one of the primary agents of socialization, the family and its role in the intergenerational transmission of religious values and practices is an apparent and logical area for further study. Evidence for both generational similarity (Acock & Bengtson, 1980) and difference (Glass, Bengtson, & Dunham, 1986) in general attitudes and behaviors has been found. Furthermore, investigations of generational influences that specifically focus on religious involvement suggest basic similarities among generations. Acock and Bengtson (1980) found basic similarity in parent-child attitudes and, irrespective of the sex of the child, that the mother's attitudes had greater predictive capacity for the child's reported attitudes than did the father's attitudes. As suggested by Cornwall (1989) and others (Acock, 1984; Glass et al., 1986), the process of parental and family socialization includes the transmission of not only basic structural characteristics (e.g., social class and religious affiliation) but also psychosocial factors and influences (i.e., parental religious beliefs and attitudes, coping strategies) that both shape the development of a comprehensive worldview and channel individuals into personal communities that serve to maintain religious beliefs and commitments. Perhaps reflecting processes of this type, Landry and Martin (1988) found that the factor structure and loadings of two scales, traditional religious beliefs and religious practice, were similar across three generations.

The investigation of levels and patterns of organizational, nonorganizational, and subjective religiosity within individual generations is an important area of inquiry. The availability of sufficient numbers of persons of different age levels within each generation will allow the investigation of the separate predictive influences of generation and age group. A related issue concerns the existence and delineation of the nature of intergenerational congruence in religious involvement. As suggested by others (Bengtson, Burton, & Mangen, 1985), the majority of studies have examined cohort or generational contrasts to the exclusion of within-lineage or parent-child continuities which are embedded within cohort comparisons. As a result, cohort contrasts often provide evidence of generational differences (generation gaps), whereas within-lineage (i.e., family) comparisons suggest basic similarities. These analyses will be helpful in clarifying which particular aspects of religious involvement are transmitted across family generations (e.g., religious affiliation versus subjective religiosity), both within various categories of African-Americans and compared with other racial groups. Furthermore, the confirmation of multidimensional measurement models of religious involvement can be performed both within family lineages and within distinct generation groups. As generational analyses addressing these concerns among African-Americans are nonexistent, these questions and issues will further our understanding of the character and content of religious socialization within African-American families.

Panel Analysis of Religiosity

Panel analysis of religious involvement among blacks and whites in which observations are made of the same persons at two or more points in time (Kessler & Greenberg, 1981) represents a fourth component of our research agenda. Conducted within national samples of respondents, it is possible to confirm measurement models of religiosity, of sociodemographic effects on religiosity, and of latent mean racial differences in religiosity using data sets containing multiple waves. Analyses of this sort represent a significant innovation over prior research, as previous panel analyses of religion and aging make sole use of single-item indicators (e.g., Markides, 1983; Markides, Levin, & Ray, 1987). Furthermore, prior longitudinal research on religion has not focused on African-Americans or on racial differences, nor have longitudinal analyses yet been conducted that make use of latent-factor models.

Panel analyses seek to assess change (Baltes & Nesselroade, 1979; Schaie & Hertzog, 1982) in the measurement structure and means of religious constructs. Procedures based on CSM will be used to examine (a) the time-invariance of the latent measurement-model structure of religious involvement, (b) the autoregressiveness or "stability" of these measurement models in terms of structural linkages over waves of data, and (c) latent-factor mean differences over time in dimensions of religious involvement. Time-invariance is a special case of factorial-invariance, and testing for this in a measurement model requires the use of simultaneous confirmatory factor analysis to determine whether the internal latent structure of a multidimensional model is invariant across two or more points in time (Liang & Levin, 1990). Without explicitly confirming the assumption of measurement equivalence over time in models of religiosity, it is possible that observed temporal changes in patterns or predictors of religiosity might be due to changes in the factor structure of religiosity over time. Time-invariance is almost universally assumed, but only rarely confirmed, thus seriously compromising the interpretability of panel findings.

Examination of the stability of structural linkages in a measurement model is a complicated issue; these and related analyses represent some of the newest developments in gerontological research (Liang & Lawrence, 1990; Liang & Levin, 1990). The analysis of latent means is a newly developed procedure by which CSM is used to test for differences in structural means of given constructs across groups (Byrne, 1989), such as over time. Therefore, used in conjunction with analyses of time-invariance and stability, one can thus more conclusively answer questions such as, "Does organizational religious involvement in older African-Americans change over time?" In sufficiently large data sets that incorporate both blacks and whites, race-invariance also can be added to the equation, such that a multidimensional, latent measurement model of religiosity can be tested for time-invariance and stability as well as for latent-mean differences across both time and race. This would represent as thorough an application of these sophisticated procedures as has yet been applied to a substantive research issue in social gerontology. An elaboration of the analytical strategies and psychometric and statistical issues that are involved is beyond the scope of this chapter.

Conclusion

We are in a propitious position in the development of knowledge with respect to religious involvement among African-Americans. Several important developments in theory, concepts, methods, and analytical approaches provide the opportunity and challenge to move in a direction that will extend and augment these important preceding efforts in this area of research and scholarship. Emergent theories and models of African-American religiosity and the black church reflect an appreciation for the multifaceted and dynamic nature of these phenomena and institutions. The conceptualization, operational definition, and measurement of religious involvement reflect increasing differentiation and incorporation of diverse aspects of religious attitudes, beliefs, and practices. Recent efforts in the development of measurement models of religious phenomena among older groups increasingly reflect these important conceptual distinctions as well as an appreciation of the effects of exogenous and health factors as they operate throughout the model.

A number of currently available national data sets addressing religious issues possess representative numbers (either individually or in the aggregate) of African-Americans and adequately reflect the distribution of major sociodemographic characteristics existing within the underlying population(s). Several of these data sets include significant numbers of items addressing religious concerns beyond the rudimentary indicators of religious affiliation and religious attendance, and thus allow for the development of multidimensional models of religiosity both within diverse groups of African-Americans and in comparison with the general population. Furthermore, several data sets contain multiple waves of information that permit panel analyses, whereas a limited number of data sets provide information on family generations that can be used to address questions of generational similarities and differences in religious involvement. Finally, these data sets allow the examination of a host of other issues in which religious factors are implicated. For example, one could examine religious effects on racial identity, electoral participation, group membership and participation, informal social support networks, and mental and physical health and well-being.

Clearly, the available data sources and proposed analyses do not address all of our information needs with respect to religious involvement among older African-Americans. We agree with Lincoln and Mamiya (1990) and others who suggest that, to varying degrees, religious considerations are often essential to understanding the various social, political, economic, educational, and social-welfare institutions and dynamics within African-American communities. Although we have advocated a particular approach and method to the investigation of these issues, research and scholarship in the areas of religious studies, political science, African-American history and culture, economic and community development, gerontology, psychology, and sociology each provide important insights on African-American religious traditions. The variety of diverse perspectives on the religious experiences of African-Americans suggests that the entire range of relevant issues cannot be elaborated or addressed by a single discipline, method, or approach. However, the social-scientific research agenda outlined here represents an important initial step in developing a more comprehensive portrayal of the character, patterns, antecedents, and consequences of religious involvement among older African-Americans. The challenge for researchers in the social sciences is to appreciate and remain responsive to the various ways in which religious phenomena permeate the fabric of African-American life. Ultimately, a research approach that both systematically and rigorously considers the nature of religious involvement among African-Americans contributes to an enriched understanding of these phenomena across time, place, and social circumstance.

References

Acock, A. C. (1984). Parents and their children: The study of inter-generational influence. *Sociology and Social Research, 68,* 151-171.

Acock, A. C., & Bengtson, V. L. (1980). Socialization and attribution process: Actual versus perceived similarity among parents and youths. *Journal of Marriage and the Family, 42,* 501-515.

Ainlay, S. C., & Smith, D. R. (1984). Aging and religious participation. *Journal of Gerontology, 39,* 357-363.

Alston, J. P. (1973). Perceived strength of religious beliefs. *Journal for the Scientific Study of Religion, 12,* 109-111.

Baltes, P. B., & Nesselroade, J. R. (1979). History and rationale of longitudinal research. In J. R. Nesselroade & P. B. Baltes (Eds.), *Longitudinal research in the study of behavior and development* (pp. 1-39). New York: Academic.

Beeghley, L., Van Velsor, E., & Bock, E. W. (1981). The correlates of religiosity among black and white Americans. *Sociological Quarterly, 22,* 403-412.

Bengtson, V. L., Burton, L., & Mangen, D. J. (1985). Generations, cohorts, and relations between age groups. In R. Binstock & E. Shanas (Eds.), *Handbook of aging and the social sciences* (pp. 304-338). New York: Van Nostrand Reinhold.

Bollen, K. A. (1989). *Structural equations with latent variables.* New York: Wiley.

Brown, D. R., & Gary, L. E. (1987). Stressful life events, social support networks, and physical and mental health of urban black adults. *Journal of Human Stress, 13,* 165-174.

Bryant, S., & Rakowski, W. (1992). Predictors of mortality among elderly African-Americans. *Research on Aging, 14,* 50-67.

Byrne, B. M. (1989). *A primer on LISREL.* New York: Springer.

Caldwell, C. H., Chatters, L. M., Billingsley, A., & Taylor, R. J. (in press). Church-based support programs for elderly black adults: Congregational and clergy characteristics. In M. A. Kimble, S. H. McFadden, J. W. Ellor, & J. J. Seeber (Eds.), *Religion, spirituality, and aging: A handbook.* Minneapolis, MN: Fortress.

Chatters, L. M., Levin, J. S., & Taylor, R. J. (1992). Antecedents and dimensions of religious involvement among older black adults. *Journal of Gerontology: Social Sciences, 47,* S269-S278.

Chatters, L. M., & Taylor, R. J. (1989a). Age differences in religious participation among black adults. *Journal of Gerontology: Social Sciences, 44,* S183-S189.

Chatters, L. M., & Taylor, R. J. (1989b). Life problems and coping strategies of older black adults. *Social Work, 34,* 313-319.

Cone, J. (1985). Black theology in American religion. *Journal of the American Academy of Religion, 53,* 755-771.

Cornwall, M. (1989). The determinants of religious behavior: A theoretical model and empirical test. *Social Forces, 68,* 572-592.

Du Bois, W. E. B. (1899). *The Philadelphia Negro.* New York: Schocken.

Ellison, C. G. (1991). Identification and separatism: Religious involvement and racial orientations among black Americans. *Sociological Quarterly, 32,* 477-494.

Ellison, C. G., & Gay, D. A. (1990). Region, religious commitment, and life satisfaction among black Americans. *Sociological Quarterly, 31,* 123-147.

Ellison, C. G., & Sherkat, D. (1990). Patterns of religiosity mobility among black Americans. *Sociological Quarterly, 31,* 551-568.

Eng, E., & Hatch, J. (1991). Networking between agencies and black churches: The lay health advisor model. *Prevention in Human Services, 10,* 123-146.

Eng, E., Hatch, J., & Cunningham, A. (1985). Institutionalizing social support through the church and into the community. *Health Education Quarterly, 12,* 81-92.

Fichter, J. H., & Maddox, G. L. (1965). Religion in the south old and new. In J. C. McKinney & E. T. Thompson (Eds.), *The South in continuity and change* (pp. 359-383). Durham, NC: Duke University Press.

Frazier, E. F. (1974). *The Negro church in America.* New York: Schocken.

Gallup, G. (1984). *Religion in America.* Princeton, NJ: Princeton Religious Research Center.

George, L. (1988). Social participation in later life: Black-white differences. In J. S. Jackson (Ed.), *The black American elderly: Research on physical and psychosocial health* (pp. 99-126). New York: Springer.

Glass, J., Bengtson, V. L., & Dunham, C. C. (1986). Attitude similarity in three-generation families: Socialization, status inheritance, or reciprocal influence. *American Sociological Review, 51,* 685-698.

Glock, C. Y., Ringer, B. R., & Babbie, E. E. (1967). *To comfort and to challenge.* Berkeley: University of California Press.

Greeley, A. M. (1979). Ethnic variations in religious commitment. In R. Wuthnow (Ed.), *The religious dimension: New direction in quantitative research* (pp. 113-134). New York: Academic.

Griffith, E. E. H. (1983). The impact of socio-cultural factors on a church-based healing model. *American Journal of Orthopsychiatry, 53,* 291-302.

Griffith, E. E. H., English, T., & Mayfield, V. (1980). Possession, prayer, and testimony: Therapeutic aspects of the Wednesday night meeting in a black church. *Psychiatry, 43,* 120-128.

Griffith, E. E. H., & Mahy, G. E. (1984). Psychological benefits of spiritual Baptist mourning. *American Journal of Psychiatry, 141,* 769-773.

Griffith, E. E. H., Young, J. L., & Smith, D. L. (1984). An analysis of the therapeutic elements in a black church service. *Hospital and Community Psychiatry, 35,* 464-469.

Hatch, J., & Eng, E. (1983). Health workers in community oriented primary care. In E. Connor & F. Mullan (Eds.), *Community oriented primary care* (pp. 138-158). Washington, DC: National Academy of Medicine.

Hatch, J., & Eng, E. (1984). Community participation and control: Or control of community participation. In V. Sidel & R. Sidel (Eds.), *Reforming medicine: Lessons of the last quarter century* (pp. 223-244). New York: Pantheon Books.

Hatch, J., & Lovelace, K. (1980). Involving the southern rural church and students of the health professions in health education. *Public Health Reports, 95,* 23-25.

Hunsberger, B. (1985). Religion, age, life satisfaction, and perceived sources of religiousness: A study of older persons. *Journal of Gerontology, 40,* 615-620.

Jacobson, C. K., Heaton, T. B., & Dennis, R. M. (1990). Black-white differences in religiosity: Item analyses and a formal structural test. *Sociological Analyses, 51,* 257-270.

Kessler, R. C., & Greenberg, D. F. (1981). *Linear panel analysis: Model of quantative change.* New York: Academic.

Koenig, H. G., Smiley, M., & Gonzales, J. (1988). *Religion, health, and aging: A review and theoretical integration.* Westport, CT: Greenwood Press.

Krause, N. (1992). Stress, religiosity, and psychological well-being among older blacks. *Journal of Aging and Health, 4,* 412-439.

Krause, N., & Tran, T. V. (1989). Stress and religious involvement among older blacks. *Journal of Gerontology: Social Sciences, 44,* S4-S13.

Landry, Jr., P. H., & Martin, M. E. (1988). Measuring intergenerational consensus. In D. J. Mangen, V. L. Bengtson, & P. H. Landry, Jr. (Eds.), *Measurement of intergenerational relations* (pp. 126-155). Beverly Hills, CA: Sage.

Levin, J. S. (1984). The role of the black church in community medicine. *Journal of the National Medical Association, 76,* 477-483.

Levin, J. S. (1986). Roles for the black pastor in preventive medicine. *Pastoral Psychology, 35,* 94-102.

Levin, J. S. (1989). Religious factors in aging, adjustment, and health: A theoretical overview. In W. M. Clements (Ed.), *Religion, aging and health: A global perspective* (pp. 133-146). New York: Haworth.

Levin, J. S., Chatters, L. M., Taylor, R. J., & Jackson, J. S. (1989, July 13). *Religiosity, health, and life satisfaction in black Americans.* Paper presented at the annual meeting of the American Psychological Association, New Orleans.

Levin, J. S., & Taylor, R. J. (1993). Gender and age differences in religiosity among black Americans. *The Gerontologist, 32,* 16-23.

Levin, J. S., & Vanderpool, H. Y. (1987). Is frequent religious attendance *really* conducive to better health?: Toward an epidemiology of religion. *Social Science and Medicine, 24,* 589-600.

Levin, J. S., & Vanderpool, H. Y. (1989). Is religion therapeutically significant for hypertension? *Social Science and Medicine, 29,* 69-78.

Levin, J. S., & Vanderpool, H. Y. (1991). Religious factors in physical health and the prevention of illness. *Prevention in Human Services, 9,* 41-64.

Liang, J., & Lawrence, R. H. (1990). *Change and stability in two dimensions of the Philadelphia Geriatric Center Morale scale.* Unpublished manuscript.

Liang, J., & Levin, J. S. (1990, November). *Panel analysis for the OARS mental health measures.* Paper presented at the annual meeting of the Gerontological Society of America, Boston.

Lincoln, C. E., & Mamiya, L. (1990). *The black church in the African American experience.* Durham: Duke Press.

Markides, K. S. (1983). Aging, religiosity, and adjustment: A longitudinal analysis. *Journal of Gerontology, 38,* 621-625.

Markides, K. S., Levin, J. S., & Ray, L. A. (1987). Religion, aging, and life satisfaction: An eight-year, three-wave longitudinal study. *The Gerontologist, 27,* 660-665.

Marx, G. (1967). Religion: Opiate or inspiration of civil rights militancy among Negroes. *American Sociological Review, 32,* 64-72.

Mindel, C. H., & Vaughan, C. E. (1978). A multidimensional approach to religiosity and disengagement. *Journal of Gerontology, 33,* 103-108.

Moore, T. (1991). The African-American church: A source of empowerment, mutual help, and social change. *Prevention in Human Services, 10,* 147-167.

Morris, A. (1981). Black southern sit-in movement: An analysis of internal organization. *American Sociological Review, 46,* 741-767.

Neighbors, H. (1991). Mental health of black Americans. In J. S. Jackson (Ed.), *Life in black America* (pp. 221-237). Newbury Park, CA: Sage.

Neighbors, H., Jackson, J. S., Bowman, P. J., & Gurin, G. (1983). Stress, coping and black mental health: Preliminary findings from a national study. *Prevention in Human Services, 2,* 5-29.

Nelsen, H. M. (1988). Unchurched black Americans: Patterns of religiosity and affiliation. *Review of Religious Research, 29,* 398-412.

Nelsen, H. M., & Nelsen, A. K. (1975). *Black church in the sixties.* Lexington: University Press of Kentucky.

Nelsen, H. M., Yokley, R. L., & Nelsen, A. K. (1971). *The black church in America*. New York: Basic Books.

Roof, W. C., & McKinney, W. (1987). *American mainline religion: Its changing shape and future*. New Brunswick, NJ: Rutgers University Press.

Sasaki, M. S. (1979). Status inconsistency and religious commitment. In R. Wuthnow (Ed.), *The religious dimension: New directions in quantitative research* (pp. 133-156). New York: Academic.

Schaie, K. W., & Hertzog, C. (1982). Longitudinal methods. In B. B. Wolman (Ed.), *Handbook of developmental psychology* (pp. 847-870). Englewood Cliffs, NJ: Prentice-Hall.

Sherkat, D. E., & Ellison, C. G. (1991). The politics of black religious change: Disaffiliation from black mainline denominations. *Social Forces, 70*, 431-454.

Stark, R., & Bainbridge, W. S. (1981). American-born sects: Initial finds. *Journal for the Scientific Study of Religion, 20*, 130-149.

Stump, R. W. (1987). Regional contrasts within black Protestantism: A research note. *Social Forces, 66*, 143-151.

Taylor, R. J. (1986). Religious participation among elderly blacks. *The Gerontologist, 26*, 630-636.

Taylor, R. J. (1988a). Correlates of religious non-involvement among black Americans. *Review of Religious Research, 30*, 126-139.

Taylor, R. J. (1988b). Structural determinants of religious participation among black Americans. *Review of Religious Research, 30*, 114-125.

Taylor, R. J. (1992). Religion and religious observances among aging black Americans. In J. S. Jackson, L. M. Chatters, & R. J. Taylor (Eds.), *Aging in black America* (pp. 101-123). Newbury Park, CA: Sage.

Taylor, R. J., & Chatters, L. M. (1986a). Church-based informal support among elderly blacks. *The Gerontologist, 26*, 637-642.

Taylor, R. J., & Chatters, L. M. (1986b). Patterns of informal support to elderly black adults: Family, friends, and church members. *Social Work, 31*, 432-438.

Taylor, R. J., & Chatters, L. M. (1988). Church members as a source of informal social support. *Review of Religious Research, 30*, 193-203.

Taylor, R. J., & Chatters, L. M. (1991a). Non-organizational religious participation among elderly blacks. *Journal of Gerontology: Social Sciences, 46*, S103-S111.

Taylor, R. J., & Chatters, L. M. (1991b). Religious life of black Americans. In J. S. Jackson (Ed.), *Life in black America* (pp. 105-123). Newbury Park, CA: Sage.

Taylor, R. J., Chatters, L. M., Jayakody, R. T., & Levin, J. S. (1993). *Race and religious participation: A multi-sample comparison*. Unpublished manuscript.

Taylor, R. J., Thornton, M. C., & Chatters, L. M. (1987). Black Americans' perceptions of the socio-historical role of the church. *Journal of Black Studies, 18*, 123-138.

Watson, W. H. (1990). Family care, economics, and health. In Z. Harel, E. A. McKinney, & M. Williams (Eds.), *Black aged* (pp. 50-68). Newbury Park, CA: Sage.

Welch, M. R. (1978). The unchurched, black religious non-affiliates. *Journal for the Scientific Study of Religion, 17*, 289-293.

Wilson, V., & Netting, F. E. (1989). Exploring the interface of local churches with the aging network: A comparison of Anglo and black congregations. *Journal of Religion and Aging, 5*, 51-60.

Wuthnow R., & Christiano K. (1979). The effects of residential migration on church attendance in the United States. In R. Wuthnow (Ed.), *The religious dimension: New directions in quantitative research* (pp. 257-276). New York: Academic Press.

Author Index

Subject Index

AARP. *See* American Association of Retired Persons
Acts, 33
Adaptation, 64-65
African-American church, 47, 111, 134-135, 144, 196-226
  and affiliation, 202-205
  and coping, 40, 209-210
  and intergenerational differences, 222-223
  and measures of religion, 211-217, 221-222
  and racial differences, 218-221
  and social resources, 25, 207-209
  models of, 200-202
  sociodemographic factors of, 24, 25, 143, 205-207, 216
  sociohistorical role of, 198-199, 202, 208
Aging problems, 23-27, 32
A Grief Observed (Lewis), 44-45
Alzheimer's disease, 24, 27
Ambiguity, 140
American Association of Retired Persons (AARP), 24, 25

American Journal of Psychiatry, 149, 183, 185
American Psychological Association, 159, 187
American Society on Aging, xvi
Anger, 37-38
Anti-tenure factor, 150-162
  and epidemiology, 155-156
  and gerontology, 159-162
  and psychology, 156-158
  and research, 150-154
  and sociology, 158-159
  treatment recommendations for, 166-173.
  See also Measures of religion; Systematic review
Architecture, 137-138
Archives of General Psychiatry, 149, 183-184, 185
Asthma, 38
Autonomy:
  and depression, 81-82
  and Judeo-Christian theology, 42, 100.
  See also Control

About the Editor

Jeffrey S. Levin, Ph.D., M.P.H., a Social Epidemiologist, received his A.B. from Duke University in 1981, graduating Magna Cum Laude and with Distinction in both Religion and Sociology. He received his M.P.H. in Health Behavior in 1983 from the University of North Carolina School of Public Health, and his Ph.D. in Preventive Medicine in 1987 from The University of Texas Medical Branch. He also completed an NIH-funded Postdoctoral Research Fellowship from 1987 to 1989 at the Institute of Gerontology of the University of Michigan and has additional advanced training in quantitative methods from the Inter-university Consortium for Political and Social Research at the University of Michigan.

Since 1989, he has been on the faculty of the Department of Family and Community Medicine at Eastern Virginia Medical School in Norfolk, Virginia, where he is currently Associate Professor. In 1991, he received a 5-year NIH FIRST Award from the National Institute on Aging for his project *Religion, Health & Psychological Well-Being in the Aged.* He is Coprincipal Investigator on a 3-year NIH grant, awarded in 1992, to study social-structural factors in religion, race, and aging. He was the first scientist to critically review the empirical literatures on the effects of religious involvement on morbidity and mortality, hypertension, well-being in the elderly, health care utilization, and other related outcomes. He is a Research Consultant to the U.S. Department of Veterans Affairs, an Inaugural Senior Research Fellow of the National Institute for Healthcare Research, and a Resource Network Member of the Family Research Council. He is the author or coauthor of more than 60 journal articles, chapters, and reviews as well as another 50 conference presentations and invited lectures, nearly all of which deal with the role of religion in physical and mental health and aging, or with maternal and child health.

About the Contributors

Dan G. Blazer, M.D., Ph.D., is Dean of Medical Education, J. P. Gibbons Professor of Psychiatry, Professor of Community Medicine, Director of the Affective Disorders Program, Head of the Division of Geriatric Psychiatry, and Senior Fellow of the Center for the Study of Aging and Human Development at Duke University Medical Center. He also is Adjunct Professor of Epidemiology at the University of North Carolina School of Public Health. A graduate of Vanderbilt University, he received his M.D. from the University of Tennessee, his M.P.H. and Ph.D. in epidemiology from North Carolina, and completed his residency in psychiatry at Duke. He has served as Principal Investigator of both the Piedmont Health Survey and the Piedmont Health Survey of the Elderly, Duke's respective ECA and EPESE projects. He also is Director of the Center for the Study of Depression in the Elderly, a member of the McArthur Program on Successful Aging, and a recipient of an NIMH Career Development Award. He is the author or editor of 10 books, and author or coauthor of more than 125 refereed scientific articles, 80 published abstracts, and 70 book chapters. He is past President of both the American Geriatrics Society and the Psychiatric Research Society, is a Fellow of several other scientific organizations, and has received numerous national awards.

Linda M. Chatters, Ph.D., is Assistant Professor of Health Behavior and Health Education in the School of Public Health, and Faculty Associate with the Program for Research on Black Americans of the Institute for Social Research, University of Michigan. After earning her Ph.D. in psychology at the University of Michigan, she completed postdoctoral study supported by both the Rockefeller Foundation and the National Institute on Aging. She is a recipient of a 5-year NIH FIRST Award Grant, through which she is investigating issues related to the use of survey data among diverse groups of black Americans. She and her colleagues have recently received a second NIH grant to study religion and aging in black and white adults.

Christopher G. Ellison, Ph.D., received his Ph.D. from Duke University in 1991 and is currently Assistant Professor of Sociology at The University of Texas at Austin. He also is affiliated with both the Center for African and African-American Studies and the Religious Studies Program at Texas. His primary research centers on the implications of religious involvement for mental and physical well-being. Other research interests include racial attitudes and political participation of black Americans, the contemporary black church, the persistence of southern regional distinctiveness, and the role of fundamentalist Protestantism in shaping attitudes toward parenting and family life. His work has appeared in *Social Forces, Journal of Health and Social Behavior, Journal of Marriage and the Family,* and *Social Science Quarterly.*

Berton H. Kaplan, Ph.D., is Professor of Epidemiology at the University of North Carolina School of Public Health, Deputy Chairman for Academic Affairs, and a Senior Associate in the Department of Anthropology. He received his Ph.D. in sociology from the University of North Carolina and has been a Social Science Research Council Fellow at Cornell University, Visiting Professor of Sociology at Stanford, and a member of the Institute of Medicine's Advisory Committee on Mental Health and Behavioral Medicine. He is the author of numerous articles, chapters, and reviews and is the author of the book *Blue Ridge.* He is the editor of *Psychiatric Disorder and the Urban Environment* and coeditor of *Further Explorations in Social Psychiatry.* He also is the cooriginator of two monographs on the family and health. He is one of the pioneering figures in the field of social epidemiology.

Harold G. Koenig, M.D., M.H.Sc., is Assistant Professor of Psychiatry and of Medicine, Duke University Medical Center. He is engaged in clinical, research, and teaching activities in the area of geriatric psychiatry and is author of two books and more than 70 articles and book chapters. He is board certified in family medicine and geriatric medicine, board eligible in geriatric psychiatry, and holds a Master's Degree in biostatistics from the Duke University Division of Biometry. His research has focused on the relationship between religion and mental health in later life, with special emphasis on disabled elders with physical health problems. He has been a research consultant to numerous pastoral care programs throughout the country and is currently on the editorial board of the *Journal of Religious Gerontology.*

David B. Larson, M.D., M.S.P.H., is Adjunct Associate Professor of Psychiatry at Duke University Medical Center and formerly was a Research Psychiatrist at NIMH. He completed his psychiatry residency, chief residency, and geriatric training at Duke, and received a 3-year epidemiology fellowship from NIH, during which he completed his M.S.P.H. in epidemiology at North Carolina. He is board certified in psychiatry, is certified as both an administrative psychiatrist and a marital and family therapist, and is an officer in the Commissioned Corps of the U.S. Public Health Service, having attained the Navy equivalent rank of Captain. His research interests include the impact of religious commitment on physical and mental health, systematic reviews of the religious research literature, provision and delivery of mental health services in primary care, and quality of care issues in the use and prescribing of psychotropic medications. He has more than 140 professional publications, and has received numerous national awards.

John S. Lyons, Ph.D., is Associate Professor of Psychiatry and Medicine at Northwestern University Medical School. He received his Ph.D. in clinical psychology and methods and measurement from the University of Illinois at Chicago in 1982. He came to Northwestern in 1984 after a 2-year National Research Service Award NIMH fellowship at the University of Chicago. He is currently the Faculty Director of the Thresholds National Research and Training Center, a U.S. Department of Education (NIDRR) center for the study of psychosocial rehabilitation for persons with serious mental illness. He has more than 100 professional publications in the areas of mental health services and the relationship of religion to health and well-being.

Heather Monroe-Blum, Ph.D., is Dean and Professor at the Faculty of Social Work at the University of Toronto. She also is Professor of Medicine and of Psychiatry, and holds status appointments in Psychiatry and Clinical Epidemiology and Biostatistics at McMaster University. She received her B.A. and B.S.W. from McMaster, her M.S.W. from Wilfrid Laurier University, and her Ph.D. in epidemiology from the University of North Carolina School of Public Health. Her research involves the application of epidemiologic methodology to the assessment of practice effectiveness as well as the study of the distribution, prevention, and treatment of major psychiatric disorders. She is currently funded by both NIMH and the Canadian National Health Research and Development Program, and is Coinvestigator on the Ontario Child Health Study Four-Year Follow-up. She is a Member of the Premier's Council on Health, Well-Being and Social Justice and maintains active membership in numerous local, national, and international planning and advisory groups in the area of health and social welfare.

Kimberly A. Sherrill, M.D., M.P.H., Assistant Professor of Psychiatry and Behavioral Medicine at Bowman Gray School of Medicine, received her undergraduate education at The University of Texas at Austin and her M.D. from The University of Texas Medical Branch. She completed residency training in psychiatry and fellowship training in psychosomatic medicine at Duke University Medical Center, followed by a fellowship at the regional burn center at the University of North Carolina. She was accepted to the Robert Wood Johnson Clinical Scholars Program at North Carolina, during which time she also completed an M.P.H. in epidemiology. She is a geriatrician and recently was awarded a Geriatric Mental Health Academic Award from NIMH for development of a program of research focused on religion and aging.

Robert Joseph Taylor, Ph.D., is Associate Professor of Social Work and Faculty Associate, Program for Research in Black Americans, Institute for Social Research, University of Michigan. After earning his Ph.D. in sociology and social work from the University of Michigan, he completed postdoctoral training sponsored by the National Institute on Aging. He received an NIH FIRST Award Grant to study family and friends social support networks across the life span, with special emphasis on the networks of older adults. He also has done pioneering work on the sociology of black religious involvement, especially among older adults, and is the Principal Investigator on a second NIH grant in which he has further explored social-structural determinants of racial variation in religiosity.

David R. Williams, Ph.D., is Associate Professor in the Department of Sociology and Associate Research Scientist in the Survey Research Center of the Institute for Social Research at the University of Michigan. He received his M.P.H. from Loma Linda University, his M.Div. from Andrews University, and his Ph.D. in sociology from the University of Michigan. His research interests include the consequences of religious involvement for health status and socioeconomic and racial differences in health. He is especially interested in ways in which both the distribution and impact of health-enhancing resources and risk factors vary by social status. His research has been supported by grants from NSF, NIMH, and NIA, and he is currently a member of the National Committee on Vital and Health Statistics.